Jack Hunt

D1594488

Growing into Goodness
Essays on Quaker Education

Growing into Goodness
Essays on Quaker Education

PAUL A. LACEY

Pendle Hill Publications
in cooperation with

Friends Council on Education

Copyright © by Paul A. Lacey
1998

Printed in the United States by Thomson-Shore, Inc.
December 1998: 1,500 copies

Cover Art: "Two Friends"
Woodcut by Wharton Esherick
used with permission from the
Wharton Esherick Museum
Paoli, Pennsylvania 19301
(610) 644-5822

Library of Congress Cataloguing-in-Publication Data

Lacey, Paul A.

Growing into goodness: essays on Quaker education/Paul A. Lacey
      p.   cm.
"In Cooperation with Friends Council on Education."
Includes bibliographical references (p. 265) and index.
ISBN 0-87574-933-X
  1. Society of Friends--Education.   2. Quakers--Education.
3. Society of Friends--History.   I. Friends Council on Education.
II. Title.
LC571.L336   1998
371.071'96--dc21   98-44919
                                                                      CIP

Dedication

*To those—teachers, administrators, staff and students—who
have gone before us, inspiring us with their example;
to our companions, whose fidelity sustains our
present work; and to those who will follow us
in service to the Teacher Within.*

Contents

Acknowledgements

I cannot name all the people and groups to whom I owe thanks for what I have learned about Quakerism and Quaker education in the last forty-seven years. My first and most lasting lessons in Quaker education began outside formal schooling. The most influential of those came through learning-by-doing in weekend workcamps in Philadelphia, which I first encountered in 1951, where David Richie and Jim Kietzman introduced me to Quakerism and became my first mentors as I tried to discover what I should do with my life.

Perhaps the single most important conversation of my life occurred as I walked with Jim along the beach on Staten Island, after a weekend painting one of the Catholic Worker houses of hospitality in New York. I had begun college planning to study law— a practical, useful profession—but had discovered how deeply I loved the study of literature, which seemed so impractical and self-indulgent. That was what I talked to Jim about, and over the years I have gratefully shared his response with many of my own students at their own crossroads moments: "The world is full of half-people, but what it needs is whole people. If you study something only out of duty, you may simply become another unhappy, unsatisfied half-person. Find whatever can help you become a whole person, and study that." His affection and wisdom freed me to pursue what has been both a precious intellectual and spiritual resource for me and the ground on which I have been allowed to meet and learn with generations of students.

I could not have been more fortunate in when and how I encountered the Religious Society of Friends. In Philadelphia in the early 1950s, the great leaders of modern Quakerism were still vigorous and influential, and they were open and responsive to even the most gauche seeker. Some of my earliest teachers included Clarence Pickett, Henry Cadbury, Walter Longstreth, Lewis Hoskins, Burns Chalmers, Steve Cary, and Dan Wilson. (I would be embarrassed by this name-dropping if I didn't know that hundreds and hundreds of people could list the same names.) They modelled integrity, patience, courage, passion for justice, living by principle, and made me want to follow their example. I learned about Quaker faith and practice by serving on committees of the yearly meeting and American Friends Service Committee with those Friends and many others similarly gifted.

Those and other important lessons were reinforced by joining Frankford Meeting (Hicksite), and by participating in the Young Friends Movement and, later, the Young Friends Committee of North America. People around my own age and the somewhat older advisers to Young Friends taught me a great deal, and I am grateful for how much Joanna Ayers, Burt Housman, Jim and Martha Kietzman, Milton Zimmerman, Sam Humes, Ruth Ferguson, Dick Taylor, Beth Leiby (Hiller), Elwood Cronk, John Kirk, Ruth and Gilbert Kilpack, Tom and Nan Brown, and Ted Benfey, among others, contributed to my growth as a Quaker.

I also learned from living writers, most notably Howard Brinton and Douglas Steere. When I came to meet each of them, I rejoiced to see how their lives and their words made a single testimony. I regularly return to Douglas Steere's *On Listening to Another* for insight and inspiration, and I could not have written these essays without Howard Brinton to guide me. Their lives also illustrated another important lesson, for the further I ventured into the Religious Society of Friends, the more aware I became not only of the magnificent original leadership provided by many women but of how rich a life of companionship between equals can be. How amazing, and how right, it is that we think of so much powerful leadership among Quakers in *both/and* language. What gifts are freed in each when a Howard Brinton finds an Anna Brinton, a Douglas Steere finds a Dorothy Steere. Such companionship among equals recommends the testimony for equality as more than a duty; it invites us to experience a great human and spiritual happiness in our own lives.

I never attended a Quaker school or college, but I am beginning my thirty-ninth year as a teacher and learner in Quaker institutions. In my second year as a teacher, I taught at Pendle Hill, and served during one term as acting director. One of the great benefits of that year was having Anna and Howard Brinton as next-door neighbors and Dan and Rosalie Wilson nearly as close. Like Thoreau in Concord, I have travelled widely in Earlham, as participant or director in many experimental programs and as administrator, but the classroom has always been my primary home. Even when I was provost and then acting president, I taught half-time, and two-thirds time during the three years that I served as director of a post-doctoral teachers program for Lilly Endowment; teaching has always been an anchor for me. Many students and colleagues have taught me about the vitality of Quaker education and sustained and challenged me in my development as a Quaker teacher. Helen and Allen Hole became dear friends and mentors from the beginning, and here I could learn again from Ted Benfey and Lewis Hoskins, this time as a colleague. Clear Creek Meeting, which sometimes seemed like the Earlham faculty gathered for prayer, made a link between the college and the Religious Society of Friends which was some-times uncomfortable, not always healthy, but at its best spiritually vital. I am grateful for the Quaker witness of my senior colleagues Hugh Barbour, Arthur Little, Jim Cope, Larry Strong, Bill Fuson, Warren Staebler, President Landrum Bolling, Dean of Students Eric Curtis, and Dean of Women

Margaret Beidler, as I began my teaching career. From those early days I have also been nourished by the dedication to Quaker education of many non-Quaker colleagues. Here I especially want to recall with gratitude the example of Leonard Holvik (who ultimately joined us Quakers!), Bill Stephenson, Jerry Bakker, Eleanore Vail and Wayne Booth. Most of all, I want to record my debt to Joe E. Elmore, for two decades the Academic Dean at Earlham, a Methodist minister who unfailingly held before us the highest expectations for what Quaker education could mean. I believe no one in my time at Earlham has done more to maintain the college's Quaker commitments. His successor, Len Clark, a devout Lutheran, continues to serve the cause of Quaker education with passionate dedication. I record, too, my thanks to Franklin Wallin for his service as president of the College.

I owe much to my contemporaries and junior colleagues (by this time, almost everyone is among the latter) on the Earlham faculty and staff. In particular, my colleagues in the English department and on the staff of the Humanities Program continually help me link my Quakerism with my professional life as a teacher-scholar of literature.

I have many people to thank for their contribution to this book. Four people especially preside over what I have written: Howard Brinton, Helen Hole, Leonard Kenworthy, and John Reader. John Reader is another whom I met first through his writing and whose friendship I cherish. Margaret and I recall a wonderful time as guests of Mary and John Reader In York, England, in 1992. They introduced us to Quaker educators in England, took us through the magnificent Yorkshire countryside, gave us glorious meals and equally nourishing conversations.

I thank Bill and Margery Oats for their friendship and for the witness of their lives as educators at the Friends School in Hobart, Australia. Bill's writings have been especially illuminating on the interplay of science and spiritual growth.

A number of friends and colleagues have read drafts of some or all of these essays, have suggested changes, pointed out errors before they got into print, and encouraged me to keep on with my task. Tom Hamm, historian and Archivist of the Quaker Collection at Earlhm, and Provost Len Clark each read the whole manuscript scrupulously and made a great many suggestions which have improved it. I especially thank Gene Mills, who took on the reading while he was engaged more than full time as Acting President of Earlham in 1996-97, and gave me many useful notes. Over several years, I have profited from on-going discussions with Kay Edstene, Foster Doan, Richard Eldridge, Tom Farquhar, Jane Fremon, Jane Manring, Stephanie Judson, Ruth Seeley, Martha Bryans, Gail Thomas, Irene McHenry, Jane Stavits, Dorothy Flanagan, Benj. Thomas, Michael Craudereuf, Jackie Stillwell, and David Bourns, growing out of weekends at Pendle Hill "in search of a Quaker philosophy of education."

As always, I owe thanks to my friends in the Lilly Library at Earlham: Evan Farber, Tom Kirk, Elaine Nelson and Christine Larson, and to Tom Hamm, Archivist of the Quaker Collection. These colleagues helped me find and get some very obscure materials. I also thank Amanda Abney, secretary to the English Department, for countless ways she has helped me, especially with the intricasies of word-processing and index-making.

I began this project while holding the D. Elton Trueblood Chair in Christian Thought and completed it while holding the College's Chair in Multidisciplinary Education, both of which allowed me leaves for research and writing. I thank then-President Richard Wood and Provost Len Clark for those opportunities. I also had a chance to teach a seminar

on Quaker education under a Knight Grant, and I thank my
student-colleagues in that seminar, Erin Seaton, Beth
Baldwin, Susanna Williams, Matt Thompson, and Jill Miller,
for the fun we had working together and the insights they
contributed to my writing.

Finally, and always, I thank my family, Margaret, Mary
(who is also my colleague in the English Department, so gets
thanked twice), Patrick and James. Their irreverent humor
gives me a sense of proportion and keeps me on my mettle;
their capacity for joy keeps me joyful, and their clear-eyed
love supports me every day of my life.

—Paul A. Lacey

Introduction

Growing into Goodness
Essays on Quaker Education

A Quaker Philosophy of Education?

I once asked a student who had graduated from a highly experimental, "alternative" high school, what she thought of her experience there. She said, 'Well, a lot of it was very good, but every term we would get together to choose a topic we were going to learn about, and then, before we could begin learning about that topic, someone would say 'how can we study this until we know what learning really is?' So we would begin talking about what we meant by 'learning'. And that would lead us to a discussion of how we know anything, to why learning is valuable, to the ends of learning, farther and farther back to first principles of learning. By the time we felt we understood enough about the nature and purposes of learning to get started on our topic, the term was almost over, so we never got very far with learning about anything but what we meant by 'learning.'"

When I have told Quaker educators that I have been studying whether there is, or has been, a Quaker philosophy of education, some of them have gotten the haunted look I imagine coming over the faces of my student and her friends each time someone asked that fatal question, what learning *really* is. Naturally, I too have gone back and back, following the path of infinite regress which opens up when we ask certain kinds of questions. Such inquiries are as enticing as they are frustrating. They take us back to those days when the big ideas always came clearest to us between two and three in the morning and after the third pot of coffee, when we *finally* knew both the purpose of life *and* whether a tree falling in the forest makes a sound if no one is there to hear it. And we miss the energy and intensity of those times, even if we are relieved that we no longer have to drink that much coffee or stay up that late for knowledge.

In these essays, I am not going to ask my readers to go that far back with me. I have to spend some time clearing the path, offering working definitions for some terms, and framing my questions, but I am emphatically *not* interested in arriving at a geometric proof that Quakers either have or have not had a philosophy of education. Instead, I want to use that question as a way of understanding what it has been like for Quakers to do education over nearly 350 years. I am less interested in abstract doctrines called philosophies than in how our predecessors in the community of faith have discerned their calling to educate their own and others' children in the daily challenges of their times and places. In such discernment, principles and the practices derived from them get enunciated which at least informally deserve the name "philosophies." I am interested in continuities and discontinuities, in what it has been like for Friends, under obedience to God's leadings as they understood them, to be educators.

My studies take their beginnings from John Reader's comment in his Swarthmore Lecture, *Of Schools and Schoolmasters,* that Friends have never had a philosophy of education, though they have thought they had. That remark, which contradicts so much conventional wisdom, has continued to work in my imagination, requiring further consideration. Certainly we might ask, if we have not had a Quaker philosophy of education, why worry about it now? Or, if there has been no shaping philosophy, has something else filled its place? Have we had an *ethos* in which teaching and learning take place, a peculiar "atmosphere"—the word recurs frequently as students and teachers describe Quaker schools in the past half-century—which is characteristic of Quaker education? If so, how can we describe that *ethos*, and what in Quakerism accounts for it?

I am one of those who always thought there was a Quaker philosophy of education, if only because, as Howard Brinton argues, our educational practice grows out of a Quaker philosophy of life. While casting about for how to get into my study, I sought out works, often anthologies of writings on education, entitled or under the subject heading "Philosophy of Education." One helpful survey of the subject scrupulously introduced each writer whose starting-point was in any way spiritual, with a variation on the phrase "not so much a philosopher as a mystic." The mystics included Plato, Comenius, Froebel, Pestalozzi, and Montessori—all good company for Quakers. Clearly, Philosophy of Education would be the poorer without its mystics, though we might not be satisfied with only a Mysticism of Education. I did not expect a Quaker philosophy of education (if there were one) to be highly systematic or the crafted work of trained philosophers, any more than our theology has been the crafted work of trained theologians. I expected it to be experiential, anchored in that cluster of openings about the nature of God and humans' encounter with God which brought the Religious Society of Friends into being. I expected that a Quaker philosophy of education (if there were one) would develop over time, in response to continuing revelation and in response to the pressures of historical events, but I thought we would be able to discern the chief hallmarks of a philosophy—clarity, coherence and consistency in fundamental principles, testing of principles against experience and the challenge of competing ideas, and adaptability to new knowledge and

xvii

insights. I thought we could find some true continuities in belief and practice from the seventeenth to the end of the twentieth century which shaped us as teachers, as founders of schools, and as parents and caretakers of the young. And I hoped that such continuities would help us conceive how to teach, how to organize and sustain schools, how to do the work of teaching-and-learning, in the future. The chief test of any philosophy is whether it lights our way from where we are to where we are going.

My colleagues in History at Earlham College have taught me a useful distinction between an historical *study* and an *essay* in history. What follows is a collection of *essays*, a work of synthesis, an attempt to come to my own understanding of a topic by reflecting on what others have said and thought, and in the process to make a contribution to the discussion. My sources have been histories of many schools, students' accounts of their experiences, memoirs and letters by teachers and headmasters, schools' missions statements, other Quakers' writings on the aims of Quaker education, and studies placing educational practice in relation to Quaker history.

In these essays, I try to address practical issues of teaching and learning from historical perspectives, to see what insights Quakerism in particular has offered, and to discover what influences have been most powerful on Quakers concerned with education. The first four essays address issues of current practice in Quaker education: the spiritual purposes of our schools, how schools interpret the phrase "that of God in everyone," the place of the meeting for worship, the business method and the testimonies in the educational project. The next three essays examine some perennial issues: finding suitable teachers, addressing the economics of Quaker education, and discovering what a "guarded education" ought to be.

The final three essays survey affinities with and influences from several philosophies of education, among them the work of Comenius, Pestalozzi, Froebel, Montessori and Dewey, and discuss the connections of ethics and *ethos* in Quaker education.

While I have been reading and writing, I have also tried to practice the craft of teaching at Earlham College, and I have sought out opportunities to learn from the practical experience of other Quaker educators. I accepted every invitation I got to visit schools under the care of Friends, and participated in a series of conferences with teachers, administrators, parents, trustees involved in Quaker education. I owe all those colleagues a great debt for what they have taught me about our common work. I have had the least opportunity to learn about what it means to be a Quaker teaching in public schools or in non-Quaker institutions in the United States, and what Quaker education is like in Africa, the Middle East, Japan and Central and South America. Most Quakers who are educators do not work in Quaker institutions, and they may well experience the most severe tests of whether there is a Quaker philosophy of education and have much to contribute to the discussion. A recent survey reported that Quaker schools in the United States connected to the Friends Council on Education are teaching around 27,000 students at present; Kenyan Friends estimate that their schools teach around half a million students.

Some Quaker educators, deeply engaged in the day-to-day work of running schools and working with young children or adolescents, have gently suggested that my starting question is not really very useful for their work. They enjoy our conversations, but for practical reasons they raise what are for them prior questions: is there a Quaker anthropology, sociology, politics, economics, psychology, or theology of education? Those are all valuable questions, but they have not seized me as *my* primary questions, and even if one's initial question is not the most useful, it may be the only means to discern and pursue better ones.

But even those colleagues who would prefer to consider other questions have supported and encouraged my work. Urging me on, my friend Bill Oats, long-time Head of the Friends' School in Hobart, Tasmania, even suggested a working title, *Toward A Quaker View of Education*. (A similar title worked well to popularize sex, after all.) The title I have chosen, Harold Loukes' phrase, "Growing Into Goodness," expresses our aspiration for Quaker education in contemporary language.

ONE

The Spiritual Purposes of a Quaker School

It is not the fault of the holy that it has become a middle-class weapon to keep children good.

The essence of education is that it be religious. A religious education is an education which inculcates duty and reverence.

Mr. Cadbury knew that wonder cannot be taught; it can only be inspired. Wonder is not a fact about something, but the joy that accompanies a connection between oneself and the world.[1]

Encountering the Sacred

Friends take it as a defining condition that a Quaker school hold a regular and required Meeting for Worship for the whole school community. We believe that Meeting for Worship is central to the life of the school, and many would expect the worship to take the form of silent waiting. What validates and *in-forms* Meeting for Worship and the practice of silence, however, are two fundamental convictions which Quaker faith and practice affirm: that God, the ultimate source of the sacred, exists, and that human beings can know and respond to God's leadings.

The sacred: what is most worthy of our focused attention and response. As Richard Eldridge and other writers remind us, the word *worth* lies hidden in the word *worship*. *Worthship* is an act of acknowledging and affirming whatever has made itself known in our lives as of ultimate worth. The sacred carries its own authentication, for it draws us into encounter with the *mysterium fascinans et tremendum*, "the fascinating and shaking mystery," which makes us feel our littleness without diminishing us because it lets us know ourselves as part of this vast whole. The sacred draws us into unity with it. Kim Hays reminds us, ". . . sacredness requires a stepping outside of oneself, an ability to lose oneself in the strength of something larger and more important than the psyche." *Wholeness, health,* and *holy* all have common roots in words meaning completeness and fulfillment. [2]

   When we encounter something which reveals sacredness, holiness, ultimate worth, whether what we encounter is *out there,* in the world around us, or *in here,* in the interior world of the soul, or in the interplay of the inward and the outward reality, the encounter calls us to respond. Sometimes our only response is a deep feeling—awe, reverence, a sense of completeness. Then it is sufficient simply to say *yes.* At other times we feel ourselves drawn to dedicate ourselves to it, to protect and preserve it, to live more purely in its presence. We feel we have been given a calling. In the presence of the sacred, we want to become better, more deliberate in our actions, more careful, and reflective.

DESCRIBING THE SACRED

For all of our nearly 350 year history, the majority of Quakers world-wide have described their experience of the sacred or Divine not only in "God-language" but specifically in Christian language. When George Fox had his great opening, it was that "there is one, even Christ Jesus, who can speak to thy condition." Quakers have believed that every human being can be so addressed, every one can have his or her condition known and spoken to, because to be human is to enter life endued with the Light of Christ. Thus the sacred is always within us as potentiality, waiting to be addressed, answered, called into fuller being. This is the Light which existed from the beginning of time, which finds its fullest expression in Jesus of Nazareth but which is known in all people, whether or not they have heard of Jesus.

Because the language through which Friends have described their experiential knowledge of the Divine has been both particularist Christian and Universalist, over time the connotations of such Quaker terms as "the Light," "the Inner Light," "that of God in everyone," have widened, and the metaphorical connections have loosened. Quaker schools, like Quaker meetings, are not of one mind on the meanings of these terms. For some Quakers, these terms are still direct metaphors for the Christian experience of God. For others, equally sincere and of good will, they are useful images, sometimes "mere" metaphors, for humanist or secular descriptions of human possibilities. "That of God in everyone" encapsulates the guiding belief of Quaker education, and is the phrase which probably appears most frequently in the mission statements of schools in the unprogrammed Quaker tradition. It has both the benefit and the detriment of being very general; its inclusiveness is the product of its imprecision. Going behind all these shorthand terms, we can affirm that the primary spiritual purpose of a Quaker school is to help prepare us to be open to the sacred, to learn how to recognize the sacred when people encounter it, and to discover their most appropriate responses to it.

The Sacred and Ritual

Humans are symbol-making creatures. We respond to the sacred by creating symbolic actions, rituals—personal or communal practices which will open us to greater awareness of the source of supreme worth, which will align us in a *participation mystique,* an inner activity which unites us with what comes to us as "unity, knowledge and power." [3] Some rituals will be prolonged and elaborate—the chanting and dancing of the Hopi, the ecstatic dancing of the Sufi, the celebration of the Mass, a hymn-sing or a performance of Bach's B Minor Mass, the Hasidim's welcoming of the Sabbath. Some will be as apparently simple as Zen "sitting," or Quaker "waiting." Each helps prepare the soul to perceive and then welcome the sacred into itself. We create forms to achieve "centering," techniques or practices of meditation, group activities which help bring us together into a gathering presence. We try to withdraw from the ordinary into the heightened awareness which glimpses of the sacred can bring, or we try to bring the ordinary into that transforming presence. Our feelings and intuitions—of reverence, awe, trust, completeness, joy, dedication, love—are first drawn toward the *source* or *center,* the *sacred occasion,* where they are focused, purified, and then redirected outward. So reverence for the source of creation leads to stewardship for the creation, love for the Divine leads to compassion for others, trust in the Divine enlarges our capacity to trust others. Knowing ourselves as God's children, as tenants in the world God created, John Woolman says, makes us want to be "answerable to the design of our creation. . . ." We "feel a desire to take hold of every opportunity to lessen the distresses of the afflicted and increase the happiness of the creation." [4]

DANGERS OF THE SACRED

Seeking the sacred can be full of dangers. The greatest danger in "being at one with something greater than the self," is receiving as ultimate what is only partial. The worst kinds of fanaticism and totalitarianism purport to embody a sacred vision, and radically isolated and wounded selves long for something absolute in which to find rest. Paul Tillich describes this as embracing the demonic, giving our centers away to what is not an "ultimate concern" but to such false gods and idols as a nation, an ethnic identity, personal wealth, or fame.[5]

The theater director and critic Peter Brook points to another danger, growing from a serious lack in the larger culture: ". . . We have lost all sense of ritual and ceremony. . . . We do not know how to celebrate, because we do not know what to celebrate." There are two climaxes of celebration, he says, loud wild applause or the climax of silence, but "We have largely forgotten silence. It even embarrasses us." Lacking healthy outlets for celebrating the sacred, we may be drawn into unhealthy ones, anxious, obsessive behavior which mimics rituals of celebration.[6]

Yet another danger is that we can make ritual an end in itself and become fixated on its perfect performance, its perfect beauty, until the ritual becomes an obstacle to knowing what it points toward. Religious communities break apart in quarrels over how their rituals should be done. Communicants simmer with anger if the priest does not say the words right, or if the words are too new-fangled, or not inclusive enough, or fail to meet some other private test. Some Quakers have private rules for how long the silence should last before someone speaks in meeting, how long the minimally acceptable time is before another person may speak, how close the messages must be to a central theme. Some have private taboos for the messages they will listen to: they must *only*, or must *never*, employ particular words or phrases.

The dangers of empty ritual, though real, can easily be over-stated. The counter-danger is that we assume that "ritual" can only be described by such modifiers as "empty," "dead," or "meaningless." It is perhaps a particular failing of Quakers that we are so quick to pronounce all ritual false and empty. Often this only means that we have both our rituals and our obsessions, but believe our freedom consists in being off-hand, careless and slovenly in performing them.

HABITS OF SILENCE AND ATTENTION

The spiritual purposes of a Quaker school require three inter-connected tasks: to help its members prepare for encounters with the sacred; to help them develop a repertoire of ways to invite the sacred more fully into their lives, to enlarge its presence in their souls, for spiritual refreshment and growth; to help them become more skillful in connecting their knowledge of the sacred presence to how they pursue their daily activities, to become more "answerable to the design of their creation." Quaker education makes its greatest contributions to this work first by introducing students to the preparatory practices of silent waiting and then to the deeper disciplines of meeting for worship, and by affirming the links between worship and our daily lives, especially in our service to others.

Describing the plans for Ackworth School in 1779, Dr. John Fothergill says "To habituate children, from their early infancy, to silence and attention, is of the greatest advantage to them, not only as a preparative to their advancement in a religious life, but as the ground-work of a well-cultivated understanding." Early habits of "silent attention" strengthen our capacity for patience and recollection.[7]

Reflecting on Quaker education up to the mid-eighteenth century, Samuel Tuke says, the "doctrine of an inward Divine Light with reference to the great duties of life," modified the character of those who received it, affected the means pursued in the moral training of young people, and had an influence on the intellectual character of the rising generation. Though pains were taken to prevent the influence of bad examples, and to fill young people's minds with "the great principles of revealed religion," in Quaker schools the greater stress was put on directing the young "to the use of their own measure of spiritual understanding—to believe that the Creator of all things was present with them, quickening them Himself in the things which were pleasing to Him, and leading them to the full acceptance of Christ as their Saviour and Governor."

Samuel Tuke emphasizes the power of the doctrine of an inward Divine Light, and Fothergill gives weight to developing habits of life which spring from that doctrine— silence, attention, patience, recollection—but they concur in believing that together the doctrine and practice exert profound influence on both the moral and the intellectual life. Tuke argues ". . . it was impossible to be habituated to self-converse without intellectual cultivation. The habit of thinking for a man's self, on the most important of all subjects, leads naturally to general freedom of thought. . . ." The influence of the doctrine led to seeing "alike the value of liberty and order."[8]

SILENCE AND THE CLASSROOM

Stressing the value of habits of silence and attention for both the religious life and "the improvement of the human mind" shapes some powerful pedagogical strategies. The teaching-

learning process changes when silence is neither an imposi-
tion, nor a punishment, nor a deprivation, but an invitation
into a milieu where time is available to pay attention to things,
to see and hear more fully. Philip Wragge reminds us that
Friends have always recognized two sources of revelation: the
inner—the Light, the Teacher, the Christ within—and the
outer—the created world, including other people. Quaker
education was always rooted in practical education because
the world was worthy to be studied. So we must learn to attend to more than one *locus* for meaning, to learn when to
center within and when outside the self, to learn when to
center on another person, a task, a calling, a text which speaks
to our condition. William Penn exhorts us to "Delight to
step home, within yourselves, I mean, and commune with
your own hearts, and be still . . ." but we furnish our home
with the peace of the created world, the love of other people,
the wisdom derived from experience, the riches of reading
and memory. In his poem "Prayer Before Study," Theodore
Roethke warns:

> A fool can play at being solemn,
> Revolving on his spinal column.
> Oh Lord, deliver me from all
> Activity centripetal.[9]

The inner and the outer must correspond, must "answer" one
another. All life is holy, but we need glimpses of the sacred to
remind us of that fact. Insight into and awareness of the
sacred may be a gift of God, but like all such gifts it needs to
be enhanced by disciplined practice. We seek "unity with
the creation" as well as within ourselves.

Quaker receptivity to the study of science, a strong characteristic since our earliest days, rests not only on the conviction that all truth is from God, and on the capacity to

trust that the sacred can be revealed through the physical world, but also on the capacity to *wait* and *attend* quietly as an observation or experiment unfolds. The child who learns how to sit still while waiting for a bird to land or a deer to emerge from the thicket is laying the foundation for greeting the sacred, for centering outside the self, for knowing herself as a part of a world of beauty and order, *as well as* for learning how to collect data. The power of this kind of silence is attested to by two former students at Germantown Friends School, recalling more than a dozen years afterwards the experience of learning science in the lower school. They write of Joseph Cadbury, their teacher,

> . . . there was something rare about Mr. Cadbury that distinguishes him in one's mind from all other teachers. He knew a lot about nature . . . , and he could explain scientific data with magnificent clarity; but it wasn't filling our heads with facts that he had in mind. We remember a strange silence that he liked to keep, as if the important facts of Nature lay beyond the reach of names and explanations. . . . When someone asked a really good question, he would roll his head from side to side, look into each of our expectant faces . . . and he wouldn't say a word. In that Silence there was something else, that no words could touch, that words if they were spoken would obscure. It was a feeling . . . that came gently at first, but grew in the Silence until it was everywhere and in everything. . . . His Silence was a way of inspiring wonder within us. . . . It was a Silence that recalls our school's greatest classroom: the Meeting House.[10]

To practice silent waiting can help create a sense of proportion about oneself and one's place in the world. Elise

Boulding stresses that children need opportunities for *solitude* in their lives, times for being alone with the self so that integration of the world outside and the interior world of the mind can occur. ". . . A sudden mastery is gained over the interior machinery which sifts, sorts, combines what comes in with what is already there. It is the first great step in spiritual development, because it involves recognition of Creator and created." Boulding tells us the fruits of solitude for children are "a sense of who and what they are, whence they came, their place in God's world. And out of this positive and secure relationship with the universe comes the freedom to 'play' with creation in the best sense of the word."[11]

Boredom, which M.H. Abrams has called the *sine qua non* of scholarship, can only be overcome by habits of patience and "silent attention." Those same habits can transform the classroom. Kim Hays wisely reminds us that, in the best *and* the worst Quaker classrooms alike, students do more of the talking than the teachers. Neither the quantity of talking, nor even the magic "one hundred percent class participation," determines the educational value of a class discussion. Discussion is educative when we practice listening thoughtfully and respectfully, when we allow pauses for reflection, when the student who needs an extra few moments of time to form an idea knows that it is available.

Observations of "discussion" classes reveal that students usually speak only a small fraction of the class time. Studies of the average length of time between a teacher's asking a question in class and then answering it him or herself, put it at about fifteen seconds. What happens if a teacher does not answer the question, but waits quietly for thirty, forty-five, even sixty whole seconds, so that students have time to entertain the question? At first, students are anxious to "break" the awkward silence, but if the teacher models patient waiting, what it means to ask or answer a question changes, from quizzing about isolated facts to organizing facts and perceptions into higher-order, more complex ideas. Joseph Cadbury's students say, "We remember someone asking once, 'Why are there stars in the sky?' It was a good question, and we knew it because it was met with Silence."[12] Such waiting can teach how to *entertain* a question, to be hospitable to it as we are hospitable to a friend. If silence is welcomed, to allow time for entertaining a question or propounding one's own, students can learn how to wait for one another to contribute to a cooperative activity. The spirit of the classroom can change. At its best, Quaker education teaches the same lesson in the classroom or laboratory, in fieldwork, as well as in meeting for worship. Thomas Farquhar, Head of Westtown School, has called this "worship across the curriculum." To create a school day which is, in Philip Wragge's phrase, "punctuated by silence," is one way we can live the principle that all of life is holy.

MEETING FOR WORSHIP

We should neither claim too much nor expect too little from meeting for worship in our schools. There are too many recollections of school or college meetings nicknamed "study hall," too many former students who remember counting windows, beams, nails, to pass the time, to allow us to overstate the impact of meeting for worship. In his *American Memoir*, Henry Seidel Canby, who graduated from Friends School in Wilmington, Delaware in 1896, is sharply critical of its shortcomings. The teachers were not educated, he claims: "They had knowledge but not knowing what to do with it, passed it on to us in the raw condition of

fact. . . . Everything was sensible, practical, and efficient except the purpose of it all which was supposed to be education
but was actually cramming under discipline. . . . *There was
no philosophy of education visible in our school, and it was one of
the best.*"[italics added] But when he comes to describe the
meeting for worship, his tone changes:

> And yet on the green-cushioned benches under the
> bare beams of that meeting house, with tree branches
> fretting at the windows, where a hundred of us young-
> sters sat in silence for most of the hour, I had my most
> pervasive religious experiences. I did not think; I did
> not knowingly feel. My meditation was wordless and
> almost without content. . . . Doors opened far within;
> the consciousness withdrew itself from externals;
> nerves, relaxed into tranquility, were of an exquisite sen-
> sitiveness.[13]

Kim Hays reports that few of the students in the three
Quaker boarding schools she studied seem to consider
either meeting for worship or required service projects as
experiences of the sacred.[14] Worship can be profoundly
educative, but we do not make it a part of school life
simply as a teaching device but as an end in itself. Those of
us who worship do so because we need to. We seek the sacred
because we need it. We recommend habits of silence and
attention for many benefits, but first of all we practice
them for their own sake, for the refreshment and renewal
they bring us. Henry Seidel Canby does not sentimentalize
his experience. Indeed, his description of meeting for worship is almost comic in its bluntness:

> I can think of no other instance where a religious
> ceremony, not respected and in the charge of the crusted

and incapable, almost meaningless in the words articu-
lated, has had so powerful an effect upon so many who
believed themselves alien. It made me in some respects
a Quaker for life.

One wishes to write in the margin next to these words,
"do not try this at *our* school," but Canby offers an important
testimony. The "crusted and incapable" Quakers who had
charge of the school, and the teachers who taught there, may
have had neither education nor a philosophy of education,
but they shared what they had, "a secret which was perhaps
the only philosophy that could protect the innermost
mind. . . . They had access to quiet."[15] Silence is not equivalent to worship, it is a milieu out of which worship can emerge.
Dietrich Bonhoeffer has written, "Right speech comes out of
silence, and right silence comes out of speech." As we must
learn to use silence in the classroom or the field, we must
learn to use it in worship. Out of deep silence, singing can
emerge, prayer or poetry, recollection or confession can arise
to be shared with the waiting group. Robert Barclay tells of
coming into the gathered meetings of Quakers and finding
the good raised up in himself and the evil lessened.
It is no wonder that he should emphasize the importance of
regularly seeing one another's faces and being part of "a joint
and visible fellowship," when we worship. [16] Susanna Williams
says that the

> core values of Quakerism are manifested variously within
> Friends schools, but the defining moment is Meeting
> for Worship. In Meeting for Worship, even more, per-
> haps, than during the hustle and bustle of the school
> day, all voices are equally valuable. The school gathers
> to share time together, to center the hive of activity

that usually consumes active learning environments.
This basis of harmony and equality builds community.
It is in this community that the foundations of a Friends
school are laid.[17]

Notes

1. Peter Brook, *The Empty Space,* New York, 1968, 45; Alfred
    North Whitehead, *Aims of Education and Other Essays,*
    1929, Free Press edition 1967, 14; Nathaniel Kahn and
    Daniel Cristol, "Joseph Cadbury," in *Studies in Education,*
    Germantown Friends School, Winter 1987, No. 52, 31.

2. See Richard L. Eldridge's essay, "Learning as Worship,"
    Friends Council on Education, 1984, and Parker J.
    Palmer's "Meeting for Learning: Education in a Quaker
    Context," Pendle Hill, 1976. Richard Eldridge makes a
    distinction between religion, "our experience of God," and
    philosophy, "the way we structure our relationships under
    God's oversight." See also Rudolph Otto, *The Idea of the
    Holy,* London, 1924, especially Chapters IV-VI for the
    classical description of the holy, and Appendix VIII,
    "Silent Worship," where he discusses Quaker worship. Kim
    Hays, *Practicing Virtues: Moral Traditions at Quaker and
    Military Boarding Schools,* Berkeley, University of California,
    1994, 208.

3. In Howard H. Brinton, *Friends for Three Hundred Years,*
    Harper Bros, 1952, Pendle Hill, 1967, 19.

4. Phillips P. Moulton, ed. John Woolman, *The Journal and
    Major Essays of John Woolman,* "A Plea for the Poor,"
    Oxford University Press, 1971, 239, 241.

5.   Hays, *Practicing Virtues*, 208; Paul Tillich, *The Dynamics of Faith*, Harper, New York, 1958, 12, 17.

6.   Brook, *Empty Space*, 45-47.

7.   Dr. John Fothergill, *A Letter to a Friend in the Country, Relative to the Intended School at Ackworth, 1779*, in *The Works of John Fothergill: with some account of his life*, 1784, 461-73.

8.   Samuel Tuke, *Five Papers on the Past Proceedings and Experience of the Society of Friends, in Connexion with the Education of Youth*, Read at the Meeting of the Friends' Educational Society, at Ackworth, in the Years 1838, 1839, 1840, 1841, 1842, 31-33.

9.   *Advice of William Penn to His Children*, Everyman's edition, 101. Theodore Roethke, *Collected Poems*, Doubleday, New York, 1966, 14.

10. Cristol, "Joseph Cadbury," 30-31.

11. Elise Boulding, *Children and Solitude*, Pendle Hill Pamphlet 125, 1962, 12-13, 30-31.

12. Cristol, "Joseph Cadbury," 31.

13. Henry Seidel Canby, *American Memoir*, 1947, 55, 59. In fairness, we should consider how faculty at Wilmington saw their situation around the time Henry Seidel Canby is describing. In 1891 the agenda for a Teachers Meeting proposes two subjects for discussion: "1. Untruthfulness in Children. 2. Are the teachers of Friends School subjected to an undue strain? If so, what is the cause?" *Friends School in Wilmington*, An Account of the Growth of the School from Its Beginnings to the Present Time with Mention of Some of the Men and Women Who Have Been a Part of It, (two hundredth anniversary) Wilmington, 1948, 40, 76.

14. Hays, *Practicing Virtues*, 211, 215.

15. Canby, *American Memoir*, 76-77.

16. Dietrich Bonhoeffer *Life Together*, Harper and Row, 1954, 78; Robert Barclay, *Barclay's Apology in Modern English*, Dean Freiday, ed., 1967, Proposition XI, Worship, 254, 243.

17. Susanna Williams, "Defining Moments: Meeting for Worship in Friends Elementary Schools," unpublished essay written for a seminar on Quaker education at Earlham College, Winter, 1995.

TWO

That of God in Every One

Every pebble is unique, but profoundly unique objects are rare.

*The spirit incarnate in the group, whether thought of as God,
His Word, or the risen Christ, could enter and transform each
member. This is education in its most profound, most thor-
ough-going aspect.*[1]

Constitutive Metaphors

We think both *in* and *through* metaphors. In order to make
ideas and experiences more coherent to ourselves, we
consciously create similitudes and comparisons. For the sake
of accommodating our explanations or arguments to our
listeners' experience, we search out metaphors appropriate
for them. Thus we consciously think *in* metaphor to accom-
modate an idea to the experience of our reader, to clarify or
illustrate what we mean, to persuade someone of the rightness of our position. We also think *through* metaphors, as we
read through eyeglasses; they provide the magnifying or
corrective lenses which are our only means for clear seeing.
In effect, they become our eyes. We may use these metaphors
to persuade another to our position, but they seem to come
to us less as consciously-created figures of speech than as

17

the only way we can say what we know. When St. Paul speaks of being crucified in Christ, for example, he is trying to define precisely what his experience of conversion was, not looking for a vivid figure of speech to catch his audience. The metaphors *by means of which* we think, are *constitutive*, and it is their nature that they seem to choose us, not we them, by embodying reality for us so fully that we take them as our only way to express reality. Because they are so important to our understanding of ourselves, belief in them as literal fact becomes for some a test of orthodoxy and faithfulness. When the constitutive metaphors die, so does a culture or tradition.

For many Friends, and so for many Friends schools, "there is that of God in every one" is such a *constitutive metaphor*, a fundamental explanation of reality, an originating, controlling image around which other metaphors and images cohere and from which they take their meaning. Canby Jones writes, "Modern Friends frequently say that 'There is that of God in everyone' is the basic Quaker teaching of Fox," though

> . . . it occurs only five times in the whole of the Nickall's edition of Fox's *Journal*. According to Lewis Benson it occurs only one hundred three additional times in the rest of Fox's published writings. By contrast 'Light' or 'Light of Christ' occurs one hundred twenty four times in the *Journal*.[2]

For some Friends, and friends of Friends, the phrase stresses the universalism which is one part of Quaker belief, and its brevity and breadth of generality provide the benefit of avoiding difficulties arising from more obviously formal theological language. For others, especially evangelical Friends, the phrase is overtly doctrinal, encapsulating the doctrines of religious liberalism. Certainly it carries the weight which we find in any concentrated shorthand phrase by which a group of people remind themselves of foundational beliefs.

"That of God in everyone" appears frequently in school mission statements and similar descriptive documents as a way of connecting a number of the school's defining beliefs, attitudes, and institutional practices to its Quakerism. Frequently, "that of God" and images of "the Light" and "the Inner Light" are used interchangeably as synonyms. Some Quaker school statements give richly textured descriptions of the term: "a Divine Spark which, when nurtured, can illumine our lives," "a Divine Light in each of us that deserves our loving attention," "a divine presence in each person which influences our decision-making, leads us to the truths we seek, and commands our highest respect." They describe the Quaker stance as "openness to the Light," and "respect for the Light in every person."

Many mission statements assert "that of God" as the source of each person's worth and dignity, the reason for self-respect as well as mutual respect between people, and the explanation for such institutional practices designed to foster a spiritual community as a weekly meeting for worship, emphasis on community service, and shared participation in decision-making. Similarly, affirming "there is that of God in every one" introduces discussions of both Quaker testimonies and attitudes toward learning in many schools' materials.

For the testimonies, it undergirds commitments to such individual character traits as integrity, simplicity, and truth-seeking; to non-violent living, peaceful resolutions of conflict, and commitments to peace and justice; to equality among people, with particular emphasis at present on racial and gender equality; and to environmental responsibility and stewardship for the natural world.

For attitudes toward learning, and pedagogical practices growing from them, the phrase is frequently cited to validate respect for each individual's uniqueness, creativity, and originality, appreciation of cultural and religious diversity, trust in others, openness to a wide range of sources for enlightenment, and an emphasis on cooperative and collaborative learning. Each person is affirmed to have the capacity to seek, and desire to learn, the truth and to achieve inner discipline. It is asserted that because "there is that of God in everyone" we each possess "unique talents and abilities," and "special gifts and abilities" which are best called forth by teaching methods characterized by individualized instruction, small, experiential classes which stress collaborative and self-paced, rather than competitive, learning opportunities.

THAT OF GOD IN STUDENTS

Who are our students? They are gentle, kind, loving, open, playful, funny, childlike, sensitive, and easily touched by others' pain. They are curious, eager to learn, conscientious and hard-working. They are also harsh, cruel toward weaker people, smug, judgmental, thin-skinned, humorless, self-centered, self-righteous. They are dull, lazy, uninterested in learning, plodding, pleasure-seeking, over-stimulated, deficient in inner resources or initiative, conformist, prey to trivial fads and fashions. One could soften those contradictions by resorting to carefully balanced "some are . . . but some are . . ." sentences. It is true: some are curious, while some are dull; and some are gentle while some are cruel, but the more complex truth is that our students live such contradictions internally, being at once curious and dull, gentle and cruel, eager to learn and deficient in inner resources or initiative. In this respect they are very much like their parents and their teachers. The gentle advice of a tract of 1832 is worth repeating: "Do not suppose they are always inattentive through design; some have slow parts, and all are giddy. . . . We were once scholars, and perhaps as dull and perverse as those we teach. . . ."[3]

Our students are different at different ages: they are perhaps gentler and more malleable when younger, perhaps more difficult to understand or influence as they get older. Teachers speak from experience of the "hormone hell" of eighth grade or the zombie-like stretches of mid-adolescence. This morning's warm, funny, outgoing student can be this afternoon's withdrawn, sour lump of misery. Developmental theory can explain, even if it can never fully prepare us for, such rapid alternations of mood, temperament, and character.

Our students are also the products of family life and social environment. Many are psychologically strong and healthy, from strong and healthy families. But many are wounded, damaged, suffering, with apparently few coping resources developed except withdrawal or anger. Half or more of our students may come from families severely strained, dysfunctional, or "broken," struggling with problems of alcohol or drug abuse. Some have their own addiction problems, have experienced psychological, physical and sexual abuse, know great wealth and great deprivation simultaneously. Some are sent to our schools as to custodial institutions. School needs to be a guarded haven, a place of safety, for all our students, but for some it is the only safe, stable place they have known, and that means it will be the place of acting out and testing as well as of trust.

Fostering the Light Within or Individualism?

In *Practicing Virtues*, Kim Hays has given us our most detailed and current study of how three contemporary Quaker boarding schools "attempt to practice a certain way of life and teach adolescents to be certain kinds of people." Many of her insights seem to be applicable beyond the three schools, describing life in both Quaker day and boarding schools and, making adjustments for their different developmental stages, younger and older students. As Hays understands our purposes, "Equality, community, simplicity, and peace are all chapters in the Quaker story of fostering the Inner Light in every individual," and the commitment to non-violence grows from the conviction among some Friends school teachers and administrators that ". . . at their core, no matter what they have done, all people are good, because, as one Friend said, 'their essence is good'—that is a basic Quaker tenet." A boarding school dean says, ". . . There is that of God in all . . . kids . . . something that is unique and spectacular and that deserves celebration," and in her own analysis Hays interchanges "that of God, or what is best in every individual."[4] "That of God in everyone" equates with individualism, which readily turns into a "culte de moi."

For most of the students at these three Quaker boarding schools, and probably at other Quaker day and boarding schools as well, "The Quaker project of bringing out the Inner Light translates into the desirability of expressing one's inner self—in other words, being different from everyone else, being a unique, special individual." Community is a high value in our schools, but in Hays' analysis, "almost always equated less with cooperation than with tolerance for individual difference." The operating assumption is that the individual is on a search for his or her own true self; when the individual has found that self and shown it to the community, "it is then the responsibility of the community to receive you lovingly and, if necessary, to adapt to your needs." Both adults and students "reject the idea of self-transformation in favor of nurturing what is already believed to be within." A student, asked what lessons she thought the school wanted her to learn, ". . . snorted with contempt."

> I don't think there are any lessons. They want you to leave [here] with yourself. I don't think they want to influence anything . . . they just want to let you develop in the way you are going to develop, and show you how to take care of yourself.

Even when teachers hope to effect changes in students, they are likely to try to do so by engaging them in projects ostensibly aimed at changing the school. "The emphasis is on improving the school, not the students." [5]

The desire to encourage the Inner Light, understood as individuality, can lead to "various forms of well-intended deception." A disillusioned young teacher says that Quakers' ". . . spiritual, very positive, pro-individual perspective" leads them to believe that "people just accidentally do bad things—it's never intended at all." Another teacher reports,

> Because of this need for each person to feel good about themselves and feel important, we praise people who are really mediocre or poor . . . I think sending people out of here thinking that they are very, very special when they are really very ordinary—that's what nervous breakdowns are based on.

For a third teacher, such over-valuing of individualism leads to a "show of favoritism toward the odd, the disturbed, and the loudly needy," while strong, competent people are poorly treated. [6]

Quaker school adults reap what they sow, says Kim Hays: ". . . they preach 'listening to your inner voice,' 'being true to yourself,' 'finding your own values,' and other anti-conformist and also anti-communal slogans." It should not surprise them that students see so little obligation to the community or should obey only the rules they think are right for them. One student complained, "They say this is a Quaker community, but then they have a disciplinary committee and all kinds of organizations to keep people in line. . . . I thought Quakers weren't supposed to impose their values on other people."

At Quaker schools, Hays says,

> . . . we find the desire for self-expression and inquiry, social conscience, openness, and relations of equality. When this combination works, the result is harmony, warmth, and mental challenge; when it fails, there is chaos, cynicism, and a deep sense of betrayal. [7]

We want to know how to make that combination work more consistently and beneficially for our students, but the crucial question is, when it fails, what makes it do so? Is it misunderstanding or confusion of our purposes, is it mistaken or unattainable promises, which turn these healthy desires incoherent or self-contradictory and create "chaos, cynicism and a deep sense of betrayal"?

GROWING INTO GOODNESS

To address these questions, we must examine what we know about our students in the light of our constitutive metaphors, to discover whether their deeper meanings and resonances can speak to our students' condition. How can we acknowledge who they are, in their possibilities and their limitations, and give them grounds for hope which are dependable because rooted in knowledge of their lives? The British Quaker and educator Harold Loukes says we must start from an affirmation of the value of the child's humanity:

> . . . not a naive belief that he is born good, but a belief that he can grow into goodness. . . . The metaphors of the light and the seed, which Quakers have so often used, are not an assertion of the simple goodness of humanity, a doctrine which is equally abhorrent to theology and to psychology; but an expression of the belief that goodness grows from within and is not added from without. . . .[8]

Through casual, unreflective use, the phrases "that of God in every one" and "the Inner Light" have become worn down and lost much of their power and precision. That is the danger in how they are frequently invoked—by students, faculty, parents, and administrators in Quaker schools—to assert that every person is naturally and inevitably good, whatever his or her actions or attitudes, that one's ultimate worth lies in being different and therefore "individual," or that the Divine Spark within oneself equates with an advertising-entertainment industry's elitist, commodified definition of uniqueness, creativity, and originality, or with what Robert Bellah calls "expressive individualism."

"That of God in everyone" has in common with a number of other phrases from Quakerism's beginnings—the Light, the Seed, the Christ Within, the Inward Teacher—that it rests on the assertion in the Gospel of John, that every human being who comes into the world comes already possessed of the Light. But this is not the same thing as saying that everybody is basically good or has some good qualities, if we only dig deep enough. That easy optimism will not stand up to the test of daily experience, as we and our students know it. In order to be a source of strength for us and them, the gathering and rallying phrase, "that of God in everyone" must also be able to address the real evil that people do, the suffering they cause one another generation after generation.

Addressing the Witness Within

A number of passages in the writings of George Fox, Isaac Penington, John Woolman, and other Friends enlarge and enrich the central Quaker metaphor of the witness within. In 1655, at a time of great persecution, George Fox writes an epistle to suggest that any Friend who feels moved by the power of the Lord to offer himself or herself in place of a brother or sister in prison should do so,

> and heap coals of fire on the head of the adversaries of God . . . Hence you may go over the heads of the persecutors, and reach the witness of God in them all. . . .[9]

Here Fox urges direct non-violent confrontation with "the adversaries of God"—a good working definition of evil-doers—with the aim of afflicting their consciences, making them blush with shame as though they felt hot coals heaped on their heads.[10] There is no suggestion that Fox thinks the persecutors are just innocently mistaken. On the contrary, they are deliberately doing rotten things, and they are going to have to quit! Fox recommends a strategy to reach that of God in these evildoers *despite* themselves, to go over their heads and reach that inward witness which will tell them the evil they do.

In perhaps the fullest discussion of what the phrase means for him, in an epistle of 1656, Fox urges Friends,

> In the power of life and wisdom, and dread of the Lord God of life, and heaven, and earth, dwell, that in the wisdom of God over all ye may be preserved, and be a terror to all the adversaries of God, and a dread, answering that of God in them all, spreading the truth abroad, awakening the witness, confounding deceit, gathering up out of transgression into the life, the covenant of Light and peace with God.[11]

Be a terror and a dread to all God's adversaries by answering that of God in them, which is another way to say by awakening the witness within them: there is a prescription for running a school! Fox may sound harsh, but even gentle Isaac Penington tells us,

> He that will truly love God, must hear wisdom's voice within, at home, in his own heart; and he that will have her words known, and her spirit poured out to him, must turn at her reproof. Prov 1, 23 . . .[12]

The witness *for* God is a witness *against* us and our actions when we do wrong. M. K. Gandhi's nonviolent campaigns for Indian independence, like Martin Luther King, Jr.'s nonviolent civil rights campaigns in the United States, were predicated on this same understanding of how the witness within struggles against the will to persist in wrongdoing. Appealing to that of God in the persecutors will throw them into confusion, Fox says. They will be divided in themselves, perhaps doing even more willful, harmful things as they struggle against the inner witness. People can hate the Light, Fox tells us, when it shows them what they do not want to see.

Later in this same epistle of 1656, Fox says, ". . . the ministers of the spirit must minister to the spirit that is transgressed and in prison, which hath been in captivity in everyone. . . ." "That of God" is waiting to be set free, but until it is freed it is transgressed and languishes in the prison created by our own transgressions. Immediately following that passage comes the great exhortation, so often quoted by itself:

And this is the word of the Lord God to you all, and a charge to you all in the presence of the living God, be patterns, be examples in all countries, places, islands, nations, wherever you come; that your carriage and life may preach among all sorts of people and to them. Then you will come to walk cheerfully over the world, answering that of God in every one; whereby in them ye may be a blessing, and make the witness of God in them to bless you.[13]

As I understand this epistle, the witness, which Fox would also call the Christ within or that of God within, remains as *potentiality*, imprisoned in the spirit, as long as we will not see and correct whatever wrong we do. Isaac Penington tells us "When the Lord reaches to his witness in men and teaching their hearts by it, the enemy keeps a noise up to over bear the witness . . ."[14] The struggle is often terrible to overcome willfulness, selfishness, anger, the spirit of revenge, our readiness to hurt others for our own benefit. Letting go of so much, around which we have built the defenses of our lives, fills us with terror and dread, while we are doing it, whatever peace and satisfaction we may ultimately feel. We know this in our own experience, as do many of our students.

From our struggle to attend to the Light Within, we may gain what John Woolman calls "a feeling sense of the

conditions of others."[15] "Answering that of God" in others
means "knowing their condition," as the basis for "speaking
to their condition." After he has his first great opening,
that the Inward Teacher could teach him, George Fox goes
through terrible tests: he feels strange impulses, has disturbing
temptations in dreams, is horrified to learn that what is in
the hearts and minds of "wicked men" can be found in his
own, as well.

> . . . And I cried to the Lord, saying, 'Why should I be
> thus, seeing I was never addicted to commit those evils?'
> And the Lord answered that it was needful I should have
> a sense of all conditions, how else should I speak to all
> conditions; and in this I saw the infinite love of God. . . .[16]

MINDING THE WITNESS WITHIN

Fox believes that we become patterns and examples by
minding or attending to our own inward witness, which then
enables us to *answer* that of God, the witness, in others. That
lonely, strangulated voice in them hears a response, a
confirming voice—yes, this is how things should be. The
image of "that of God" is always associated with listening,
and answering, paying attention so that the pattern or
example will be able to speak to our need or condition.
Answering that of God in another is always speaking the
truth in love. A witness to the truth desires to speak with the
greatest accuracy about what we know or perceive and makes
an identity between what we say and our inner self. To want
to speak the truth in love requires being vulnerable to
learning our limitations, even to learning that we are wrong.
The truth is not merely accurate facts, though we must be as
correct in our statement of them as possible, but an inner
coherence. Friends have tended to use the terms "truth" and

"light" interchangeably as synonyms. If we come into the truth as though it were light, we are searched by it, required to look at ourselves and what we are saying in its clear radiance. We are strengthened, comforted, and warmed into life by it. Truth is healing, like the light; our motive in speaking it in love is to help healing to occur, in ourselves as much as in those we address. No matter how painful the truth, its dependability and the dependability of love give the hearer hope.

This examination of the language and practice of early Quakers does not imply that we can, or should, limit our understanding of such phrases as "that of God in everyone" and "the Inner Light" to their historic meaning. Trying to wear early Friends' ideas ready-made is no more use than trying to wear their clothes. But nothing is lost, and much gained, by enriching our casual use of their words with the psychological and spiritual wisdom their experience taught them.

The Light We Have in Common

Understanding them may help us deal with the over-emphasis on individualism, for example, for "that of God in every one" testifies far more to our *sameness* than to our individuality. It is the supreme gift of God which all humans have in common. We differ in "the measure" of our light, as age and experience give us more to work with, or in the degree to which we are obedient to the light we have been given, but every human who comes into the world has received the light. Michael Polanyi has written,

> Every pebble is unique, but profoundly unique objects
> are rare. Wherever these are found (whether in nature

or among the members of human society) they are interesting in themselves. They offer opportunity for intimate indwelling and for a systematic study of their individuality.[17]

It is true that William Penn praised George Fox, after his death, as "an original, no man's copy," but if we are to be, or follow, patterns and examples, what is usually called originality is not of great value.

Every teacher and administrator in a Friends school has come up against a student, or a parent, who, having failed to get his way after pulling every string imaginable, going over some people's heads, manipulating others, complains loudly "I thought this place cared about the *individual*." Quaker schools seem to be perpetually in the middle of a great allegorical drama, *The Tragical Conflict of the Individual and the Group*, in which the Individual plays a role like John Bunyan's Christian and the Group plays the part of all the wicked tempters and evil opponents. The assumption seems to be that *only* the individual is sacred, and that groups of individuals, no matter how hard they work at community, lose some degree of sacredness with every added soul. But Howard Brinton reminds us that the Light comes not only to individuals but to the waiting group, where, if way opens, it produces unity, knowledge, and power which in turn create behavior characterized by community, harmony, equality, and simplicity, which he identifies as the chief Quaker testimonies.[18] It can be an intensely frustrating experience to deal with such misreadings of Quakerism as rampant individualism, a "culte de moi," but part of caring for the individual is to keep reminding the self-centered and immature that *they* are not the only individuals in the world.

Clearer understanding of Quaker principles may help us achieve more of the benefits of collaboration and cooperation as expressions of community. It may help us to avoid over-praising modest accomplishments and practicing other "'well-intended deceptions" which actually demean our students. What a relief it can be to recognize that being worthy of respect does not depend on being different, odd, original, creative, or unique. Those are personal characteristics, often defined by wealth or social position, or the fads of lifestyle cliques or sub-cultures, attractive but easily inflated and over-valued, often as transitory, pretentious, and embarrassing as another generation's dress-styles. Every cliché of thought, speech, or style was once original. Someone has said, "In our society, everyone wants an A for originality." Bell bottoms, Nehru jackets, double-knit blazers, earth-shoes, lava lamps, kidney-shaped desks, executive toys—the list of things hailed as "original," "creative," even "unique," is as long as it is amusing.

Though all of us are attracted to physical beauty, cleverness, wittiness, and intelligence, the Quaker affirmation that there is that of God in each person asserts that being worthy of respect does not depend on possessing attractive qualities or skills. Until we can respect another person without any justification except that he or she is a child of God, it is not really respect.

From these insights, we may also want to give closer scrutiny to why and how we value diversity. Diversity and community are not easily reconciled values. The student who found his school's anti-drug programs "un-Quakerly" because "I thought Quakers weren't supposed to impose their values on other people," underlines the point. Kim Hays asks "Can one teach Quaker principles and open-mindedness at the same time?"[19] Based on experience, the answer would appear to be: not if we confuse the two. If Quakerism is treated as a blank sheet, to be inscribed any way one wishes, we must expect some contradictory and unpleasant graffiti. A school which is no more than the lengthened shadow of an adolescent has little to offer, educationally.

NOTES

1. Michael Polanyi, *The Study of Man*, Chicago, University of Chicago, 1958, 85; Howard Brinton, *The Pendle Hill Idea: a Quaker Experiment in Work, Worship, Study*, Pendle Hill pamphlet 70, 1950, reprinted 1970, 11.

2. T. Canby Jones, ed., *"The Power of the Lord is Over All" The Pastoral Letters of George Fox*, Friends United Press, 1989, Introduction.

3. "An Address to Those Who Have the Care of Children," Tract 21, Tract Association of Friends of Philadelphia, 1832, 2.

4. Hays, *Practicing Virtues*, 3, 44-45, 80-81.

5. Hays, *Practicing Virtues*, 30, 80, 104, 105.

6. Hays, *Practicing Virtues*, 82-83.

7. Hays, *Practicing Virtues*, 30, 126, 174.

8. Harold Loukes, *Friends and Their Children*, London, George Harrap and Co., 1958, 26.

9. John L. Nickalls, ed. *Journal of George Fox*, Cambridge University Press, 1952, 221.

10. John Lampen, ed., *Wait in the Light,* London, Quaker Home Service, 1981, 48, quotes a relevant passage from Fox, *Journal:* "So I looked him in the face. And the Witness started up in him and made him blush when he looked at me again. For he saw that I saw him."

11. Fox, *Journal,* 263.

12. *Letters of Isaac Penington,* from the second London edition, Philadelphia, Nathan Kite, 1842, 204.

13. Fox, *Journal,* 263.

14. Penington, *Letters,* 306ff.

15. John Woolman, *On Schools,* in *The Works of John Woolman. In Two Parts,* Philadelphia, Joseph Crukshank, 1774, 30.

16. Fox, *Journal,* 19.

17. Polanyi, *Study of Man,* 85.

18. Brinton, *300,* 42.

19. Hays, *Practicing Virtues,* 120, 126.

THREE

Roots and Fruits:
Quaker Decision-Making

Fellowship among students and with faculty, not arbitrary exercise of authority, makes for the discipline which comes from within.

The discussion that followed was not altogether harmonious, but the discord was muted. The secretary was reminded of a sentence from Schopenhauer: "We live like hedgehogs in a bag, in close and prickly contact."

Working for Quakers is a triumph of process over task. [1]

Roots and Fruits

Quaker schools today rightly pursue the values of pluralism, multi-culturalism, and inclusiveness, both for their own sake and on pragmatic grounds, since our schools continue a long historical pattern of being able to recruit only small numbers of Quaker students, faculty, and staff and their outreach to other people diffuses Quaker principles and practice into the larger society. But heightening the importance of those values does not require that we minimize essential qualities of Quakerism. We need not minimize the peculiarity of its

35

roots—for example, its origins as a Christian communion, and the dependence of our decision-making process on the meeting for worship and on the conviction that we can be led by God—in order to emphasize the attractiveness of such *fruits* as its affinities to political and religious liberalism and social activism.

Howard Brinton distinguishes three classes of doctrines of the Religious Society of Friends: "The primary doctrine concerns the Inward Light, the secondary, the meeting for worship and the meeting for business, and the tertiary, the outreaching social implications of the type of community life expressed through these meetings." As his terminology indicates, from the primary come the secondary doctrines, while the tertiary, the social testimonies of the Society, derive from the secondary. Only in the secondary doctrines, which are embodied in the meeting for worship and the meeting for business, he argues, is Quakerism "unique and clearly distinguished from other sects and opinions." In both meeting for worship and meeting for business "the individual experience of God's light and leading becomes a group experience by which the Divine Presence in the midst operates as a uniting or coordinating Power."[2] The primary and secondary doctrines are the roots of Quakerism, and the social testimonies are the fruits. As the organic metaphor asserts, they are inextricably joined together; each will shrink and die, cut off from the other.

When schools have found it difficult to talk about worship as directed toward the sacred or divine, however, they have tended instead to define their Quakerness more in terms of the fruits of Quaker worship—by social service undertaken as an expression of the social testimonies, and by how widely students, parents, teachers, administrators, and trustees participate in a common search for decisions.

Schools have also tended to focus on shared decision-making, usually called working toward "consensus," primarily as a reflection of particular Quaker social testimonies. The process has come to be cited as primary evidence for Friends' commitment to the testimonies on equality and community, as expressions of respect for the individual, and as affirmations of "that of God in everyone" as a metaphor for personal creativity or individualism. Thus connecting Quaker decision-making so thoroughly with experiments in "participatory democracy" and with the social and political activism of the testimonies, over-simplifies Quaker history and consequently loses sight of some of Quakerism's deepest strengths.

THE SPIRITUAL BASIS FOR MEETING FOR BUSINESS

A child in First-Day School, told that we are put here on earth to serve others, asked, "Then what are the others here for?" Part of the job for everyone involved in a Friends school is to help answer that question. Robert Greenleaf suggests two key questions which we might ask about our schools:

1) How can an institution become more serving?
2) Do those being served grow as persons: do they, while they are being served, become healthier, wiser, freer, more autonomous, more likely themselves to become servants?[3]

These are superb questions for focusing on issues of caring and service, in the curriculum and the life of the institution. They also have relevance for how we explain Quaker decision-making and governance. People looking in from the outside sometimes speak of the Quaker decision-making process as a wonderful method to keep peace in a group and to avoid the conflicts of majority rule. Various writers have written about the method as embodying some of the most positive features of group therapy, as being the fullest expression of democratic governance, and as the way to get the most effective decisions. Many good practices can come out of Quaker business method which are nonetheless not of its essence; it may have a number of wonderful side-effects, but its validity as an expression of religious faith rests ultimately on its being another way we can hear and respond to the sacred.

It is also often said that the Quaker decision-making process rests on the belief that each of us has a part of the truth, but we must come together and pool our knowledge to gain a fuller truth. That understanding rests on a concept of truth as a complex pattern of information which must be assembled like a giant jigsaw puzzle or multi-faceted scientific experiment, and it has much to recommend it. Certainly arriving at a wise decision requires assembling and testing information, but Quaker decision-making conceives of truth as more than accurate data (though God's truth cannot be discerned by falsifying data) and of the business meeting as more than a means of processing information. Instead, the business method works from the expectation that an opening from God can come to anyone and the conviction that every person is capable of knowing the truth and participating in the search for it, not that we already come in with a bigger or smaller piece of it in our possession. All of us in the meeting for worship in which business is transacted are engaged in a common search, and each of us can be led to express with greater or less clarity, according to our own *measure*, or portion of knowledge, wisdom, skill, what God is calling us all to do. We bring our concerns, understanding, and opinions into the Light, believing that the Light itself will guide us, increase our *measure*, and make us more capable of being led by it. Certainly the method rests on respect for each person as a child of God and a sense of the equality of all people before God.

It is not self-evident that the best way to operate an institution is to wait for the whole faith-community to hear a single leading from God, but that is the foundational premise of a Quaker business meeting. The Quaker meeting for business, which ought to be the starting-place (but *only* the starting-place) for institutionalizing decision-making processes in a Quaker school, does not operate on the premise that many voices are good to hear from; it operates on the premise that *one* voice is to be sought, the voice of God. "The ministry", says Barclay, "is not monopolized by a certain kind of men, set aside as clergy, . . . while the rest are despised as laymen. Instead, it is left to the free gift of God to choose anyone [God] may deem appropriate, whether rich or poor, servant or master, young or old, yes, even male or female."[4] God chooses whom God wills to minister, but that is not one-person-one-vote democracy, nor even consensus democracy—both of which are enormously important in our larger political life and may also have relevance to how a Quaker school is governed.

History of Governance in Quaker Schools

Some may wish it were otherwise, but the historical facts are clear: far from being the centerpiece of school life and symbol of Quaker process we now wish to make it, widely-shared decision-making has been rare in the past. W. A. Campbell-Stewart says of British Quaker schools in the period 1660-1779, "There was no attempt to decide important matters in schools by Quaker methods, and it is true to say that the influence of the Business Meeting in education

as far as the children went was indirect and residual."⁵ Until
very recently, in fact, school committees or trustees made
the key decisions and delegated little authority to faculty
and even less to students. Nor was a voteless search for the
sense of the meeting the common way to arrive at decisions
in board, committee, or faculty meetings. "A hundred years
ago Roberts Rules of Order were seen as a civilized, Quakerly
way to bring fairness and order to decision making. They
were used in faculty deliberations and taught to the students."⁶
What is said here of George School could also have been
said of most Quaker schools and colleges.

Heads of Quaker schools and presidents of Quaker
colleges in the United States were far more authoritative,
if not authoritarian, until after the Second World War,
when a new generation of leaders in education emerged from
Civilian Public Service camps, to become simultaneously
jewels in the crown and thorns in the flesh of their heads or
presidents. A single example may serve as illustration. When
Thomas E. Jones became President of Earlham College in
1946, he introduced two features which have since come to
be thought of as quintessentially Quaker: group decisions
arrived at by seeking the "sense of the meeting" rather
than by voting; and the practice of students, faculty, and
administrators addressing one another by first name.

Until 1946, the patterns of governance at Earlham were
hierarchical. In 1860, when the Earlham faculty was first
organized for business, it decided matters by majority vote.
In 1871 it adopted Roberts Rules of Order, "the standard
which remained in place for seventy years."⁷ Tom Jones'
experience administering Civilian Public Service, where
the participants made group decisions according to a consensual model, led him to recommend the new approach to
decision-making in the College. (That second new feature

was the lengthened shadow of Jones' own personality. A typical response when he was introduced to someone was for him to thrust out his right hand and say, "I go by Tom.") In 1951, a report on Earlham for Lilly Endowment, Inc. noted as significant "the very full participation in policy-making by all members of the staff."[8] Yet in 1955, an internal report, growing out of a national Ford Foundation project, called for the Earlham faculty to choose its own presiding officer in place of either the president or academic dean. This recommendation marked a major departure from past practice, which at first Jones resisted strenuously, though ultimately he became a strong advocate of the change. The same report called for the creation of a faculty committee to advise the president on hiring, renewal, and tenure policies for faculty, the beginning of such formal, regular participation in personnel matters at the college.[9]

After the Second World War, faculty and staff participation in decision-making increased in the same ways in other Quaker schools and colleges, and perhaps for the same reasons. In 1946, at a national conference on education at Earlham College, the Headmaster of Friends Central School, Richard McFeely, suggested "We can achieve greater unity in the school by giving teachers a greater participation in school administration."[10] In 1950, Howard Brinton describes the adult educational center Pendle Hill as

> . . . an *integrated community* in the sense that there is no formal distinction between staff and students. The staff consists of the more permanent residents who, because of greater experience, exercise greater weight in the councils of the group. At the Meeting for Business, a session in which any problem connected with the community life may be considered, all residents, including

sojourners who have accepted pilgrim accommodations, take part. Decisions are arrived at, according to the Quaker method, on the basis of unanimity without voting.

He substantially qualifies this statement, however, by cautioning that ". . . the initiation of change resides in a group more inclusive than that which is in residence at any one time. It involves Pendle Hill as a whole, that is, the Board of Managers, students past and present, staff, and also the financial contributors." Brinton also stresses the importance of *weight,* vested more substantially in staff, the permanent members of the community who are assumed to bring greater experience to any decision. The statement carries the strong implication that the Quaker decision-making process works best when those in the position of greatest responsibility are also those of the greatest weight.[11]

Another substantial change in patterns of decision-making and participation in governance begins to appear in the political and social turmoil of the late 1960s and 1970s. Only then did Quaker schools and colleges begin systematically to include faculty observers in trustee meetings or student members on faculty committees, and in some cases only after considerable struggle. It became widely expected that hierarchical organizations would become flatter and that many, if not most, decisions would be arrived at through broadly participative methods. Such changes were occurring in many schools and colleges and some experimental colleges initiated patterns of participatory democracy which went well beyond the patterns of Quaker governance.

A pioneer in these developments among Quaker schools, The Meeting School, which opened in 1957, was created on the model of the Friends meeting for worship and for business, and named a Clerk in place of a Principal or

Head of School. Friends World College, founded in 1965, eventually conceived of its chief administrative officer as the moderator of a presidential council rather than as a president. In 1974 Pendle Hill restructured its administration to dispense with a directorship and replace it with "a constellation of five department heads and an executive clerk," a change intended to ease the strain on the head as an individual and to remove "the image of personal dominance which provoked resentment in many students."[12] More recently, Pendle Hill changed the title of its chief administrative officer to executive secretary, and Friends World College ceased independent existence and became a program of Long Island University.

Examples from three different Friends schools illustrate similar developments:

* In 1963-64, the "vigorous centralizing of authority" which a new Head of Sidwell School had undertaken was criticized for undermining "what had become the school's consensus style." The Head remained only two years. In 1967, when a board member with long experience working with Quaker groups became Board secretary, he

> . . . adopted a system of minute-keeping which highlighted the consensus decision-making that is at the heart of the process. . . . The next year, the principle was established permanently that the Sidwell Friends Board conducted its affairs after the manner of Friends— by consensus.[13]

* At George School, in 1969, the faculty "demoted the Head of School from his seat at the head of the faculty," displacing him from a traditional responsibility, and began to elect its presiding officer from among its own members. ". . . The faculty even took it upon itself to draw up job

descriptions for the Head and other administrators, so 'they would know what the faculty expected of them.'" Twenty years later, one of the leaders of the change justifies the "dethronement" thus: ". . . putting a Head of School, inevitably and rightly a power wielder, into a Quaker clerkship, *by design a powerless position,* (italics added) creates a contradiction sure to corrupt Quaker process."[14]

*At Friends Seminary, a rebellion against a Board-mandated "house-cleaning" undertaken by a new school Head in 1975 resulted in the unionization of the faculty. The Head was called "dictatorial" and it was said of his actions that "They violate fundamentally Quaker educational philosophy and practice." The Head resigned in his second year.[15]

THE PRACTICE OF DECISION-MAKING IN FRIENDS SCHOOLS

What is generally meant when people talk about decision-making on the basis of consensus in a Friends school reflects 1960s ideas about participatory democracy conflated with ideas about Quaker testimonies on equality and community. From that perspective, "process" becomes sacralized in itself by a rhetoric which detaches the Inward Light from the religious roots of Quakerism and identifies it solely with personal insight and individualism. The most anti-hierarchical approaches seem to grow out of a sentimental notion of how a monthly meeting operates and a desire to create a community simply by fervently announcing that it exists. When this confusion of ideas is uncritically accepted as Quaker decision-making, serious difficulties arise. People become disillusioned and cynical about a business method they have burdened with expectations it cannot possibly meet.

Current practice in many Quaker schools, in fact, represents a substantial modification of the Quaker meeting for worship for business, and that is probably as it should be.

If, in the day-to-day operation of a school, we find it valuable to solicit ideas and opinions as widely as possible, to share governance with as much of the community as possible, it is important to recognize that the success of such a process depends very directly on our capacity to trust one another's motives as well as wisdom. The process, as schools have developed it, is above all a way of establishing, maintaining, and extending trust among all parts of the institution. For such trust to occur will depend directly on two things:

1) Each person's sense that information is as widely, accurately, and willingly shared as possible. If one is fully a part of a consultative or decision-making process, one should not have to pry information out of school offices or from colleagues. Knowledge really is power, and withholding information which people need and have a right to have, is an abuse of power. It is *never* an incentive to greater trust. Keeping good, accurate, open minutes is an essential aspect of business process. Minutes are arrived at together and, once approved, are binding on the group.

2) That there are sufficient times and occasions for people to be consulted about decisions which are to be taken, even if they are not going to be the ones who make the decisions, so that their views can have appropriate impact on the final decision. Consultation should begin early and go through enough iterations that people get a chance to reflect and to modify their views in the light of new information. While information should be as public and accessible as possible, people reflecting on complex issues must not be prematurely forced into taking stands, so consultation must also provide

for appropriate kinds of confidentiality. Imposing a seal of confidentiality on information which needs to be generally known manipulates decisions and undermines trust, but so does depriving people of the chance to season their views in private. Too much secrecy is a threat to good decision-making, but so is a violation of confidences.

It is *not* a requirement or expectation of the process that everyone be equally involved in making every decision. Weight, official and delegated responsibility, expertise, and the like are all important considerations in determining who makes a final decision. Though there should be as much clarity as possible about who is responsible for a decision, it is *never* a satisfactory explanation for a bad or injurious decision that somebody had the right to make it. Likewise, it is not sufficient to say that a decision was arrived at by consensus, if consultation was not taken seriously or was not wide enough or undertaken soon enough to have its proper effect. That everyone in a room agreed to do something is a definition of criminal conspiracy as much as it is of consensus. It is not enough that people were given a chance to speak; they need to have good evidence that decision-makers were seriously listening to what they had to say.

What is being described here as effective consultation and decision-making is not peculiarly Quaker in structure or process, but it is what we would expect from any institution which claimed to take shared governance seriously. Such a process needs a clear and publicly-known structure of information-gathering, consultation, and review, with individuals and groups clear about how they participate in the decision, *including what limits there are in their participation*, to meet expectations of fairness, efficiency, legitimacy. What we want from a decision-making and consultative structure is maximum clarity about who will make any final decision, within what guidelines, and with what information from what sources. We want to know what constitutes legitimate and illegitimate influence on the decision. When we have a legitimate stake in a decision, we expect to be carefully listened to, and if the structure and process we are committed to give us weight in the decision, we expect that weight to be considered.

At its best, the decision-making process of a Friends school or college ought to go beyond the kind of good democratic and consultative process described above. Of particular importance for a school, the method of arriving at decisions can be *educative*, teaching individuals how to listen with discernment to others and to oneself, how to discover the *measure* within oneself and in others, how to treat uncongenial views respectfully, how to test self-interest against the interests of a community, how to take disagreement and conflict into silence, how to wait in silence, to let conflict mature, perhaps to transform, into clearness. The method can teach a community how to hear the leading of the Divine.

Whenever the business method is misused, turned into simply another way to manipulate groups and individuals to do what the most aggressive (or passive-aggressive) people want, it is destructive and *miseducative*. When people are most unhappy or cynical about working for Quaker organizations, they tell us it is because they feel taken for granted, treated like hired hands by a thoroughly benevolent matriarchy/patriarchy, while being assured that they are equals in the religious community, or left uninformed or gently misinformed for their own good. Undoubtedly some who speak this way misunderstand their part in the decision-making out of self-interest, but mature people know when they have been heard, even if they have not persuaded their listeners to their point of view, and this kind of criticism is too widespread to be discounted.

John Reader says the great challenge is to incorporate the spirit of compassion into the structure of an institution. Caring means enabling and empowering people by helping them develop skills and confirming them in their competence. The meeting for worship in which we attend to the business of the fellowship is where we try to discern God's leadings for us in quite focused and practical matters. Roger C. Wilson says: "To determine what shall be done and the quality of spirit in which ends shall be pursued is a moral responsibility; to determine how that shall be done and to see that it is done, is an administrative responsibility within the moral framework."[16] Both the business meeting and the governance structure in a Quaker school should be infused with the spirit of worship, the expectation that the most practical matters have their roots in the sacred. At the most practical level, the decision-making process in a Quaker school has as its purposes arriving at good decisions and helping people become more skilled at sharing responsibility for decisions. It aims to serve people and help them become better servants. The report of the 1946 conference, *Quaker Education Considered,* says that "One great contribution of the Quaker school or college comes as it teaches the art by which men live together in harmony." At its best, the Quaker business meeting places on each participant the responsibility to share in discerning, and then enacting, the group's will as it emerges from deep seeking for the Divine will. It sensitizes each of us to ways of testing our own limited self-interest, and turns each of us inward, to find what is more than our own will. "Fellowship among students and with faculty, not arbitrary exercise of authority, makes for the discipline that comes from within."[17] The business meeting is an invitation to us to learn how to grow in clarity, in determination, and in goodness.

NOTES

1. *Quaker Education Considered,* Report of Friends Conference on Education, held at Earlham College, November 21-22, 1946, Greensboro, Guilford College, n.d., 23; Eleanore Price Mather, *Pendle Hill: A Quaker Experiment in Education and Community,* Pendle Hill, 1980, 98. The quotation comes from the minutes of the Pendle Hill Board, January 16, 1971; said by a participant in a conference on Quaker personnel policies.

2. Howard H. Brinton, *Quaker Education in Theory and Practice,* Pendle Hill, 1940, fourth printing, 1967, 11-12.

3. Robert K. Greenleaf, *Servant: Retrospect and Prospect,* Center for Applied Studies, 1980, 3, 22. Robert Greenleaf refers the reader to *The Servant as Leader,* where these two questions were first raised.

4. Barclay, *Apology,* Proposition X, Worship, 210.

5. W. A. Campbell Stewart, *Quakers and Education As Seen in Their Schools in England,* 1953, reprinted Kennikat Press, 1971, 36.

6. Kingdon W. Swayne, *George School: The History of a Quaker Community,* George School, 1992, 80.

7. Thomas D. Hamm, *Earlham College: A History, 1847-1997,* Bloomington, University of Indiana Press, 1997, 76.

8. Opal Thornburgh, *Earlham, The Story of the College,* Earlham College, 1963, 358, 366.

9. Hamm, *Earlham College,* 228-29.

10. *Quaker Education Considered,* 21.

11. Brinton, *Pendle Hill Idea,* 16, 27.

12. Mather, *Pendle Hill,* 107.

13. William R. MacKaye and Mary Anne MacKaye,
     Mr. *Sidwell's School: A Centennial History 1883-1983*,
     Washington, 1983, 187, 209-10.

14. Swayne, *George School*, 39, 126.

15. Nancy Reid Gibbs, *Children of Light: Friends Seminary
     1786-1986*, New York Friends Seminary, 1986, 166-82.

16. Roger C. Wilson, *Authority, Leadership and Concern*, London,
     Quaker Home Service, Swarthmore Lecture , 1949, 45.

17. *Quaker Education Considered*, 23.

Four

⟫⬦⟪

THE TESTIMONIES

Can a Quaker educational community be conducted on the principles of the Quaker meeting for worship or for business with the consequent embodiment of the social doctrines of community, harmony, equality and simplicity?

Do not even the most important of our testimonies, say on such subjects as war and simplicity of life, lack power because we are content too often to repeat the phrases of a former day, and too idle or too cowardly to give them present day point and force?

A process of translation must occur if a tradition is to become accessible on a daily basis.[1]

"LET YOUR LIVES SPEAK "

In addition to holding a regular meeting for worship and sharing decision-making widely, Friends schools point to programs of community service and service projects as expressions of their Quaker faith and practice. Quaker service emerges as an expression of what Quakers have called their "testimonies," a word which has had very broad and general meanings in the past. Initially it referred to a personal witness, an enacting of an opening or revelation from God,

51

or a concern which arose within one as a response to a leading. John Punshon asserts that the testimonies arise from the Light of Christ within, working in the conscience to bring about "convincement" of the Truth. They "begin as matters of individual decision when people decide to take personal responsibility for something." But they are also a form of communication, to "proclaim how the world ought to be, and thus, by implication, what other people *ought* to do."[2]

"Witness" and "testimony" carry with them the aura of the courtroom, where one is expected to tell the whole truth and nothing but the truth. When we testify, we assert an identity between what we affirm to be true and our own integrity. We stand behind what we say. A Quaker testimony, then, is always, in the strongest sense, an expression of personal integrity, an identification of the deepest self with a belief or principle, and an enacted witness to Truth, to God's will for the world. It may therefore be an action against, or in favor of, concrete patterns of behavior or institutions. It is such a testimony *because* it is first of all a truth-affirmation about God and a witness to God's relation to humans and to the created world. Hugh Barbour and Arthur Roberts argue, ". . . early Quaker behavior arose from a radical experience of Christ and the Spirit rather than from humanitarianism. . . . Quaker social ethics was never a mere sum of particular concerns and protests; always it was part of a totally opened life." Caroline Stephen calls Quaker testimony "practical witness-bearing to a stricter obedience to the teaching of Jesus Christ than is thought necessary by the mass of those who are called by his name. . . ."[3]

George Fox characteristically announces such an act of witness, or testimony, in such phrases as " I was moved of the Lord," "I was commanded" or, when something offended his understanding of the Christian life, "it struck at my life."

John Woolman characteristically speaks of a leading or "draught" to an act of witness as arising as a "motion of love." Some actions require inexplicable or embarrassing behavior as a "sign," "witness," or "testimony," such as Fox's walking barefoot through the streets, crying "Woe to the bloody city of Lichfield," and other Friends' walking through towns naked,[4] On many occasions, Fox invited more severe prison sentences or otherwise complicated his life because he insisted on "clearing his conscience " by affronting the pride of judges and other authorities, in cases where a worldly-wise person would have left well enough alone. Belief in human perfectibility leaves no place for "well enough," however.

In another common use of the term, after Fox's death, Margaret Fell Fox writes a a memorial which describes, affirms, and celebrates his ministry, which is called a "testimony " to his life.[5] "Testimony " is still used in this sense of testifying to the faithfulness of a departed Friend's life-work. Social testimonies are not different from the fundamental religious witness to the Truth of Christ, they are a particular expression of it. Fox describes an experience in Mansfield, in 1648, perhaps his first public testimony to a social concern, when "it was upon me from the Lord to go and speak to the justices that they should not oppress the servants in their wages. . . ." When Fox says he is called to bring people away from false religions, ". . . that they might know the pure religion, and might visit the fatherless, the widows, and the strangers, and keep themselves from the spots of the world . . . ," he draws a significant conclusion about the consequences which would follow: "And then there would not be so many beggars, the sight of whom often grieved my heart, to see so much hard-heartedness amongst them that professed the name of Christ."[6] In the phrases Fox quotes from the General Epistle of James [1:27], we find imbedded a scrip-

tural rationale for the Quaker testimony for social justice, as
we will find rationales for the peace testimony [4:1-2] and
the testimony for equality [2:1-9, 15-16] and against oaths
[5:12-13] in the five brief chapters of James' Epistle.

Over time, "testimony " has largely shifted from referring
to the individual, in some cases inexplicable or idiosyncratic,
witness for God (though it never loses that meaning), to
defining *corporate* discernment of how Quakers should
act. In 1651, when Fox refuses a captaincy in Cromwell's
army, he does so because ". . . I lived in the virtue of that
life and power that took away the occasion of all wars, and I
knew from whence all wars did rise, from the lust according
to James's doctrine." [James 4:1-3] This is Fox's personal
testimony, his response to God's command to him. Not until
1660/1661 does this personal testimony become something
more, when, in the Declaration to the King, as Michael J.
Sheeran points out, "A dozen prominent Friends took it upon
themselves to declare that pacifism was a central Quaker
tenet. . . . to define Quaker belief with an absoluteness
uncharacteristic of the movement."[7]

> We know that wars and fightings proceed from the lusts
> of men (as Jas. iv. 1-3), out of which lusts the Lord hath
> redeemed us, and so out of the occasion of war. . . . All
> bloody principles and practices, we, as to our own par-
> ticulars, do utterly deny, with all outward wars and strife
> and fightings with outward weapons, for any end or un-
> der any pretence whatsoever. And this is our testimony
> to the whole world.

As this brief survey illustrates, the testimonies of Friends
are not easy to describe or define. Certainly they have
changed substantially over time. When George Fox sums up
everything he understands himself to be called to testify

about, in calling people to pure religion, the list seems disproportionate, crotchety, and diffuse. He tells us he was forbidden by the Lord to put off his hat to anyone and commanded to "thee " and "thou " all men and women, without respect to their social status. He was also forbidden to say "good morrow " or "good evening " to anyone. He was exercised to go to courts and cry for justice, and to warn public-house keepers not to let people have too much drink, "and in testifying against their wakes, or feasts, their May-games, sports, plays, and shows. . . ." In fairs and markets he was made to declare against "deceitful merchandise and cheating and cozening" and call people to speak and act honestly. Moreover, "I was moved also to cry against all sorts of music, and against the mountebanks playing tricks on their stages. . . ." He was exercised with school-masters and school-mistresses, fathers and mothers, masters and mistresses in private families, that they should care for educating children and servants, ". . . to train them up in the law of life, the law of the Spirit, the law of love and faith. . . ." "Likewise I was exercised about the star-gazers," and about hireling priests, whose steeple-bells "struck at my life."[8]

In *The Rise and Progress of the People Called Quakers* (1694) William Penn lists twelve testimonies, ranging from truth-telling, loving one another, loving enemies, addressing everyone as "thee," not saying "good morrow " or "good evening," to not drinking healths to people and particular practices in marriage, naming children, and burial of the dead.[9] And John Punshon cites the index to Britain Yearly Meeting's current *Christian Faith and Practice,* where "Testimonies " has references to "betting and gambling, capital punishment, conscription, 'hat honour,' integrity in business, oaths, peace, penal reform, plain language, relief of suffering, slavery, social order, Sunday observance, temperance and moderation, times and seasons, and tithes." The testimonies, John Punshon says, "are religious, ethical, collective, demanding, developing— and vague."[10]

Whether Fox's, Penn's or Britain Yearly Meeting's, lists of testimonies in themselves tell us only of the letter, not the spirit. In their apparent over-scrupulosity, lack of priority or sense of proportion, they cannot help reminding us of that famous hero of the school-child's essay who "jumped on his horse and rode off in all directions."

Time itself has winnowed out some testimonies, at least as originally understood, and modified others. Barbour and Frost call attention to five points about four traditional testimonies, truthfulness, simplicity, equality, and peace: 1) each has a truth-element; 2) each has double roots in the Bible and religious experience; 3) each has support in a social class or regional custom; 4) each served as a spiritual weapon in "the Lamb's War"; 5) and in each case, the testimony "became a uniform and united stand among Quakers and then a badge of loyalty that Friends upheld even when its truth and shock value were gone."[11]

The testimony against judicial oaths had great power in the first generation of Quakerism, when abiding by it would assure that one would be imprisoned and quite possibly deprived of all one's property. Now, when affirming in court is accepted, and there is no shock value in refusing to swear, the testimony may merely be a "badge of loyalty " to Quaker tradition, except when government bodies try to exact "loyalty oaths " from citizens and employees. Likewise, one form of the testimonies for plain speech and equality, addressing everyone as "thee " or "thou," initially had enormous impact when such behavior could prove costly. In 1895, Philadelphia Yearly Meeting (Hicksite) "urged Friends to continue the use of plain language among themselves, not as a testimony against social rank, but because 'it is the language of love,—of affection,—of the home.'"[12] Now the "plain speech" is used primarily in families wishing to use an intimate form that English has lost and, as testimony, is at best a quaint survival of a tumultuous past.

QUAKER EDUCATION AND THE TESTIMONIES

From the beginning, a fundamental purpose of Quaker schools has been to preserve the testimonies, as they and the forms they take are known at the time, and to inculcate them in each new generation. Samuel Tuke claims that the testimonies shaped both content and form in early Quaker education, when the chief testimonies to be inculcated were those against oaths and the payment of tithes, the testimony for plainness, which included the testimony for personal integrity but increasingly came to be identified with plain dress, and the testimony against war.[13]

In the twentieth century, the most influential writing about the place of the testimonies in Quaker education is Howard Brinton's, who was variously professor of mathematics, physics, philosophy, and religion at Guilford, Earlham, and Haverford Colleges, long-time Director of Studies at Pendle Hill, and a prolific writer on Quaker topics. In a series of works, most notably *Quaker Education in Theory and Practice*, 1940, *The Pendle Hill Idea: A Quaker Experiment in Work, Study, Worship*, 1950, and *Friends for Three Hundred Years*, 1952, he offers explications of four cornerstone social testimonies. In *Quaker Education* he says,

> For the sake of clearness which is obtained at the price of over-simplification, four social doctrines are here singled out for consideration. Let us list them as com-

munity, harmony, equality, and simplicity. Obviously in such a classification there is much over-lapping.[14]

In *Friends for Three Hundred Years*, he describes a process in which Light from God streams down to the waiting group, where, if way is open to it, the Light produces three results: unity, knowledge, and power. From them we have the kind of behavior

> . . . which exists as an ideal in a meeting for worship and a meeting for business. Because of the characteristics of the Light of Christ, the resulting behavior can be described in a general way by the four words Community, Harmony, Equality and Simplicity, though these are not to be taken as all-inclusive.[15]

Brinton connects the testimonies with the forms and types of relationships "with God and one another " which originate within the meetings for worship and for business. The social actions which express the testimonies grow out of "the practice and form of the meetings. . . . The individual becomes slowly sensitized to the world's needs." "The meeting both creates and exemplifies the kind of behavior which ought to prevail everywhere. It is therefore both a laboratory and a training ground for the desired social order."[16]

The emphasis and weight which Brinton gives these four doctrines or social testimonies, in relation to one another, shift somewhat as he focuses on the Religious Society of Friends itself or on Quaker schools. Stressing that the Quaker school in the past emerges from the life of a meeting whose members were both a religious and economic unit, spiritually, socially and economically interdependent, he appears to be alone in identifying community itself as a social doctrine and testimony, rather than as a product of the Quaker form of worship and the testimonies for truth-telling and integrity, peace, justice, equality and simplicity.[17] He always offers his list with a degree of tentativeness, emphasizing that he limits his discussion to these four doctrines, social concerns, testimonies (he uses all three terms) for the sake of clarity and at the risk of over-simplification. The wisdom and powerful insight of his writings have been so influential, however, and so germane to the mission of Friends schools in the period leading up to and after the Second World War, that his formulation has essentially defined our understanding of the testimonies for two generations.

THE TESTIMONIES IN FRIENDS SCHOOLS TODAY

Some sampling of school mission statements and recruitment materials will show the impact of Howard Brinton's formulation of the testimonies. When it reopened in 1944, Scattergood School adopted these four testimonies exactly as organizing principles, and its recently-published history analyzes much of the life of the school under the four categories. The mission statement of State College Friends School announces that its educational program is grounded in the principles of equality, community, simplicity, and harmony, each of which it carefully explicates. The Friends School in Atlanta says that the school manifests the Quaker values of simplicity, community, justice, equality, and peace. Oakwood Friends School describes itself as "guided by Quaker principles of tolerance and inclusion, the peaceful resolution of conflict, simplicity and social justice, and the recognition of the worth of each individual."

Many schools have translated these four testimonies into their own preferred language: for harmony, by which Brinton meant both peacemaking and concern for social justice, schools have substituted such terms as peaceful resolution of conflict, non-violence, cooperation, non-violent resolution of conflict, harmony with others and with nature, seeking ways to foster peace and understanding, nonviolent social justice, and stewardship of the environment.

Though frequently mentioned in mission statements, simplicity is often left unexplicated. Sometimes it is interpreted as simplicity in time management, an inner awareness where people can find centeredness and escape clutter, a challenge to the inequalities of wealth, avoidance of materialism, a life centered in the spirit, a constant search for truth and for the genuine, reliance on one's own creative resources, and speaking plainly, clearly, and honestly.

The testimonies for equality and community are frequently described in overlapping terms. In explicating the testimony for equality, schools emphasize gender equality, respect for differences, multi-culturalism, tolerance and inclusion, respect for each individual, appreciation of human diversity, high regard for tolerance, accepting and respecting uniqueness and diversity, and the belief that there is "that of God in everyone."

Community and caring for and cherishing the worth and dignity of each individual are frequently linked in school statements. The hallmarks of community are often described as respect for differences, tolerance and inclusion, appreciation of human diversity and the uniqueness of each individual, cooperation, and especially an expression of belief in "that of God in everyone." Two particular aspects of school life are often cited to illustrate the commitment to community: a community meeting where decisions are made on the basis of consensus, and participation in work programs or community service projects which encourage caring service to others.

In addition, Quaker schools frequently speak of inculcating ethical values not obviously comprised in the four testimonies (though all of them are implicit if not explicit in Brinton's discussions of the testimony for simplicity)—most notably integrity, truthfulness, responsibility and self-discipline. These tend to be less elaborated on and explicated, perhaps because they seem so obvious for any community, particularly an educational community, that discussion seems unnecessary.

TESTIMONIES AND THE TEACHING-LEARNING PROCESS

Clearly a crucial contribution of Quaker education is that it tries to recommend, by precept and action, forms and patterns of behavior which Quakers believe should characterize the whole society. Our schools are a significant force for demonstrating how people ought to live, how we ought to behave toward others, what attitudes and actions, "virtues " we believe should shape our social order, nationally and globally. Kim Hays describes such schools as "self-consciously moral." They are "places where adults deliberately attempt to practice a certain way of life and teach [children and] adolescents to be certain kinds of people."[18] Every teacher and parent knows that listing virtues to be practiced or testimonies to follow, like drilling students on what people used to do in the old days, is easy, but discovering how to teach, model, and reinforce the habits which express testimonies, how to encourage people not only to learn about testimonies but to make them their own, is extremely difficult. Yet it is also the very essence of moral education.

These issues raise a number of pedagogical questions: how can we best conceptualize, express, and teach the Quaker testimonies to school-age people today? Is it enough to expand and elaborate Brinton's formulation, or are there other formulations, new testimonies, which can better speak to our needs? What patterns of behavior and forms of organization can best serve to educate in the testimonies?

Since teaching is always, in large part, a process of accommodating concepts and information to the understanding of the hearers, making things clear to those who are under our care, how, in teaching the testimonies, do we preserve the integrity of the tradition? How do we translate historical meanings into relevant contemporary witness? And how do we deal with the conflicts which always accompany projects intended to change behavior? What are the chief obstacles to, or pedagogical problems in, teaching the testimonies? What practical witnesses do we wish to represent? Can we teach by exemplifying the testimonies in the way we approach all subjects? Can we teach the testimonies across the curriculum, as we hope to incorporate worship across the curriculum?

Teaching the Conflicts

John Punshon reminds us, "Traditions are the lifeblood of civilizations, cultures and religions. They are ways of exploring and questioning human life at its deepest level. . . ," and dialogue or controversy are inseparable from and essential to any tradition. It follows, then, that life in Quaker school communities will not be orderly but filled with conflict, as Hays tells us, because a living tradition must always be undergoing translation, and two necessary aspects of the process are the practice of virtues and the acceptance of conflict. She cites Alistair MacIntyre: "A living tradition . . . is an historically extended, socially embodied argument, and an argument in part about the good which constitutes that tradition."[19]

Students of literary, philosophical, and spiritual texts recognize that each generation must translate such texts afresh in order to make them its own. It is commonplace to say that to translate is to betray, and that things are always better in the original, but translating afresh does not merely mean updating the vernacular so as to make ourselves comfortable with what an uncongenial text or tradition says. It is not to impose what one *wants* to be the equivalence between words in two languages, but to search out what are truly their most nearly common meanings, their denotative as well as connotative meanings. Translating is not an exercise in wishful thinking, but a dedicated search for the most accurate, truthful, and vital rendering of another age's experience and understanding. To be a translator is above all to be an honest broker between one time and another, one culture and another, preserving the integrity of what is being translated as a means of maintaining one's own integrity. In the process, it is often to discover uncongenial meanings, or to recognize that, because of the pre-occupations of one's own time, a previously-submerged theme rises to prominence and speaks to us in new accents.

THE TESTIMONY FOR INTEGRITY

Such a submerged theme rises as we translate the testimonies in Quaker education today—the need to restore to its previous centrality the testimony of integrity. Discerning the importance of a commitment to truth-telling, to keeping one's word, to living with integrity, has the double advantage of comprehending the historical weight of a testimony and addressing a profound developmental need for young people, particularly adolescents, for whom the struggle to find personal identity and a place in a group *is* the struggle for per-

sonal integrity. The adolescent, Erik Erikson tells us "looks
most fervently for men [women] and ideas to have *faith* in,
which also means men [women] and ideas in whose service it
would seem worth while to prove oneself trustworthy."[20]

Modeling and teaching integrity as wholeness are difficult
in any situation, but the tasks are especially difficult with
adolescents. The developmental stage, at its healthiest, is
characterized by a continual testing of limits, even an abso-
lutist demand that, for example, every rule be administered
perfectly or be entirely abandoned. "Hypocrisy " and "hypo-
crite " become adolescents' favorite words for describing the
adults they know and the social structures they live in.
Erikson speaks of faith and hope as strengths or "virtues "
which emerge from a sense of basic trust, which he calls
"the first and basic wholeness." But such a wholeness cannot
be assumed in the lives of the students we teach, for it is
absent or hard to find in the lives of many adults. Lacking
wholeness, each of us is likely to reach for an inadequate
substitute. Erikson tells us, "When the human being, because
of accidental or developmental shifts, loses an essential wholeness, he restructures himself and the world by taking recourse
to what we may call *totalism.*"

> Totality . . . evokes a Gestalt in which an absolute
> boundary is emphasized: given a certain arbitrary
> delineation, nothing that belongs inside must be left
> outside, nothing that must be outside can be tolerated
> inside. A totality is as absolutely inclusive as it is utterly
> exclusive. . . .

Wholeness, however, connotes "an assembly of parts, even
quite diversified parts, that enter into fruitful association and
organization," as suggested by terms like wholeheartedness,
whole mindedness, and wholesomeness. "As a Gestalt, then,

wholeness emphasizes a sound, organic, progressive mutuality between diversified functions and parts within an entirety, the boundaries of which are open and fluid."[21] Wholeness embraces flexibility, openness, and change. Under conflict, it is therefore always vulnerable to wearing down and losing definition. Totality requires absolutes, over-scrupulosity, rigidity. Under conflict, it is therefore always in danger of shattering apart. Totalism is a desperate, unhealthy attempt to restore a lost or false wholeness.

Wilmer A. Cooper lists four key marks of integrity: 1) truth-telling; 2) authenticity, genuineness, and veracity in personhood; 3) obedience and faithfulness to conscience illumined by the Light Within; 4) Wholeness.[22] Whatever a testimony's particular focus, together they cohere around commitments to personal fidelity, to discovering what is worth trusting and becoming someone whom others can trust. For young people on the brink of adulthood, needing to negotiate commitments and life-choices in a society characterized by ethical and moral instability, self-indulgence, untrustworthiness, this witness for coherence, consistency, and integrity is perhaps the most important aspect of the testimony for plainness and simplicity.

Identity without integrity is false consciousness. To give greater attention to integrity as a hub of Quaker education will not reduce the tensions and conflicts in which a school operates, but it might make them more intellectually, ethically, and spiritually fruitful.

THE MEANING OF COMMUNITY

Placing integrity at the hub of our testimonies opens up some fruitful ways to reconceive how a school can become a community. In 1940, when Howard Brinton first published *Quaker*

Education, the homogeneous life of Quaker meeting and school was disappearing: "the hedges were down." At the same time, the kind of coherence which such economically, socially, and religiously interdependent communities had known, and which the larger society most needed, was becoming attenuated by economic depression, the violence of the mass movements of nationalism, fascism, and communism, and world-wide preparation for war. Then, as now, people longed for true community. Its importance was so great that Brinton described community itself as a testimony, rather than as a set of conditions shaped by Quakers' religious convictions and practice.

As we ask how to create the conditions in which Quaker education can best flourish today, it may be useful to take a step back from Howard Brinton's formulation and think of the school community first as a *product* of the meeting for worship, the meeting for business, and the testimonies for integrity, peace, justice, equality, and simplicity. As an outcome of Quaker practice, rather than an entitlement provided by teachers and staff, community would depend on how well its members learned, practiced, and improved the arts of living together. It would depend on learning how to practice group discernment and hold one another to discipline.

A community, defined in what the authors of *Habits of the Heart* call a strong sense, is

> a group of people who are socially interdependent, who participate together in discussion and decision-making, and share certain *practices* that both define the community and are nurtured by it. Such a community is not quickly formed. It almost always has a history and so is also a *community of memory*, defined in part by its past and its memory of its past.[23]

An intentional community always requires a novitiate, a time of intense education and training for the would-be member in the purposes, beliefs, and practices of the group, a probationary period during which the individual and the group decide whether they belong together. In such a community, the newcomer has to learn and earn his or her way into full membership. The community is an established entity which the newcomer joins on its terms, not a blank sheet to be inscribed as the newcomer chooses. In the early Christian church, a convert had to be accepted into the fellowship, and was by that act acknowledged as a *member* of the Body of Christ, but each member had a dignity and responsibility according to his or her measure or seasoning in the truth. Though membership was far more fluid in the early Society of Friends, *convincement* was a process of submitting to learn from and obey the Inward Teacher, and the worshipping fellowship was responsible for discerning the gifts and measure of its members. One of the crucial tests which the meeting applied to any individual's leading was whether it increased the fruits of the Spirit within the fellowship, "tender love, unity, grace and good order . . . a sweetness and harmony of life, unity, and subjection to one another, and a preserving one another in the Lord."[24]

That kind of understanding has been lost in the promise of instant intimacy, instant equality, and support of "expressive individualism" frequently attached to notions of community today. In Quaker schools, such notions reflect an uncritical confusion of Quakerism with American middle-class individualism. "Our verbal homage to community is only one side of a deep ambivalence that runs through the American character," says Parker J. Palmer, "the other side of which is a celebration of unfettered individualism." Robert Bellah and his associates tell us that ". . . the ties one

forms in the search for meaning through expressive individualism are not those of the moral community of the calling."
They are rather the ties of what, following *Habits of the Heart*,
we might call the lifestyle enclave, which tends to be both
fundamentally segmental—involving only a segment of each
individual and including only those with a common
lifestyle—and also to celebrate "the narcissism of similarity."
"Members of a lifestyle enclave express their identity through
shared patterns of appearance, consumption, and leisure
activities, which often serve to differentiate them sharply from
those with other lifestyles." [25]

As Kim Hays interprets practice in the Quaker boarding
schools she studied, the emphasis falls on changing the
community to meet members' needs, not on transforming
individuals. She argues that the Quaker virtues of equality,
community, simplicity, and peace "describe an environment,
not an individual." But there can be no such environment,
no *ethos* characterized by those virtues, except as people continually create the conditions by their own enacted principles.
Communities *are* what they *do,* and, as Gerard Manley
Hopkins says, "The just man justices." Environments do
not remain static; they improve or degrade according to how
we inhabit them. Community is not an entitlement but an
opportunity and a responsibility. For a Quaker school, the
goal is to find "the moral community of the calling."

EQUALITY

The Quaker testimony for equality of all people roots in the
Christian doctrine, symbolically represented in Peter's dream,
in *Acts* 10, from which he concludes that God is no respecter
of persons, and enunciated by St. Paul in *Galatians* 5:27-28,
that in Christ there is neither Jew nor Greek, bond nor free,

male nor female. This asserts, in the first instance, that every person has the capacity to know Christ, be converted, and thus become a new being, after which, the distinctions of race, class, gender—to use our contemporary terms—will no longer matter. For Quakers, convinced that the Light of Christ is to be found in every person, the equality obtains whether or not the individual has become part of the body of Christ, the church. In the first generation of Quakers, the testimony for equality was, like the testimony for simplicity, an assault on human pride. In class terms, it was essentially a leveling *down*, as the political, social, and economic influences which foster democratic institutions intertwined with religious convictions. More particularly, the conviction that men and women were to share in the ministry and to be *helpsmeet* to one another, as in the days before the Fall, which George Fox repeatedly asserts as the justification for setting up women's and men's monthly meetings, sets a very high standard for equality between the sexes.[26]

As Quakers prospered and their socio-economic status rose, their understanding of the direction in which equalizing would operate inevitably became more complicated. What was implicit in the testimony becomes more clearly focused: equality within the Religious Society of Friends would be "represented in the meeting by the equal opportunity for all to take part in the worship or business regardless of age, sex, or official position."[27] As a testimony to the larger society, it would manifest itself primarily through reform movements and charitable services for oppressed or less fortunate people, to help them prosper and improve their position in the world. Any radical *leveling down* equality there might have been in the early Society became transformed into a good-hearted, patriarchal benevolence, aimed at helping people reach modestly *upward*.

Howard Brinton cites two broad educational policies which have been shaped by the testimony for equality: equal education of both sexes and equality of education of races and classes.[28] Certainly, Quakers in America have an honorable history of setting up schools for Native Americans and African-Americans, where there were few opportunities for education, and in the eighteenth century, some schools admitted both black and white children. Quakers were also deeply invested in schools for freed slaves. The concern to help people gain opportunities to develop their talents, and thus prosper, was informed by the conviction that all human beings are children of God, but it did not challenge the social distances created by class. Commenting on the "limits of Quaker reform," however, Jean R. Soderlund concludes:

> After 1780, individual Quakers, not the Yearly Meeting or a political presence of Friends in state government, worked for an end to slavery through the Pennsylvania Abolition Society and similar groups. Under their influence, the white abolitionist movement continued forward into American history the gradualist, segregationist, and paternalistic policies developed for almost a century within the Society of Friends.[29]

One consequence of Friends' anxious desire to maintain their own purity, arising from the series of shocks represented by the Seven Years' War, the American Revolution, and the Separation, was a withdrawal into what Soderlund describes as clannishness and "tribalism " in reform. Soderlund and Philip S. Benjamin have argued that the attempt to maintain separate, "select " schools, by making a virtue of exclusivity also made racial integration of Quaker schools harder. Certainly Quakers in the twentieth century were slow to admit minority students, particularly African-Americans, into their own schools. The agitation to integrate Quaker schools became stronger after the Second World War, but many school histories reflect prolonged and hard struggles with parents, school committees, and other constituents before that could happen. Thomas D. Hamm suggests that Friends west of the Appalachian mountains were probably more open to African-American students than Friends in the east. The midwestern Friends academies that survived into the 1920s and 1930s, he says, while they may not have been easy places for African-American students, at least did not *exclude* them.[30]

If reaching out beyond their historically homogeneous constituency to bring a wide diversity of students into Quaker schools is an expression of the testimony for equality, it must be said that the schools, however slow they were to change, have accomplished far more than most Friends meetings. At present in some schools, people of color make up as much as a third of the student body.

The deeper struggle to raise consciousness about gender, racial, and ethnic inequalities, to learn how to practice equality when people of different races and classes live in close association with one another, now engages Quaker schools, as it must engage the larger society. Equality of opportunity has little meaning unless a school is willing to shape curriculum to the needs and experiences of new constituencies.

As an educational goal today, the testimony for equality requires confronting and holding in a creative tension the values of both *difference* and *unity*. In the past, equality has always assumed blending diversity into some transcendent and stronger unity. Indeed, most notions of community presuppose such a transformation from the many to the one. The ancient world's categories of Jew and Greek, slave and free, male and female, distinguished inferiors from superiors, but Christianity promised to obliterate such distinctions in favor of an organic body made up of divergent parts. Likewise, in the democratic ideal of the melting-pot, the supposed weaknesses of narrowly provincial identities and tribal separations which perpetuated racial, cultural, and class hatreds would be dissolved and reforged into a new, strong alloy, the American. In each case, difference was to turn into unity, and with it equality, through a process like dying: a crucifixion with Christ, for St. Paul, and the smelting of metal ore, in the American vision.

Neither Christianity nor the secularized version of religion, American democracy, could fulfill its promise to achieve equality through blending into unity. But if their metaphors have failed us, the homely new metaphors of society as like a rainbow, or like a tossed salad, where each part retains its own essential nature, are inadequate to describe our twin needs for meaningful equality along with the strength and power of commonality. In American society today, the goal of such a transcendent unity is in dispute. Instead, the premise of multi-culturalism is that the struggle for equality is the struggle of separate identity-groups to define themselves and to claim their share of power. Equality will consist of rights negotiated among such independent and separate cultural and political groups.

In such an analysis, there is no center to aspire to join, only mal-distributed power and a multiplicity of endangered margins to protect. As Todd Gittlin argues, "A people against whom boundaries were drawn respond by fortifying those very boundaries." Life on the margin can have the comfort of self-confirmation and at least has the safety of familiarity.

It is not clear how the understandable desires for validation through multi-culturalism can be addressed, nor how the testimony for equality should be expressed in relation to them. What is clear is that our schools must be deeply engaged in trying to discover the answers to those questions. Gittlin warns us, "to recognize diversity, more than diversity is needed. The commons is needed. . . . Mutuality needs tending."[31] To learn how to be faithful to the testimony for equality, and to express it through building a school community in harmony with the goals of greater diversity and multicultural sensitivity, will engage Quaker schools profoundly.

"I Wish I Could Live More Simplistically "

So a student said, innocently and earnestly. She is not the only person to confuse the terms "simple " and "simplistic, " and the confusion itself is a useful entry to reflect on the place of simplicity in Quaker education. If living the testimony with integrity is a problem for us today, the difficulties have always been there. It has meant freeing ourselves from trivialities or luxuries so as to have time and energy for essentials, but even in the first generation that had become reduced to the "poor gospel " that only drab colors were fit for a Quaker to wear. "Plain dress " might be very expensive, so long as it lacked collars for men and adornment for women. Worldliness increased as a hat's crown rose and rounded. As the tests became more and more focused on the badge of loyalty, which was literally a vain show of plainness, simplicity became simplistic.

Even William Penn and Robert Barclay leave us troubled by their interpretations of the testimony. William Penn sees an issue of justice and what we now call the right use of resources as aspects of the testimony: "The very trimming of the vain world would clothe all the naked one." But if Penn's clothes were untrimmed, his mode of living was not; he set a lavish table and generally lived beyond his means. David E. Shi says of him,

> . . . Like many other upper-class spokesmen for the simple life, then and now, Penn saw no contradiction between his espousal of material moderation and his own princely style of living. . . . For the masses he advised austerity; for himself and a few others like him, he supported enlightened gentility.[32]

Barclay argues that simplicity must be understood in relation to social position:

> If a man dresses quietly and without unnecessary trimmings, we will not criticize him if he dresses better than his servants. For it is probably a greater act of mortification for him to abstain from fine clothes than it would be for his servant. His worldly estate and education have accustomed him to things which his servant has never known.[33]

"Mortification" is worth noticing in Barclay's comment. Plainness was a way of challenging the pretensions of other people through blunt speech and refusing the niceties of language which expressed respect to some persons more than others. The target for mortification, then, was not always the advocate of simplicity, whose stark dress and demeanor might conceal the splendid robes of self-righteousness.

The testimony for simplicity has still to be enunciated for our time, free of play-acting at ostentatious plainness. Simplicity is comprised neither in flat old-time hats nor artfully torn and patched jeans. The first style of dress is an exercise in sentimental nostalgia; the second pretends to a poverty which insults the truly impoverished, who would never willingly wear tattered, patched clothing. Playing "simpler than thou" is as enticing as it is morally dangerous. Living simplistically is actually rather easy; it is living simply that is hard.

Certainly the testimony must find expression in how we use things, for the sake of economic justice, the right use of resources, and protection of the environment, but it cannot be reduced to lists of what is permitted or proscribed. Perhaps a rule of thumb can be: when an object or a practice reduces the clutter and unnecessary business in our lives, at no unreasonable added cost, so we have more time and energy for what we think is truly worth doing, when our lives are so filled by satisfying work and recreation that fads, styles, and trivial amusements have no attractions, when we can enjoy living with less so that others can have enough, we are living simply. But when we brag about that as simplicity, we are being simplistic. Rufus Jones writes, "Unclouded honesty at the heart and center of the man [woman] is the true basis of simplicity."

PEACE AND JUSTICE

According to John Punshon, the testimony of simplicity is as fundamental as the peace testimony and, like it, rests upon compassion.[34] Compassion, feeling-with another, also lies at the heart of the testimony for justice, but justice further derives from principles of fairness and integrity. The prophet Micah tells us we are to *love* mercy, but at the minimum to *do* justly. If we typically associate compassion with the heart and the emotions, justice must always involve the head, the reasoning faculties. As a Christian, if I owe someone my compassion, the degree and form tend to be prescribed only by my capacity to feel care, affection, and responsibility. If I owe someone justice, however, the terms of my obligation are far more precise. To *do* justly, I must meet minimal standards of behavior, tested against a plumb line. We experience acts of compassion as free-will gifts and acts of justice as paying debts. If I fail in compassion, others will think my character is flawed; if I fail at justice, someone is injured who may demand restitution. A judge can merely excoriate my lack of compassion, but she is entitled and required to punish my doing unjustly. The classical image of Justice is as a blindfolded goddess, holding in one hand a set of scales for discerning equity and in the other a sword to punish wrongdoers. When calling on judges to give justice, George Fox invariably cited the precept that "the magistrate is not to bear the sword in vain." Images for compassion might be of such sufferers-with or sufferers-on-behalf-of human beings as the Compassionate Buddha or the Sacred Heart of Jesus. Compassion cannot be blindfolded; justice must be. Justice is adjudication between conflicting claims, striking a balance. Compassion continually seeks to transcend mere balance, to go beyond justice.

The origins of the Quaker peace testimony lie in "vocational pacifism," a sense that we are specifically called *not* to fight with carnal weapons. Particularly in response to the Second World War, genocide, and weapons of mass destruction, however, Quakers have had to recognize that merely withdrawing from violence is not sufficient. Conditions and institutions which produce violence must be identified and corrected. We accept Reinhold Neibuhr's dictum that there can be no peace without justice, and add that neither can there be justice without peace.

Teaching the intertwined arts of peace- and justice-making is perhaps the greatest challenge in Quaker education, for it requires educating both the cognitive and the affective faculties, heart and head, through what is studied and how it is studied, through the interplay of curriculum and co-curriculum, and in the administration and governance of the school. It incorporates all the separate testimonies and every aspect of school life.

Peace-making begins on the playground and in the earliest grades, in the style of teaching and with practice in elementary conflict-resolution techniques, but it must grow in sophistication as conflicts become more complex. Not all conflicts rest simply on innocent misunderstanding or lack of personal acquaintance, nor is justice found equally on all sides of every issue. Good will and compassion are always necessary but rarely sufficient for achieving peace with justice, for the deepest, most intractable conflicts arise from the clash of economic, social, political interests exacerbated by tribal, cultural, and religious differences. A peace-maker must be a truth-seeker, always pursuing a comprehensive grasp of relevant facts, for spiritual truths grounded in misinformation lose their character and become platitudes or falsehoods. Reconciliation is not merely a matter of splitting the differences between opponents. The solution for the lower school playground will not suffice in Northern Ireland or the Middle East. The assumption that the truth always lies somewhere in-between sends us looking for it in only one place. But truth may be found on one side or the other, in the middle, or at the margin of a conflict; we cannot know until we have been humbled enough to seek it where it resides. Neither is social justice simply equivalent to what the political left (or right) wants. A peace-maker must learn how to gather, test, and analyze information, and have the courage to pursue evidence wherever it leads.

A peace-maker must be a truth-teller, for adversaries who hate, fear, and distrust one another must know they can trust the integrity of whoever would negotiate between them. A peace-maker must listen and interpret faithfully what has been said, not what he or she wishes had been said. A peace-maker must be an honest broker, a reconciler who communicates accurately what each side believes its rights to be, and a prophet who speaks forthrightly to each about its shortcomings.

The skills for such peace-making can be taught in how Quaker schools teach history, social studies, science, languages and literature, in the topics chosen, the assignments given and the questions entertained. Courses might focus on how particular wars have begun, or what conditions have preceded negotiated settlements of conflict, for example, or on the development of particular non-violent methods for confrontation such as the sit-down strike, the picket line, or the boycott. Interdisciplinary courses organized around multiple and conflicting narratives of conflicts can help students develop the mix of compassion and detachment required for being a mediator.[35] Peace-making skills can be refined by direct experiential learning in social service projects outside the school. They can be modeled in the ways that teachers and students treat one another and in how the school rules are made and administered. John Reader asks how we can incorporate the spirit of compassion into the structure of an institution. Speaking from many years' experience as head of Friends School, Great Ayton, he says

> It is comparatively easy to show understanding and love if we are not in a position of authority; it is a challenge that exists in any age to build humanity and charity into the life of an institution and to reconcile the function of government [governance] with the exercise of love and friendship.[36]

What he calls compassion incorporates both clear knowledge and a care for justice. Its institutional style is marked by clear rules and firm control and an emphasis on restitution rather than retribution for wrong-doing. Restitution " heals the wrong-doer at the same time as it demonstrates to the community disapproval of anti-social behavior. Moreover, restitution leaves the way more open for the exercise of love toward the offender than does retribution." A student abusing drugs was required to leave his Quaker boarding school to enter rehabilitation, and told he would be welcomed back when he was drug-free but could return on no other terms. Speaking of the effect on him of the school's firmness, he said, "They saved my life." Reader says, "Compassion includes many forms of insight, from pity for suffering to the posing of a sharp challenge to those, like the rich young ruler in the gospels, who need it."[37]

A Training Ground for the Desired Social Order

Erik Erikson says that as a teacher—which in a Quaker school includes administrators and staff—translates the rudiments of hope, will, purpose, and competence, she or he ". . . conveys a logic much beyond the literal meaning of the words [s/he] teaches, and . . . outlines a particular world image and style of fellowship."[38] A primary purpose of a Quaker school is to recommend the testimonies for their own sake. They represent how Friends believe people should live with one another. Their educative power cannot be over-estimated, for they establish the *ethos* in which the formal curriculum is imbedded. Without becoming dogma, they help determine not only the courses to be offered but the topics to be examined and the spirit of the classroom. How a teacher makes assignments, how she evaluates tests, papers, and homework, can model trust in students' integrity and the values of coop-

eration, mutual respect, and freedom which are integral to
the testimonies for peace, justice, and equality. To study history not as a series of heroic wars and conquests, or as the
lives of great men, but as an inquiry into why wars happen
and how they are brought to an end, and what the lives
of ordinary men and women are like from age to age, is to
approach a traditional discipline respectfully and with fresh
questions influenced by the testimonies. To study the natural world from the perspective of loving stewardship instead
of mastery, to read literature with attention to a multiplicity
of voices and a widened understanding of humans' conditions, is to experience learning enriched by the values of the
testimonies.

As they help form the curriculum, the testimonies also
determine the Quaker school's style of administration—
establishing rules and expectations with clarity, emphasizing
restitution rather than punishment for wrong-doing,
modeling compassion as both forgiveness and sharp challenge
to those who need it. Equality can be addressed in something more than the superficial form of addressing everyone
by first name; listening well and patiently, speaking forthrightly and patiently, making information as widely available as possible, and sharing decision-making can shape a
style of companionship predicated on being seekers together,
expecting to learn from one another. Our goals in Quaker
education are two-fold: to encourage people to make the world
better, to become informed, skilled agents of positive social,
political, economic, and educational change, devoted to the
fullest possible expression of the particular world image and
style of fellowship represented by the Quaker testimonies;
and to help our students learn to make their contributions
from lives which are spiritually centered, fulfilled, and happy.
Amid all the abundant reasons why movements for social

justice are so often fueled by fear, anger, resentment, and envy, the testimonies offer other motives to act. The particular contribution of Quaker education is to help our students conceive of new opportunities, new richness, new styles of fellowship, rooted in spiritual strengths.

NOTES

1. Brinton, *Quaker Education*, 21; W. C. Braithwaite, "Has Quakerism a Message to the World Today?" in *Report of the Proceedings of the conference of members of the Society of Friends, held by direction of the Yearly Meeting in Manchester, from eleventh to the fifteenth of eleventh month, 1895, 1896,* 45; Hays, *Practicing Virtues*, 5.

2. John Punshon, *Testimony and Tradition: Some Aspects of Quaker Spirituality*, London, Quaker Home Service, Swarthmore Lecture, 1990, 27-28.

3. Hugh Barbour and Arthur Roberts, eds., *Early Quaker Writings 1650-1700*, Grand Rapids, William B. Eerdmans, 1973, 353, 434 ; Caroline Stephen, *Quaker Strongholds*, in Douglas V. Steere, ed., *Quaker Spirituality*, New York, The Paulist Press, 1984, 255.

4. Woolman, *Journal*, 23; Fox, *Journal*, 71-72.

5. *The Testimony of Margaret Fox concerning her late Husband George Fox, 1690*, in Mary Garman, Judith Applegate, Margaret Benefiel, Dortha Meredith, eds., *Hidden in Plain Sight: Quaker Women's Writings 1650-1700*, Pendle Hill, 1996, 233-43.

6. Fox, *Journal*, 26, 35-37.

7. Fox, *Journal*, 65; Michael J. Sheeran, *Beyond Majority Rule: Voteless Decisions in the Religious Society of Friends*, Philadelphia, Philadelphia Yearly Meeting of Friends, 1983, 15.

8. Fox, *Journal*, 36-39, 399-404.

9. Frederick B. Tolles, and E. Gordon Alderfer, eds., *The Witness of William Penn*, Macmillan, New York, 1957, 21-29.

10. Punshon, *Testimony and Tradition*, 19-20.

11. Hugh Barbour and J. William Frost, *The Quakers*, New York, Greenwood Press, 1988, 41.

12. Philip S. Benjamin, *The Philadelphia Quakers in the Industrial Age: 1865-1920*, Philadelphia, Temple University Press, 1976, 28.

13. Tuke, *Five Papers*, 34-35.

14. Brinton, *Quaker Education*, 15

15. Brinton, *300*, 119. In *Pendle Hill Idea* Howard Brinton describes the integrating idea of Quakerism as based on experience and secondarily on historical events; "In determining the character of an educational group this idea has four important social consequences which have been listed as Equality, Simplicity, Harmony, and Community. These are the four social doctrines of the Society of Friends," 29.

16. Brinton, *Quaker Education*, 14-15.

17. Brinton, *300*, 126-29; *Pendle Hill Idea*, 31.

18. Hays, *Practicing Virtues*, 3-5.

19. Punshon, *Testimony and Tradition*, 17 ; Hays, *Practicing Virtues*, 5-6.

20. Erik H. Erikson, *Identity: Youth and Crisis*, Norton, New York, 1968, 128-29.

21. Erikson, *Identity*, 80-81.

22. Wilmer A. Cooper, *The Testimony of Integrity in the Religious Society of Friends*, Pendle Hill Pamphlet 296, 1991, 18-21.

23. Robert N Bellah, Richard Madsen, William M. Sullivan, Ann Swidler, and Steven M. Tipton, *Habits of the Heart: Individualism and Commitment in American Life*, Berkeley, University of California Press, 1985, 333.

24. Sheeran, *Beyond Majority Rule*, 27.

25. "Expressive individualism holds that each person has a unique core of feeling and intuition that should unfold or be expressed if individuality is to be realized. This core, though unique, is not necessarily alien to other persons or to nature." *Habits of the Heart*, 333-34; Hays, *Practicing Virtues*, 81, speaks of expressive individualism in Quaker schools; Parker J. Palmer, *A Place Called Community*, Pendle Hill Pamphlet, 8 ; *Habits of the Heart*, 7-72, 335.

26. Jones, *The Power of the Lord Is Over All*, Epistle 264 (1669), 254-55, Epistle 291 (1672) 286.

27. Brinton, *Quaker Education*, 16.

28. Brinton, *Quaker Education*, 41.

29. Jean R. Soderlund, *Quakers and Slavery: A Divided Spirit*, Princeton, Princeton University Press, 1995, 187.

30. Soderlund, *Quakers and Slavery*, 151, 186; see Benjamin, *Philadelphia Quakers*, Chapters 2 and 6, esp. 145-46; Hamm to Lacey.

31. Todd Gittlin, *The Twilight of Common Dreams: Why America Is Wracked by Culture Wars*, New York, Holt, 1995, 153 , 236.

32. Barbour and Frost, *The Quakers*, 44; David E. Shi, *The Simple Life: Plain Living and High Thinking in American Culture*, New York, Oxford University Press, 1985, 35-36. Shi is citing *No Cross, No Crown* in Penn, *Works* I, 432.

33. Barclay, *Apology*, 405.

34. Punshon, *Testimony and Tradition*, 61-64.

35. I have in mind here a specific course taught by Franklin Wallin on how wars end, a course on war and literature regularly taught by Tony Bing, and a course I team-teach at Earlham with historian and Vietnam veteran Chuck Yates on event and narrative in the Vietnam War, all at Earlham College.

36. John Reader, *Of Schools and Schoolmasters*, London, Quaker Home Service, Swarthmore Lecture 1979, 13.

37. Reader, *Of Schools*, 63-64, 68-69.

38. Erik H. Erikson, *Insight and Responsibility*, Lectures on the Ethical Implications of Pschoanalytic Insight, Norton, New York, 130-31.

Five

⟫•◆•⟪

"Owing to the Want of a Suitable Teacher . . ."

It is not very difficult to draw out a fair scheme of management for an academy, but to find the people to carry it out in its various parts, is far from easy.

Nothing presents less of an obstacle than the perfecting of the imaginary.[1]

In 1695, London Yearly Meeting's epistle urged "that schoolmasters and mistresses, who are faithful Friends and well qualified, be encouraged in all counties, cities and other places, where there may be need. . . ." Concealed behind that gentle advice lies a fundamental and perennial problem for Quaker education, the lack of qualified teachers who are also members of the Society of Friends to teach in our schools, and the consequent need which a document of 1697 bluntly defines for "breeding up schoolmasters." By that year, W.A. Campbell Stewart tells us, schools in local meetings are either being closed or not being opened—among the latter, in Bedfordshire, Cambridgeshire, Berkshire, and Derbyshire—because there are not enough qualified Quaker teachers to teach in them.[2] After the very earliest period of Quakerism, when significant numbers of university-educated men came into the Society and were

85

available to set up schools because deprived of other professional outlets for their training, the Religious Society of Friends began to experience a dearth of qualified Quaker teachers which has never since abated. In Britain, according to D.G.B. Hubbard, the period from 1695 to 1725 "must be regarded as the high-water mark of the Society' s interest in its schools . . . By 1725 the time of almost reckless enthusiasm for founding schools was over. . . . "[3]

Until it became required and state-supported, education of children depended primarily on the resources and ambitions of their parents. (In the United States, starting around the first third of the nineteenth century, later in England, where the Education Act of 1870 first established compulsory, universal education, but free universal education was not fully available until the Education Act of 1944.)

The perennial problem for Quaker schools is not merely lack of Quaker teachers but lack of Quaker students as well. A "Testimony" issued from New England Yearly Meeting in 1708 urges

> . . . That Friends do their endeavors to gett Friends School-masters or Mistresses. And in want of Such to have their children Taught att home. Not send them to Such as are not Friends because of the Danger of being Corrupted with the hurtfull Conversation of Other Youth or other wise.[4]

Though official bodies of the Society continually exhort Friends *not* to send their children to schools and teachers outside the supervision of Friends, the frequency of the exhortation only confirms the persistence of the practice. Some parents look for the cheapest possible education for their children. Some are dissatisfied that the schools do not show sufficient Quaker influence. Some assume that a Quaker school should be both fully staffed by Quakers *and* very inexpensive.

For many reasons, then, including some which are both short-sighted and self-serving, by as early as 1695 we find the familiar pattern: Quakers do not send their children to Quaker-sponsored or -supervised schools; there is then not enough tuition or direct meeting *per student* support to give teachers adequate salaries. Quaker teachers are not available, and sometimes those who are—Quaker or not—are poorly qualified to teach. That makes the schools less attractive to parents, who therefore send their children elsewhere, which further reduces the tuition and meeting support to pay teachers adequately. Instead of seeing these as separate problems, we might better speak of them as constituting a *syndrome*. The school in Waterford, Ireland in and after 1742 epitomizes the situation:

> . . . at times the school appears to have been suspended, at others, no friend suitably qualified offering as teacher, one of another profession had to be employed, the number of pupils was sometimes discouragingly small, and at length, on this account the school was thrown open to the children of those of other professions.[5]

Friends Seminary's experience is also instructive. In 1781, the School Committee wrote to the Two Weeks Meeting in London requesting a "young man, unmarried, a member of our Society, of an exemplary life and conversation" who was to be a very good penman, "well-vers' d in arithmetic and with a competent knowledge of English grammar." Hearing nothing from London for two years, they found a teacher closer to home who lasted from 1784 to 1793; two different teachers served in 1793, and one in 1794; the school closed from 1798-1800, "owing to the want of a suitable teacher."

In 1810, the school's Trustees asked the Meeting's permission to hire teachers "who were not members of the Society, but would conform with the Quaker teaching methods" and the Meeting agreed the following year.[6]

According to the 1760 report on the state of education to London Yearly Meeting:

> . . . in some counties there are no Friends' schools, . . . in others they are for the most part mixed; . . . the number of able and well qualified teachers amongst us is very small; and, from the difficulty there is in pro-curing suitable instructors, where they are wanted, it would seem that the number of scholars they produce, of reputation for learning, is very inconsiderable.[7]

Samuel Tuke reports that these schools were estimated to be teaching about 630 Quaker children, less than half the number who needed schooling. Helen G. Hole describes the teachers as "miserably underpaid."[8]

From the seventeenth well into the nineteenth centuries, on both sides of the Atlantic, Quaker education is comprised of a combination of meeting-supported schools and private ventures undertaken by individual Friends and more or less overseen by the meeting's education committee. In January 1777, a committee report to Wilmington Monthly Meeting lists one school under the care of a Preparative Meeting which is headed by a Friend, "one Woman's or Mistresses' School under the direction of Women's Preparative meeting to which some Friends children are sent, the Mistress not a Friend, two Master's schools to which Friends children are sent, one of the masters belonging to Friends but neither of their schools under the direction of the meeting."[9] In 1784, Philadelphia Monthly Meeting's Overseers directed five schools associated with the public school system and "five schools taught by Friends or persons believed to be members of the Society but not under the care of Overseers."[10] In 1836, there were only 37 teachers in New England Yearly Meeting and only about one-seventh of its 300 children in Quaker schools.[11]

"The Cheaper the Better"

Given what they thought they could ask of their teachers, and offer them in salary, it is hardly surprising that these schools could not find enough Quakers and had to turn to people of other religious persuasions to teach for them. What is surprising is how little Quakers seemed to care about the qualifications of their teachers." I do not know how it is amongst you," Anthony Benezet writes Samuel Fothergill in 1758, "but here, any person of tolerable morals, who can read and write, is esteemed sufficiently qualified for a schoolmaster . . ."[12] Writing to David Barclay in 1787, Moses Brown describes as "neglected" New England Friends' "discipline in regard to promoting of Schools." Few Friends were schoolmasters and the children who got any education were sent to other schools to get it.

> The general Method . . . now is, for Neighborhoods to hire a person a few months in the winter season to Teach School, the greater part of those thus hired are not able to teach with the propriety, or Accuracy of a Teacher, they having but a bare Qualification to do common business, and some not even this . . .[13]

Describing Wilmington, Delaware in the 1780s, Benjamin Ferris is much harsher.

. . . in country places, it was then common to employ as school master, any tolerably decent looking traveler who would apply for the office. The first and most important inquiry was, at how low a price would he teach a child for three calendar months. If that question was satisfactorily settled, and it was found that he could 'read, write and cipher,' the bargain was concluded. It most frequently happened that the applicant was a foreigner who spoke English (if it can be said that he spoke it at all) with a broad, uncouth accent, or vile brogue, announcing that he had just come ashore from some passenger ship; and it very often turned out, that he was an habitual drunkard, who spent a goodly portion of his time during school hours in sleep. To such teachers it was common to expose the morals of children.

Though Benjamin Ferris says that "things were not so bad" in the town of Wilmington, the best he can say is that "the teachers were frequently good moral characters, though often very deficient in other respects." In those early days, Wilmington Meeting had as many as ten schools under its care, some maintained by the Meeting and others run as private ventures by members. "The minutes often recorded that most of these schools were closed because of lack of the right kind of teacher."[14]

In *Some Necessary Remarks on the Education of the Youth in the Country-Parts of this and the Neighboring Governments,* Anthony Benezet argues that if a boy "be only designed for the common offices of life," it is thought enough for him to be taught

. . . to read and write, with a little arithmetick, and that often but imperfectly; no matter by whom, but the cheaper the better.

Thus it happens, that persons, every way, disqualified, both in learning and in morals, are, for the sake of having it done cheaper, entrusted with the education of children; by which means, the youth are deprived of learning, and instead of improving in virtue, which ought to be the main design of instruction, rather become proficients in vice.

It is small comfort to know that the lamentable quality of school-masters was general, not unique to Friends, in this period.

DEALING WITH DEARTH

There are only a few ways to respond to the dearth of qualified Quaker teachers: Close the School; Do Without and Make Do; Breed Our Own. In earlier days it happens now and again that a school is closed because it cannot find a Quaker teacher, and though that decision has great appeal for the purist, it does not solve the problem of providing Quaker youth with education. At best, it acknowledges the grim fact of failure. But it leaves students with no alternative except to be taught in a non-Quaker setting by non-Friends. As Friends Central School' s Committee described the challenge of competing with Philadelphia' s developing public education in 1845, "Temptation is now strongly presented to surrender the plastic mind of infancy to the forming hand of the stranger."[15]

DO WITHOUT AND MAKE DO

Making Do may lead in several directions—some more appealing than others. It can mean accepting that the schools will have to be "mixed" that is, having non-Quakers and Quakers together in staff and student body. Then a school can look for well-qualified, pious people, "close in profession" to Friends. In Philadelphia, the school Overseers report in 1801,

> . . . so great a slackness is evident among those who have the care of children that, for want of numbers to attend such schools sufficient to afford the teachers the means of a maintenance, we have been . . . under the necessity of again opening a door for allowing a mixture . . . [in schools intended to be 'select'].[16]

Ackworth School was fortunate enough to find a Quaker for its first teacher. Recommending Joseph Donbavand for the position, John Fothergill says he wishes he could put Donbavand under the instruction of a drill sergeant for a fortnight, "to teach him only how to walk." In one of those exercises of plain speech as close to rudeness as it is to ingratitude, the Committee minuted, "as no other suitable person offers he is appointed." Donbavand stayed for 38 years.[17] Ackworth's second teacher, George Lomax, was an attender but not a member of the Society. His appointment suggests "a great paucity of well qualified teachers among Friends at that time" says the historian of Ackworth's first century.[18] In addition to his teaching duties, Lomax was put in charge of keeping track of how much small beer and ale were made for the students.[19]

Other strategies for making do lead to hiring excellent teachers, even if they are not particularly pious or in profession with the Society. From the first third of the nineteenth century to the present day, we find some schools making the decision to hire the best trained teachers and later the most specialized teachers. When this happens, it is so the schools can be as attractive to students and their parents as possible. Wilmington minutes in 1829:

> The general improvement of schools in the mode of teaching and by the introduction of numerous useful branches of instruction . . . make it necessary that Friends seminaries should in some good degree keep pace with this improvement in order to deserve and insure the patronage of our own members.[20]

This choice to Make Do is full of compromises. A good, decent school influenced by Quaker principles and practices surely appears to be a better way to Make Do than to give up in despair and hire the cheapest drunkard who comes along, or to send children to state schools because they are less expensive than Quaker ones. As Nancy Reid Gibbs says of the choice available to Friends Seminary in the nineteenth century, it "was not between a partially Quaker school or a purely Quaker school; it was between a partially Quaker school or none at all."[21] For the purist, half a Quaker school is *not* better than none at all. But anyone who reads the history of Friends' education carefully will have to give up the sentimental notion that there has ever been such a thing as "a pure Quaker school" in any meaningful sense.

BREEDING OUR OWN

The means which the early Society entertained for addressing the dearth of Quaker teachers tell us a great deal about why it remained a problem. For almost a hundred years, from 1695 to 1778, documents from London Yearly Meeting, Ireland National Meeting, and Philadelphia Yearly Meeting propose essentially the same kinds of actions: Seek out "poor children of Friends [who] are of a proper genius for learning," to be trained as teachers. In 1715, minuting that ". . . the want of proper persons amongst Friends, qualified for school-masters, has been the occasion of great damage to the Society in many places. . . " London Yearly Meeting urges monthly meetings to "assist young men of low circumstances, whose genius and conduct may be suitable for that office, with the means requisite to obtain the proper qualifications; and when so qualified afford them the necessary encourage-ment for their support."

A plan of 1762 further proposed that ". . . lame and infirm persons, of competent abilities" be encouraged and assisted "to be qualified for the office of teacher."[22] In Philadelphia, in 1778, Anthony Benezet and Isaac Zane recommend training "lame children, and such, who in other respects, may be in-capable of supporting themselves by labour, to be educated and qualified to serve as School-Masters; a consideration well worthy our particular care, as well from duty, as interest."[23]

Significant attitudes toward teaching lie imbedded in these recommendations. Perhaps it speaks well for Friends that they recognize another way education is a Quaker social concern— teaching *may* be a means of comfortable subsistence, if not much upward mobility, for the children of the poor, or for lame or otherwise infirm people who cannot compete for more strenuous, more remunerative jobs. But the fundamental as-sumption is that anyone who can make a living some other way than teaching, will do so. In short, for Friends, as for the larger society, teachers are necessary but not honored.

As the details of these proposals make clear, to be a teacher in the eighteenth century required accepting a subordinate and dependent position in society. One of the most sophisti-cated plans, coming out of York Quarterly Meeting in 1762, proposed that five or more persons be engaged, each to be placed in one of the Particular Meetings most in need of a teacher. "It was expected that some friend of ability would give [each such teacher] his board and lodging for instructing his children and servants." Each schoolmaster would stay in a place for four to six months, teaching the children of poor Friends gratis, receiving payment from those who could pay, keeping an evening school for "servants and young people, who were deficient in learning, and to be cured of bad and unbecoming habits in reading." He would then move on to another location and repeat the work, including trying to improve "the qualifications of the masters and mistresses, who may happen to be stationary, and whose attainments were deficient." After a few years, when these itinerant teachers had improved the level of instruction in these several places, "they themselves were to settle down, in their honourable calling" where they might be of most service.[24]

Though this experiment was never tried, what the proposals took for granted deserves to be underlined. First, these teachers were not expected to have a home life or family of their own for at least the five years of their service. Second, they were to be dependents on the meeting, to move around every four to six months in those five years and to earn their room and board—in someone's home—by extra teaching. Third, it would appear they were to be engaged in teaching every waking hour: to keep school for poor children for free, to charge only those able to pay for their teaching, *and* to keep evening school—with no fee arrangements mentioned—for servants and young people "deficient in learning" and with "bad and unbecoming habits in reading." In their spare time, they were to raise the level of qualifications for local schoolmasters and mistresses.

Immediately after describing the duties expected of these teachers, Samuel Tuke notes that "Lame and infirm persons, of competent abilities, were to be encouraged, to place themselves under the care of the committee, to be qualified for the office of teacher, . . ." agreeing to place themselves under the committee's direction after they had qualified. Is it too suspicious to suggest that juxtaposing attention to the lame and infirm with the outline of these expectations of teachers reveals attitudes about teachers as people who should always be dependent on the charity of others?

In 1778, Benezet and Zane note that Friends think themselves under the necessity "of hiring no other but a single person, for a Master, on account of boarding him, from one house to another, amongst themselves; hence they are induced to bargain with transient persons, often of doubtful characters. . . ." Some of those appointed have been men of corrupt minds, but even where they have been moral, "yet they are seldom likely to remain in the service any longer than some employ more agreeable to support themselves offers. . . ." Their Committee makes a radically different proposal for meeting the needs for schoolmasters, which is never acted upon:

> That within the compass of each Meeting, where the settlement of a school is necessary, a plot of ground be provided, sufficient for a garden, orchard, grass for a cow, &c. and that a suitable house, stable, &c. be erected thereon. . . . Such a provision would be an encouragement to a staid person, with a family, who will be likely to remain a considerable time, perhaps, his whole life, in the service, to engage therein.[25]

Teaching as Ministry

In every generation, there are people who understand that they are called to teach as a ministry. John Stroud tells us that when the Society as a whole in England had lost interest in the schools, responsibility for Quaker education fell on a small number of devoted schoolmasters who ". . . alone kept alive the spirit of an earlier enthusiasm during the period of decline which set in at about the first quarter of the eighteenth century and lasted until the establishment of Ackworth in 1779."[26]

The larger Society of Friends has enjoyed a reputation for dedication to its schools which really belongs to small numbers of teachers, parents, and school committee members. Anthony Benezet is one of those devoted teachers in the American colonies. For him, educating and training young people "both with relation to time and eternity" is, "next to preaching the Gospel . . . the greatest and most acceptable service we can offer to the great Father and Head of the family of the whole earth, and the most exalted duty a Christian mind can be engaged in." Writing just at the time Quakers have withdrawn from governing Pennsylvania, Benezet holds out teaching as a particularly appropriate calling for people prohibited by principle from "meddling with offices, &c." Quakers, he says, are "a people, rather than others, to serve God and our country in the education of the youth."

"Shake Hands with the World"

Precisely because he is so devoted a teacher, what Benezet says about the profession's standing carries weight. He acknowledges that for younger Friends to dedicate themselves to teaching will mean "to shake hands with the world and all its enticing prospects, seeking and expecting nothing from it but dread and trouble. . ."

It is worth recalling that, in 1778, Benezet and Zane exhort Friends of means to support improving the circumstances of Quaker teachers by invoking "our blessed Saviour's express command, '*Lay not up for yourselves, treasures on the earth . . .*' " None of their recommendations bear fruit. Writing twenty years earlier to Samuel Fothergill, Benezet acknowledges that, if the good health of Quaker education requires sacrifice, a disproportionate share of the burden will always be borne by the teachers.

> And although by engaging in the education of the youth we should be deprived of some of those things so desirable to nature, which we might better enjoy and accumulate in the way of trade, and thereby look upon ourselves under affliction, yet may we not hope that it will be termed for righteousness' sake, and therefore should not we have thereat to rejoice, and be exceeding glad, and even leap for joy![27]

For the person who already knows herself or himself called by God to teach, Benezet' s words would be deeply inspiring. As an argument to recruit those who are unsure, those with a possible "genius" for teaching, or poor or physically impaired persons, however, an encouragement "to serve Christ in a station generally so little regarded, where the labour of love . . . is much hid" might be far less appealing.

Benezet testifies from his own experience "that it is a great mistake to think that the education of youth is toilsome and disagreeable . . . except to such who from a desire of gain, take upon them the care of more children than they ought. . . ." But since a common recommendation for improving the pay of teachers, on both sides of the Atlantic, was to establish a per-student rate the meeting would contribute above tuition, in some cases leaving the teacher free to bring in additional tuition-paying students, Benezet' s strictures against teachers who try to teach too many children seem unduly harsh. John Woolman, who himself kept a small private venture school for a time, recognizes that teachers can find it difficult to support their families without taking on too many students to give each the appropriate spiritual and educational attention:

> But where the straitness of a man's circumstances, joined with the small wages set on teaching children, proves a temptation and so enters into his heart that he takes charge of too many for the measure of his gift, or where the desire for wealth so corrupts the heart of any that they take charge of too many, here the true order of a Christian education is lost.[28]

Given what we know about teachers' pay, the phrase "desire for wealth" seems unduly alarmist.

By the end of the eighteenth century and early in the nineteenth, Quakers in both England and the United States were increasingly feeling the weight of responsibility to provide better education for their children and, as a means to that end, to provide more substantial support for training school teachers. (Most frequently, the plans speak of training "masters" though The Mount is early in developing a teaching apprentices program for its own needs.) New England Yearly Meeting, in establishing the school at Portsmouth which would become Moses Brown School, identified the first priority as creating a school or schools "for the Education of our Children & Youth, in order to Qualify, not only a sufficient number of Instructors and School Masters; But that the Poor Children, and others of the Society, may receive Necessary Learning, to Qualify them for Business."[29]

With the creation of Nine Partners (later Oakwood) School, Moses Brown, Westtown, and later the schools which became colleges (Haverford, Guilford, and Earlham), and

Swarthmore, the first Quaker institution created specifically
as a college to train teachers, American Quakerism may be
said to have begun to address its long-term need for Quaker
teachers in a substantial way. In England, first at Ackworth,
later at Sidcot, Islington, and Wigton in the early nineteenth
century,[30] teacher-apprentice programs arose to deal with the
same problem. "For well over a century," according to Elfrida
Vipont Foulds, "Ackworth apprentices formed the backbone
of the teaching profession in the Society of Friends."[31]
Though the first apprentice teacher was engaged at Ackworth
in 1782, it was not until 1848, when a bequest established
The Flounders' Institute, ". . . for the education of the sons
of poorer members of the Society of Friends with a special
view to render them competent to undertake the education
and instruction of youth . . ." that English Friends made any
set provision for training teachers.

APPRENTICESHIPS AND OTHER WAYS
TO GET TEACHING FOR FREE

For Benezet and Woolman, the call to teaching was inevitably also a call to voluntary poverty. For each of them, that
dual call was a joyful gift from God. For other Friends,
perhaps especially those too busy making money to attend to
the needs of Quaker schools, it was convenient to subscribe
to the same view. Campbell Stewart says the pattern of
service, poverty, intellectual limitation, and strict Quaker
plainness "lay on Friend apprentices and on most Friend
teachers in the first forty years of the [nineteenth] century."[32]

Not until 1804 did the Ackworth Committee give up
"the idea that only a voluntary Superintendent could serve
Ackworth with a truly religious sense of concern," and pay
its newly-appointed fifth superintendent a salary. Early on at

Wigton and Rawdon, no regular salaries were paid the Superintendents, but 'gifts' were occasionally given. At the Mount, successive Superintendents not only received no salary but even paid "handsomely" for their residence at the school. Moreover, "when there was a deficit . . . , these generous people were expected to pay it."[33]

The first Ackworth apprentice was given an extra year's schooling and articled to remain at the school for six or seven more years. His perquisites, in addition to room and board, included sixpence a month for the first three years and a shilling a month for the final three years. Subsequent apprentices, ages fifteen to seventeen, had heavy responsibilities, including having to take charge of classes of 60 or 70 boys outside of classtime. Not surprisingly, at Ackworth, Sidcot, and Islington, many of the apprentices did not remain to serve their full terms.

In 1836, The Mount tried an apprenticeship system to train the women teachers it needed. Four or five girls a year—increased to ten after 1857—were to be admitted at lower fees, given training and an extra year of schooling, then engaged for several years as junior teachers at the school. According to Campbell Stewart, ". . . girl trainees received a meagre professional training at The Mount from 1866 to 1902, and none at all for thirty years up to 1866."[34] Lydia Rous, Superintendent at The Mount from 1866-1879, gave greater emphasis to the intellectual development of apprentice teachers.

By the latter third of the nineteenth century, the apprentice system was in fact harming its participants' professional prospects. The 1879 Education Conference report notes that apprentices at The Mount receive training "not sufficient to enable them to matriculate or gain any certificate of recognized value." At age twenty-one they are free to matriculate if they can afford to forgo earning a year' s salary. By contrast, the young woman who enters The Mount as a regular student "receives uninterrupted systematic instruction for two or three years; matriculates at the London University, and at the age of nineteen is probably in a situation where she is gaining 40 or 50 [pounds] per annum."[35]

By the beginning of the twentieth century in England, responding to the need to train teachers for state-supported schools, training colleges became widespread. In order for Friends' schools to compete with these schools, their teachers needed to be certified by some external system. The Flounders' Institute course of study was adapted to the examination requirements of London University in 1858 and became connected with Leeds University in 1904. In 1909, the Flounders Institute ended and the endowment was used to give direct grants to Quakers to study at other universities and training institutions. In England, "in the twentieth century, Quakers have come to rely on the established training courses at universities or training colleges, for, except for the few at Woodbrooke, Friends could not independently afford to train students to that standard."[36] In the United States, where small church-related colleges dominated higher education until after the Second World War, it was natural for Quaker colleges to establish education departments which prepared students either for Quaker schools or for certification as public school teachers. In addition, during the depths of the Depression, Friends Council on Education sponsored an Interne Council from 1935 to meet emergency needs in the schools and for new, inexperienced teachers. "Each school acted independently and quite individually with offers to accept interne teachers, many as observors, some as apprentices, others as part-time, and still others as dormitory assistants. The remuneration ran from zero to about 300 dollars."

Describing the "apprentice plan" in 1940, the Friends Council says ". . . Friends' schools can make a contribution to education as a whole by endeavoring to train, with as sound a professional program as possible, the type of teacher desired in Friends' schools and which the best modern schools require." Rachel Letchworth acknowledges that ". . . the internes of 1935 were defending a system which in better times financially would have come close to exploitation." The Interne Program, begun under John Lester, later developed under Irvin C. Poley into a program which also granted education credit through the University of Pennsylvania.[37]

"Perfecting the Imaginary"

We Quakers seem to treat any bad news about ourselves as though it were a sore tooth to enjoy biting down on. At the same time, of course, we cannot help taking comfort from believing that some other Quaker is more at fault for the bad news than we are. Ranking our schools and other Quaker institutions from "Pure" through "Real" to "Not Really" is one of our great indoor sports. "More Quaker than Thee" is another. Each has the advantage that the rules and scoring are completely subjective.

It is commonly argued that schools cannot claim to be Quaker unless they have a "critical mass" of members of the Religious Society of Friends among both students and faculty. If this argument rests on the premise that there was a time when our schools deserved to be called Quaker because they had such a "critical mass" to shape the school life, the historical record casts doubt on such a confident conclusion. Certainly some schools have had more Quakers as a percentage of students and faculty than others. Day schools have perhaps had to struggle more than some boarding schools to recruit Quaker students and faculty. Some yearly meeting schools have been, or tried to be, more homogeneous than others. And certainly we can see that the Quaker presence on school committees or boards has, in the past, been maintained at very high levels. But that is only to say that official author-ity and ultimate control of the schools have remained in the hands of Quakers, even while financial support from meetings and individual Friends continually diminished and the num-ber of Quaker students and teachers continually shrank.

Helen G. Hole says, "In the past, Quaker education has had a vitality which came from its being a living expression of a religious life and a part of the ongoing growth of that life." She then asks, "Can we honestly say that this is still true?"[38] The historical record shows a far more ambiguous development. Even if we choose to believe that everything that happened in Quaker education from the founding of the first Quaker schools in 1668—about which we know very little—was perfect, we cannot escape the fact that by 1695 all the problems we now face were already evident. These subsequent three hundred years have been a continual, and largely unsuccessful, struggle to win Quakers to support their schools and their teachers adequately. Campbell Stewart claims that education did not really become a "concern" for the whole Society or its regions in England "until the late eighteenth and early nineteenth centuries, but was, before that, the 'concern' of individuals or small groups."[39] Even after becoming a matter of wider interest, however, Quaker education has been sustained by very small numbers of people—sacrificial teachers, headmasters and headmistresses, dedicated committee members, and parents—while the larger body of Friends manifests what Anthony Benezet and Isaac Zane call a "backwardness . . . to contribute." "If this had not been the case," they add, "a matter of so great importance, as the virtuous education of our youth, would not have lain neglected, for so long a course of years."[40]

If there were giants in the earth in former days, their numbers have always been too small to argue either the vitality of Quaker education or an organic connection with the Religious Society of Friends, whose passing some writers mourn. Each age has had to struggle with the same grinding daily problems to sustain Quaker schools. Each school has to find ways to attract Quakers as well as others who are prepared to live sacrificially according to Quaker principles. There is not a school in the Religious Society of Friends whose history does not celebrate great souls whose devotion has made Quaker principles live for generations of students but who have not themselves been Friends. Many of the giants have been, or are, non-Quakers.

This history may teach different lessons to different people. That there have not been enough Quaker students or teachers for virtually the whole of Friends' history may lead some to despair of seeing Quaker education fulfill its promise. The discovery that there has not been a golden age in the past may be heartbreaking for some. For others, this history of struggle, rising and falling and rising again over a few years or decades, is far more inspiring than the picture of a golden age to which we can no longer aspire. Even if our best days are not in the future—and they may be—why should we not live as though there are still good days ahead for Quaker education, good work to do, students to teach, companions in the common quest to find and cherish?

My reading of this story leads me to hope, for it shows me that those who accomplished much in the past were enough like me that I can hope to learn from and emulate their example. My favorite stanza from the hymn "For All the Saints" reads:

Oh blest communion, fellowship divine,
We feebly struggle, they in glory shine.
Yet all are one in Thee, for all are Thine,
Hallelujah, Hallelujah.

Quakers struggling to find enough teachers and students
to sustain their schools, improvising ways of training new
teachers and educating the students they had, piecing
together the scanty resources they had to teach each new
generation, can be made to shine in a sentimental light, a
false glory. They can be used to afflict us because we take the
feebleness of our struggle as evidence of our unfaithfulness.
Or we can see in them the blest communion, the fellowship
of those who feebly struggle to do God's work in the conditions in which they find themselves. Our call is not to
become an earlier generation but to be as faithful as possible
in our own. Quaker education is hanging on by a thread, as
usual. We can deplore the hanging on, be grateful for the
thread, or take hope from the *as usual*.

Notes

1. Tuke, *Five Papers*, 65; Hippolyte Taine, quoted in Richard Pipes, *The Russian Revolution*, Vintage Books, New York, 1991, 121.

2. Brinton, *Quaker Education*, 95-96.

3. D.G.B. Hubbard, *Early Quaker Education, 1650-1780*, M.A.Thesis of University of London, 1939, 161, quoted in Campbell Stewart, 46.

4. R. W. Kelsey, *Centennial History of Moses Brown School: 1819-1919*, Moses Brown School, Providence, 1919, 8-9.

5. Report Concerning Friends Schools in Ireland, Appendix to Tuke, *Five Papers*, 11.

6. Gibbs, *Children of Light*, 20, 24-25, 27.

7. Tuke, *Five Papers*, 50.

8. Helen G. Hole, *Things Civil and Useful*, Friends United Press, Richmond, Indiana, 9.

9. Author unknown, *Friends School in Wilmington*, Friends School, Wilmington, Delaware, 1948, 4.

10. Carol H. Brown, ed., *A Friends Select History*, Friends Select School, Philadelphia, 1989, 13.

11. Hole, *Things Civil and Useful*, 9.

12. Benezet, Anthony, "Letter to Samuel Fothergill" (Eleventh month 27th, 1758) in *The Friends Library*, Vol. ix, Philadelphia, Joseph Rakestraw, 1837-50, 220-22.

13. Kelsey, *Moses Brown School*, 10-11.

14. *Friends School in Wilmington*, 6-7.

15. Clayton L. Faraday, *Friends Central History 1845-1984*, Friends Central School, Philadelphia, 5.

16. Brown, *A Friends Select School History*, 18.

17. *So Numerous a Family: 200 Years of Quaker Education at Ackworth*, Ackworth School, England, 1979, 12.

18. Henry Thompson, *A History of Ackworth School During Its First Hundred Years*, Ackworth, England, 1879, 36.

19. Thompson, *Ackworth School*, 36. One of the complaints leveled against the school in 1789 was that there was "insufficiency in the supply of beer . . ." 82. In 1795 a visiting committee trying to save money expressed concern about the expenditure for malt and thought that "one hundred gallons of table beer and fifty gallons of ale were a large quantity to be consumed weekly." 89. Elfrida Foulds' *History of Ackworth*, 1959, tells of continual complaints about the quality of the beer served at the school. ". . . The boys had even grumbled to Joseph John Gurney about it and he had dealt with them promptly and firmly. 'You should throw your heads back,' he had said, 'and give your minds to it!'" The school ceases to serve beer after 1842, the year the Inn became a Temperance Hotel. This note has little to do with the breeding of Quaker teachers but is offered as a reward to the dedicated reader.

20. *Wilmington School History*, 9.

21. Gibbs, *Children of Light*, 198.

22. Tuke, *Five Papers*, 13-14, 44-45, 53.

23. "Some Observations Relating to the Establishment of Schools, Agreed to by the Committee, to be laid for consideration before the Yearly-Meeting," signed on behalf of the Committee by Anthony Benezet and Isaac Zane, 29th 9th Month, 1778, forwarded from Yearly Meeting to the attention of Quarterly, Monthly and Preparative Meetings by James Pemberton, Clerk of the Yearly Meeting, 10 Month 2nd, 1778.

24. Tuke, *Five Papers*, 53-54.

25. Benezet, *Some Observations*, 1788.

26. L.J. Stroud, *The History of Quaker Education in England, 1647-1903*, M. Ed Thesis, University of Leeds, 1944, 60, quoted in Campbell Stewart, 47.

27. Letter to Samuel Fothergill, Eleventh month 27th, 1758.

28. John Woolman, "On Schools," printed as Chapter Fourteen of *A Plea for the Poor* in Moulton, 265.

29. Kelsey, *Moses Brown School*, 16-17.

30. Campbell Stewart discusses other boarding schools after the founding of Ackworth, 60-75. They are: Sidcot (1808), Saffron Walden (1811) (previously at Islington and Clerkenwell), Wigton (1815), Bootham (1823), The Mount (1831), Rawdon (1832), Penketh (1834), Ayton (1841), and Sibford (1842).

31. Foulds, *History of Ackworth*, 42

32. Campbell Stewart, *Quakers and Education*, 96-100.

33. Foulds, *History of Ackworth*, 55; Sturge and Clark, *The Mount School*, quoted in Campbell Stewart, 96-97.

34. Campbell Stewart, *Quakers and Education*, 97, 110.

35. Campbell Stewart, *Quakers and Education*, 98-99.

36. Campbell Stewart, *Quakers and Education*, 110.

37. Rachel K. Letchworth, "Yesterday, Today—And Tomorrow? Friends Council on Education, 1931-1981", 1981, 7-10; "Internships in Friends' Schools: A Development in Teacher Training," 1940, 4.

38. Hole, *Things Civil and Useful*, 1.

39. Campbell Stewart, *Quakers and Education*, 41.

40. Benezet, *Some Observations*, 1788.

Six

⟹◆⟸

"A LIBERAL, GUARDED AND RELIGIOUS EDUCATION ON MODERATE TERMS"

Pedants sneer at an education which is useful. But if education is not useful, what is it?

We have abstained at the present time from introducing views calculated to increase the expenses of instruction; yet, we desire that the attention of Friends may be turned to a more enlarged consideration of the subject, and be prepared to act thereon, as way opens.

. . . The greater the Quaker presence in the school, the greater its financial peril.[1]

TENSIONS AND CONTRADICTIONS

In 1667, when George Fox urged setting up two boarding schools, one for boys and one for girls, where they might be instructed "in all things civil and useful in the creation, " he set a plumb line for Quaker education. "This brief but comprehensive phrase," Samuel Tuke says, was designed "to include every branch and department of knowledge which can shed any truly beneficial rays on the condition of man."[2]

111

It reflects the hopefulness about human possibilities and confidence in the power of education which remain characteristic of Quakerism.

A phrase equally pithy and relevant, though less stirring, appears in 1823, in Bootham School's announced purpose to provide: "a liberal, guarded and religious education on moderate terms." This phrase sums up the mixture of goals Quakers have expected of their schools and identifies most of the tensions and contradictions which Quaker schools must address. The tensions cluster around two kinds of issues, educational and socio-economic. The first kind is represented in some of the key terms we encounter to define the particular educational goals of Friends schools: "liberal," "literary," "religiously guarded." These have to do primarily with what is taught and how the teaching and learning are organized.

The second kind of tension is nicely captured in that bland phrase "on moderate terms." The fundamental economic problem in establishing schools is how to pay for them, because the fundamental social problem is how to make education available to those who cannot pay for it themselves. It would be embarrassing to mention something so obvious, except that obvious problems are often the hardest to solve and are therefore those we would most like to blame on someone.

EDUCATION AS SOCIAL CONCERN

The 1832 Philadelphia "Report of the Joint Committee of Four Monthly Meetings to Consider the Subject of Select Schools," touches on all the themes to be explored in this essay:

> As it should be the purpose of these schools to afford to our youth a liberal as well as a guarded education, they

should be well furnished with apparatus and other requisite facilities. . . . The price of tuition . . . should be so graded as to be adequate to meet the salaries of the teachers, the rent of rooms and other incidental expenses. . . . But . . . it is desirable that moderate prices should be maintained so as to place the benefits of the schools within the reach of Friends generally. . . .[3]

The rich and well-to-do have always been able to educate their children, by hiring tutors within the family or by paying for excellent schools. That has not changed, even with the development of public education. The richest and most racially and socio-economically segregated education now available in the United States is in public education in very rich suburbs, where the tax base can provide such education. The same pattern obtains at the "flagship" campuses of state universities, where the students' family median income is so high. If, as has always been the case within the Religious Society of Friends, the social concern for education is to make it as widely available as possible, so as to liberate as many people as possible, a basic question will always be how to provide education for the poor. Answering that question will have significant influence on every aspect of a school's life— who the students will be, who the teachers will be, what the course of study will be, sometimes even what the food and housing will be like.

JOHN BELLERS' *Proposals*

One of the earliest Quaker attempts to address education as a social concern is John Bellers' *Proposals for Raising a Colledge of Industry of All Useful Trades and Husbandry* in 1696. Bellers' proposals are remarkable for their comprehensiveness but also for what they leave out. He offers his proposals to both the Society of Friends,[4] and the wider society, though he presents slightly different arguments to the two populations. In his Epistle to Friends in 1718, Bellers argues, from the premise that the two commandments are to love God and to love our neighbor as ourselves, and from the words of the Apostle James that "pure religion and undefil'd before God and the Father is to visit (or Relieve) the Fatherless and the widows in their Affliction, and to keep unspotted from the world", that

> Therefore a Virtuous Education that may keep the YOUTH unspotted from the world, and a sufficient Provision for the imployment of the Able POOR, with a charitable Subsistence from the Disabled, is one of the most Essential visible Parts of the true Apostolick Christian Religion.

Here, in the briefest compass, is an attempt to address both sets of issues which press Quaker education—how to give a virtuous education which will keep the young "unspotted from the world," a goal which in a later generation will be described as offering "guarded" or "religiously guarded" education—and how to give useful education leading to gainful employment to those who cannot afford it, in this case the poor and the disabled. Bellers acknowledges that there are good Quaker schools near London, costing eighteen or twenty pounds a year, and schools in the North at eight or ten pounds a year, for "such whose Parents are able and willing" to pay. But there are many Friends who can afford neither, and "keeping their Children at Home, and sending them daily to what School is nearest them, . . . may be of very Pernicious Consequence, by the Company and Conversation they may meet with either at School or out of it."[5]

The "College" he proposes will board students cheaply, teach them "all sorts of Learning and Languages" as well as "all sorts of Handicraft Trades," and provide paid work for the children in order to reduce costs for their parents. Bellers insists this would not be a Workhouse or a Hospital, "the first sounding too much like a Bridewell, and the second like an Almshouse," but a College, which "bespeaks a more *Liberal education.*"[6]

ADDRESSING THE ECONOMIC PROBLEM

Bellers appeals to enlightened self-interest in addressing the wider English society through Parliament and "The Thinking and Publick-Spirited": "It's the Interest of the Rich to take Care of the Poor, and their Education, by which they will take Care of their own Heirs, for . . . who knows how soon it may be his own lot, or his Posterities, to fall poor?" His educational plan proposes three aims: "First, Profit for the Rich, (which will be Life to the rest). Secondly, A plentiful Living for the Poor, without difficulty. Thirdly, A good Education for Youth, that may tend to prepare their Souls into the Nature of the good Ground." All this, he asserts on his title-page "will be Advantage to the Government, by the Increase of the People, and their Riches."[7]

Bellers ingeniously attempts to solve a number of apparently disparate problems in one grand plan: to provide basic and practical and "virtuous" education to the children of the poor, to teach them a livelihood and put them to work, to provide for the elderly and infirm poor, to make the school self-sustaining and provide a profit for its Founders, thus modeling solutions to these problems throughout society. On the title-page of the *Proposals* appears the motto, "Industry Brings Plenty" followed by the lines "The Sluggard shall be

cloathed with Raggs. He that will not Work, shall not Eat."
If those words seem intended to appeal to the rich, in the
body of the proposal Bellers emphasizes, "This Colledge-
Fellowship will make Labour, and not Money, the Standard
to value all Necessities by. . . ."

Finishing the Second Creation

A clear philosophy and theology underlie Bellers' proposals.
Since humanity fell, he argues, God has "continued a second
Creation" whose end is to "produce from Men a Creation of
Angels, or beings equal to them." Citing the example of
"the children, called The Black-Guard"—the idle poor,
unemployed and unemployable—he says:

> They are capable of being Saints on Earth, and as
> Angels in Heaven; How much is owing to Birth and
> Education, that hath made the difference between
> them and us? Was it our Vertue or their Vice that
> made that Difference? Had we any Capacity before
> we were born?[8]

Education is a means by which human beings participate
in and serve that "second Creation." Through humanity's
improvement over time, brought about by God's grace and
the effects of education, we may become "Angels, or beings
equal to them," but in this life we must know how to make
our living, to earn our food, clothing, and shelter. In this life,
the human soul and mind are housed in the human body,
and we cannot meet the needs of one unless we meet the
needs of all three. Helping to put people into good ways of
earning a living "will be instrumental in finishing [God's]
Creation. . . ." In *Some Reasons for an European State*, 1710,
He argues:

Imposing Religion, without reaching the Understanding, is not Leading Men to Heaven. Men will not be sav'd against their own Wills. Neither can a Man firmly believe what he is not convinced of. Where ideas are Clear and Understood Artists don't differ about them. There is no need of a Rack to force a mathematical Demonstration; nor to make a Mechanick to be a good Workman.[9]

Bellers' proposals represent more than a curiosity in Quaker history. Though he offers them for a number of years without response, and they are never fully enacted, in 1702 they bore fruit as a laboring school which ultimately became the Quaker boarding school Saffron Walden. From their first appearance in print they had the signed support of a number of Quaker leaders, among them George Fox and William Penn. We have warrant, therefore, for believing that they expressed some shared assumptions about education among Friends.

Whose Need Lays An Obligation On Us?

Some features of Bellers' analysis of educational issues and recommendations for addressing them deserve particular notice. The curriculum was to be eminently practical. The school was to be what in the nineteenth century is called a "laboring school"—it required four hours of study and four hours of labor each day—later an important feature in a number of Quaker schools and, in the form of "cooperative education," a defining characteristic of a number of experimental colleges in the United States today.

What is most significant for our understanding of Quaker education, however, is how precisely Bellers identifies a population whose need for education laid a religious obligation on Quakers. In the first instance, it is the children of poor Friends, but that, though a constant theme in the history of Quaker schools, very early broadens into a social concern for other groups who are deprived of opportunities for schooling—e.g. children of their fellow prisoners and their persecutors, Blacks, American Indians, the daughters of poor people not members of the Society of Friends, even the children of parents who were disowned by Friends.[10]

In recent years we have seen the same kind of commitment to education as a social concern expressed through the creation of schools specifically for students with learning differences or who are underachievers in traditional schools, for example, The Quaker School at Horsham, Delaware Valley Friends School, Stratford Friends School, the Mary McDowell Center, and Thornton Friends School. Detroit Friends School, the first intentionally integrated school in Michigan, was founded *not* for Friends' children but "at the behest of civic leaders looking to set up an inclusive school."

"To Teach the Rudiments . . . To The Poor"

Thomas Budd's proposals for education, published in 1685, share many of Bellers' assumptions. In *Good Order Established in Pennsylvania and New Jersey in America* he recommends that laws should establish "that all Persons inhabiting in the said Provinces, do put their Children seven years to the publick school, or longer, if the parents please," that boys and girls be instructed in reading, writing, arithmetic, Latin, and other useful languages, as well as some " Art, Mystery, or Trade," and that

... to the end that the Children of poor People, and the Children of *Indians* may have the like good Learning with the Children of Rich People, let them be maintained free of charge to their Parents, out of the Profits of the school, arising by the Work of the Scholars. . . .[11]

In his earliest versions of the Frame of Government for Pennsylvania, William Penn set forth the principle that education was the function of the civil authority. One article of the Charter for the "public" school whose descendant is the William Penn Charter School, provided for "poor children to be taught and educated in good literature until they be fit to be put apprentices . . ."[12]

Friends in Wilmington, Delaware set up a school in 1748, "to teach the rudiments of reading, writing and 'ciphering' to the poor of the neighborhood." The Meeting seems to be remarkable for its sense of responsibility for educating poor children who were not Quaker as well as for educating black and white students together. In 1772, Benjamin Ferris left the meeting 25 pounds, the interest from which was to be applied yearly to the "Schooling of Poor Children either White or Black, who are not under the care of any Society, at the School that is under the Inspection of Friends;" in 1783, David Ferris left money for "the Schooling of Poor Children White or Black, that have no right in any religious Society;" and in 1794 John and Mary Dickinson left 200 pounds for poor children or children not in affluent circumstances, "without distinction of religious profession." A minute of 1813 records that money from funds is "principally expended on Poor Children not of our Society whom we have sent to several Schools taught by Women Friends not under the inspection of any committee."[13]

"With Relation to Time and Eternity"

Perhaps no one embodies dedication to the interwoven aims of Quaker education more fully than Anthony Benezet (1713-1784). One of the great and early anti-slavery activists in the Religious Society of Friends, friend of John Woolman, whose *Journal* he saw through the editorial process to publication, writer and publicist on the evils of slavery, he was, by life-long calling, a teacher. In a letter to Samuel Fothergill dated Eleventh month 27th, 1758 he asks, "Ought not the educating and training up of youth, both with relation to time and eternity, next to our more immediate duty to God, be the chief concern of every one that really desires the welfare and enlargement of the borders of Zion?"

With relation to time and eternity captures the double calling of education: to offer practical learning—"literary" in that it taught the skills of reading and writing and introduced "good literature," "liberal" in that it taught such useful and broadening knowledge as the natural sciences, foreign languages, mathematics, as well as crafts and trades,—and "guarded" or "religiously guarded" education in that it offered a framework of "virtuous" learning in which practical education could take place.

Schools for Black People

A revealing test case for Quaker education as social concern is the commitment to educating Black people in America, both slave and free, which emerges very early among Friends. In his Letter to the Governor of Barbados in 1671, George Fox urges educating the Blacks and Tawnies. Schools for Negroes are recorded in the minutes of Quaker meetings in

North Carolina as early as 1787. A minute from Eastern Quarterly Meeting of North Carolina Friends in 1787 speaks of assisting preparative meetings to promote schools for Black people, and in 1818 Deep River Quarterly Meeting records concern for "the Care of people of Colour . . . to be instructed in School learning to fit them for business, and in useful employment in life. . . ." The first Quaker school in the Commonwealth of Virginia was founded by Robert Pleasants in 1782, specifically for "blacks and people of color." It was short-lived, but other attempts to offer schooling to black children were made until the legislature forbade them in the 1830s. In 1826, Linda Selleck reports, Indiana Yearly Meeting convened its first committee on Concerns of People of Color. This committee made sure that black children "were either taught by black teachers with Quaker financial aid, or enrolled in the local Quaker schools."[14]

In addition to his teaching at the Girls' School, Anthony Benezet kept an evening school for Black children in his home for twenty years before the concern matured in 1770—largely through his influence—into a commitment of Philadelphia Monthly Meeting to start a school ". . . for the instruction of negro and mulatto children in reading, writing, and other useful learning suitable to their capacity and circumstance, . . . clear of expense to their parents. . . ."[15] The school was open to boys and girls and classes were taught co-educationally. The first appeal for "subscriptions" or donations to support the work describes it as a "concern for the religious instruction of many who now remain in ignorance, and deprived of the valuable blessings others enjoy." *A Brief Sketch of the Schools for Black People*, 1867, says the intent was that the students "should receive such a religious and literary instruction as would qualify them for the proper enjoyment of freedom, and for becoming useful and worthy citizens." In an early report to the Meeting about the school, the Committee writes:

> . . . As we have had frequent opportunities through the course of this service, for observing their capacity for learning, to be equal to other children, we are confirmed in our apprehensions that it is our duty and true interest as men and Christians, to promote and support this school; and hope that in other places, a concern of the same kind will be raised, as the good effects of our care become known and observed.

Anthony Benezet's will, leaving his estate to the school, specifies that it is to employ "a religious minded person, or persons, to teach a number of negro, mulatto, or Indian children, to read, write, arithmetic, plain accounts, needle work &c . . ." and that preference be given to "an industrious, careful person, of true piety, who may be or become suitably qualified. . . ." For Benezet, as for other Friends of his time, practical education *is* religious education, when the teaching is done "with relation to time and eternity."[16]

In 1837, Philadelphia Quakers established The Institute for Colored Youth, which later became Cheyney State College in Cheyney, Pennsylvania, "for the education of colored youth in higher learning." The Institute reversed the usual pattern in Quaker-founded schools, starting with advanced literary education and only later focusing on practical training. Fanny Jackson-Coppin, who was for thirty-six years associated with the Institute as teacher and principal, describes teaching Caesar, Virgil, Cicero, Horace, Xenophon's *Anabasis*, and New Testament Greek, as well as Normal School training in English, teaching theory, and methods. The School offered equally demanding programs in science and Mathematics. After the Centennial Exhibition of 1876, she reports, the school expanded from its higher educational studies to offer mechanical, industrial, and agricultural courses. Explaining why it was so important that an Industrial Department should be added to the Institute, Fanny Jackson-Coppin says, "The only place at the time where a colored boy could learn a trade, was in the House of Refuge or the Penitentiary!"[17]

Other schools serving black educational needs in Philadelphia before the Civil War included the Adelphi School, which, starting in 1808, offered instruction, "for black girls and infants of both sexes," the Joseph Sturge Mission School, which offered Bible classes, and the Beehive School, which offered elementary subjects and practical arts such as sewing and knitting from 1865 to 1888. The Association for the Free Instruction of Adult Colored Persons began in 1789 and offered night-school education until 1890.[18]

After the Civil War, Philadelphia Friends took active part in founding schools for freedmen in the South. In 1869, the Hicksites "were maintaining ten schools with a student enrollment of 632." In the same year, under Orthodox Friends, "3,700 black students received instruction in thirty-seven schools in southern Virginia and North Carolina under the aegis of the Friends' Freedmen Association of Philadelphia." The Baltimore Association is credited with re-establishing education in many parts of the South. Of the sixty schools it founded in North Carolina, some admitted black students from the start. In 1867 the Baltimore Association reported six day and twenty-two Sunday Schools for blacks, serving an estimated 1600 to 2000 students. Indiana Yearly Meeting established and supported Southland College, an industrial and teacher training school for black people in Arkansas for sixty years. With the end of Reconstruction, Friends' schools in the South became harder to sustain, but "as late as 1880 the Orthodox group continued to sustain eighteen schools and was spending $10,000 a year to maintain them."[19]

Not all Quaker-influenced work for black education occurred under the supervision of Quaker organizations. While she gave Philadelphia Yearly Meeting (Hicksite) $20,000 for freedmen's schools, Anna T. Jeanes donated a million dollars to establish a fund for developing "rudimentary education, moral and spiritual refinement for rural, community, or country schools for Southern states." According to Philip S. Benjamin, "the educational philosophy to which the Quakers subscribed in the nineties was that of Booker T. Washington, the black accommodationist whose Tuskeegee Institute set the pattern for Negro schooling for decades." The Quaker emphasis on practical education made Washington's approach especially congenial. Influenced by the Tuskeegee model, the Jeanes Fund supported industrial and vocational education and sponsored special supervising teachers, but what is especially important is its role in developing African-American teachers. "Jeanes teachers were members of the black race who worked on a county-wide basis to help improve schools and community life for blacks." In South Carolina alone, from 1908 to 1964, 180 Jeanes teachers worked in 52 counties.[20]

Failing financial support forced Friends' Freedmen Association to give up its elementary schools before the end of the century and focus on preparing black students to become teachers at The Christiansburg Institute, later the Christiansburg Normal and Industrial School, in Virginia. By 1887, the entire faculty at Christiansburg was black, and the Institute for Colored Youth (Cheyney) had always had black faculty and administration. The first two black women to receive bachelor's degrees in the United States, (from Oberlin College) one of them Fanny Jackson-Coppin, both taught at the Institute for Colored Youth. Seven of the seventeen teachers supported by Hicksite Friends in 1871 were black; the Orthodox had twelve, six teachers-in-charge and six assistants, out of a staff of thirty-six in 1875. Philip S. Benjamin argues ". . . Quaker readiness to hire black teachers can be explained more in terms of practicality than social understanding. Friends had a difficult time finding white teachers to work for the modest salaries they offered." Though we may wonder how Benjamin can so confidently determine Friends' motives, we may also note that one positive multiplier-effect of Quaker parsimony in providing schools for black students is that a significant number of black teachers were trained and employed. In this case, as always, concern for finances had a direct impact on efforts to find and train good teachers.[21]

Benjamin stresses that Friends after the Civil War were part of a major melioristic effort made by Northern churches to provide education for freed persons, "but the Quaker contribution was out of all proportion to their numbers," and in their work many Quakers held tenaciously to a concept of "the just debt" owed to black people. What is sad and undeniable is that, like most white Americans in the nineteenth and early twentieth century, Quakers "regarded Negroes as a class apart. It never occurred to them to integrate black youth into the schools they provided for their own children." Bishop Richard Wright, Jr., of the A.M.E Church excused this segregation, believing Friends wanted to "'encourage independent action' and foster 'self-confidence and opportunity.'" That may have been a fortunate consequence of narrow views, but if we are unhappy that, with so much far-sightedness about education for the poor, disadvantaged, and oppressed, our predecessors lacked our insight into the evils of class-bias, we must also pray that our own blind spots will be no more grievous to our successors one or two hundred years from now.[22]

ACKWORTH: "A SAFE AND HEALTHY RETREAT"

Dr. John Fothergill identifies "the children of Friends not in affluent circumstances" as the particular objects of English Friends' concern in founding Ackworth School in 1779, ". . . the children of such persons, as must either provide for their offspring a very cheap education, or none at all." Such parents, he says, have been unable to "find any means of obtaining a safe education" for their children, so have kept them at home, "where it was impracticable to keep them at all times from corrupt company."[23] The school will provide "for the *subsistence* of great numbers of children of both sexes, in a safe and healthy retreat" and "for their *orderly* and *Christian education*."

Some key terms here are "safe education," "safe and healthy retreat," and "orderly and Christian education." London Yearly Meeting of 1777 had been concerned "to revive former Advices respecting the Education of Youth," especially that "they may be prevented from mixing with those not of our religious Persuasion, which so often leads into hurtful Habits, from which they are not easily reclaimed."[24] The home setting is not safe from dangerous company, often identified in this period as servants or those one meets in city living; moreover, as Fothergill's letter warns, "Too few are the parents who can honestly say, that 'they train up their children in a godly conversation, in plainness of speech, behaviour and apparel, and in frequent reading the Holy Scriptures.'"

Speaking of the shortcomings of the Bellers-inspired school at Clerkenwell, Fothergill says, "We need not any proofs of the difficulty of educating our youth in great cities." The boys at the school have been permitted too much of the freedom of the city, and they have been allowed to visit friends and relations "not always the most exemplary in their conduct." Some of "the ancient poor" who live in the school "may have been brought thither, by deviating from the principles of our profession" and are therefore not good examples to the students.

> Perhaps there is not an institution existing, upon which more labour, and disinterested endeavours, that every thing might be managed with order, economy, reputation, and general benefit, have been employed, than in this house [at Clerkenwell]. . . . In the progress of this undertaking experience has proved, that the benefits derived from it have not been, in every respect, adequate to the hopes and expectations of those who have been engaged in its support; too few of the youth therein educated, the number considered, having turned out useful or reputable members of society.

Ackworth was to be paid for by direct subsidy from the Yearly Meeting, from donations and annuities, and from tuition (subsidized in part or full). Such guaranteed financial support would seem to assure, at least at the beginning, that the education can be "guarded" from the wrong kinds of experiences and influences. To use a phrase singularly inapposite to Quaker education at the close of the eighteenth century, who pays the piper calls the tune.

Friends Seminary: Free Schooling for Quakers

Friends Seminary, a day school founded in New York City in 1786, offers a useful comparison to Ackworth. The author of its history says the school was born of a promise and a threat. "Friends offered a way of life . . . that could be left to their children only through a faithful home and a guarded education. . . ." So the Seminary was designed, in the immediate circumstances of the American Revolution, "not so much to instruct as to protect." At first, Friends Seminary was open only to Quaker children, but "this rule proved perishable; the school would not otherwise have survived the decade." The Quaker population in New York city was too small to support its educational goals, especially the goal to educate the children of poor Friends. It was "soon obvious that the school must open to non-Quaker children, whose fees would permit the trustees to admit poor Quaker children for free." After the Orthodox-Hicksite Separation of 1827-28, Friends felt even greater pressure to make education available to *every* Quaker child, so all children of the Monthly Meeting became eligible for free schooling. As a direct consequence, the school could never again afford to be strictly Quaker. In order to remain solvent, *and* allow for the free education of Quaker children, it had to admit non-Quaker children. In 1877 and following, Friends Seminary had deficits as a result of attracting more Quakers. "The greater the Quaker presence in the school, the greater its financial peril." This had significant impact on curriculum, staffing, and pedagogy.[25]

ECONOMY AND PEDAGOGY: THE LANCASTRIAN SYSTEM

A single example of the impact of economy on pedagogy will illustrate the point. In the first half of the nineteenth century, a number of Quaker schools, among them Ackworth and Friends Seminary, experimented with the "monitorial system" of teaching created by Joseph Lancaster, a Quaker educator. It was used in the first "free schools," the schools for black children set up by Friends which eventually become the New York public school system. William Allen introduced the system into schools in Russia, and Thomas Scattergood introduced it through "The Association of Friends for the Instruction of Poor Children," which supported a school for "moral and literary instruction" to destitute children in Philadelphia from 1809-1818.

The Lancastrian system was designed to teach large numbers of children in a pyramidal arrangement. A single teacher would instruct older student "monitors," who would in turn be responsible for teaching the younger children. (Anyone who has ever taken introductory lecture courses with a connected "discussion section" at a large American university has experienced a more sophisticated, though frequently no more satisfying, version of the system.) To keep students working, or at least under control, when the teacher was not watching over them, the "monitorial system" depended on "rivalry, shame and acquisitiveness to educate." Tickets were given out for good behavior, which students could accumulate and then redeem for prizes.[26]

What is most important to note about the "monitorial system" is what it is intended to accomplish. Joseph Lancaster devised his version of the system in order to handle the responsibilities of being the only teacher in a school with 350 students. Though there are arguments that the older child learns more effectively who helps another, this is an afterthought. The system is not an attempt to solve problems of instruction but of instructional *expense*. Its only virtue is that it can give some basic schooling to large numbers of people who cannot afford anything better.[27]

"The Quaker Conscience Cut All Profit to the Bone"

The Lancastrian system represented false economy and bad pedagogy, but the problems it sought to address were real. Increasingly, in England and the United States in the nineteenth century, Quaker schools had to deal with a tension which threatened to become a contradiction. W. A. Campbell Stewart says of Quaker schools in England that, though the general upward trend in wages and prices in the nineteenth century forced school fees up, Friends raised fees with great reluctance and were ". . . particularly firm in the first sixty years of the century, when the classes for whom the schools were founded were kept clearly in mind (that is during the period of 'guarded' education) . . ." Campbell Stewart assures us that "economies in the schools were such that life was extremely rigorous, but the Quaker conscience cut all profit to the bone." Later, when non-Quakers were admitted in greater numbers, charges were increased so that "the contributions of those not in affluence were balanced by those in greater affluence." When Rawdon School opened in 1832, a scale of fees was established: parents from the founding Meetings paid what they could afford, subsidized by the Meetings; higher rates were set for those who were not from the Meetings which founded the school. In 1871, when children with no ties to the Society of Friends were admitted, they were charged at the higher rate. Other Friends schools followed Rawdon's example.[28]

Meeting the Competition

Particularly in the United States, as free public education became widely available, to offer a Quaker education meant struggling with how to be simultaneously "guarded" and academically competitive. Wilmington Friends School Committee minuted in 1829 that "The general improvement of schools in the mode of teaching and by the introduction of numerous branches of instruction not formerly attended to, make it necessary that Friends seminaries should in some good degree keep pace with this improvement in order to deserve and insure the patronage of our own members . . ." and proposed changes ". . . in order to establish a school under the care of Friends which, from its intrinsic excellence as a seminary of useful instruction, will command the respect of parents and guardians, and be the means of inculcating on the youthful mind a due estimate of our religious testimonies. . . ."[29] Writing in 1866, Edward Parrish says, "The policy of confining these schools to members of the Society has generally, of latter years, been superseded by that of excluding no pupils of good character who are willing to conform to the rules. . . . It has the advantage of securing larger remuneration to the teachers and improved facilities for instruction. . . . " Eli Lamb, Head of Baltimore Friends School, "concluded that, if Friends education was to survive, Friends schools would have to admit substantial numbers of students of other religious backgrounds." In 1880, fewer than 30 of 300 students in Baltimore Friends were Quaker.[30]

What Price Quaker Schools?

It is time to explore the obvious further. There are only a limited number of ways a religious body can pay for its schools: by assessment of its members and direct appropriation from the parent body, by appeals for "subscriptions" or donations from interested individuals, by establishing endowments through gifts and wills from such people, by charging tuition, by designing features of the schools to generate income or make a profit. The Religious Society of Friends has tried them all, in one combination or another, with varying degrees of success. Paying for education becomes more complex, the more a group sees itself under religious concern to promote the welfare of people—its own members or others—who are either denied educational opportunities or are unable to afford schooling. The more accessible educational opportunities are made to people in need, the more complex budgeting and fund-raising activities must become.

The purist might ask, what price is too high for preserving Friends education? Indeed, the question is asked all the time, sometimes searchingly, sometimes rhetorically. If we look to our past for guidance, we discover that there has rarely been a time when circumstances have not made both the question and the possible answers very complex. There has always been a concern for educating the children of the meeting, though the number of years such a concern repeatedly comes down from London or Philadelphia Yearly Meeting may be an index of how *little* is happening, rather than how much. Those many expressions of concern always stress two things: that children need the support of formal education, and that such education is ineffective without spiritual nourishment in the family.

Who Are the Children of the Meeting?

Arthur Little, late professor of drama at Earlham College, argued that the work of Quaker education has always been to educate the children of the meeting, and that the job of each generation of Quakers is to discover who the children of the meeting now are. From very early on, the concern for education reaches beyond the narrowest definition of "children of the meeting," to encompass those whose need of the liberating effects of education was greatest—poor children of no religious affiliation, Indians, blacks, slave and free, among others.

It was always taken for granted that schooling was to help children keep themselves "unspotted from the world," a favorite phrase for George Fox, taken from that distillation of the social implications of Christian faith, the *General Epistle of James*. As it became harder to maintain such distance from "the world," Friends created some "select" schools exclusively for Quakers, to provide the "guarded" education which they hoped would help the Society of Friends maintain its defining "peculiarity." Some of those schools remained "select" for a long time; others very quickly had to open to non-Friends, simply because there was no other way to stay open.

As more and better educational opportunities became generally available, Friends schools had to decide how to attract and hold the children of the meeting by the "intrinsic excellence" of their educational offerings. Friends schools had therefore to be academically as good as, even better than, other schools.

Excellence on Moderate Terms

Rising expectations bring rising expenses. Many Quakers value education highly but are not eager to pay a lot for it. In this they are like a great many other people. Like our predecessors, we want some equivalent of "a liberal, guarded and religious education" for our children, "a school . . . which, from its intrinsic excellence . . . will command the respect of parents and guardians, and be the means of inculcating on the youthful mind a due estimate of our

religious testimonies . . ." and we want it "on moderate terms."
We must not be surprised if trying to accomplish all that requires flexibility, compromise, accommodation, and settling
for something less than perfect.

NOTES

1. Alfred North Whitehead, *The Aims of Education, and other
    essays,* 1929, New York, New American Library 1963, 2;
    Indiana Yearly Meeting committee on education, 1829,
    quoted in Thornburg, *Earlham,* 30; Gibbs, *Children of
    Light,* 73.

2. Tuke, *Five Papers,* 11.

3. Cited in Brown, *A Friends Select History,* 26.

4. In "An Epistle to the Quarterly-Meeting of London and
    Middlesex," 1718, and in addresses "To the Lords and
    Commons Assembled in Parliament," and "To The
    Thinking and Publick-Spirited" 1696, in George Clarke,
    ed., *John Bellers, His Life, Times and Writings,* London,
    Routledge and Kegan Paul, 1987.

5. Clarke notes that Bellers points out that more than half of
    the members of the Society are poor.

6. Clarke, 224, *Bellers, An Epistle...1718.*

7. Clarke, 50, *Bellers, Proposals.*

8. Clarke, 228, *Bellers, Epistle, 1718.*

9. Clarke, *Bellers,* 147.

10. Among such schools we may note early provision in wills
    for educating Negroes, poor whites, Indians in the schools

kept by Friends in Wilmington, Delaware, the school kept for Negro children by Anthony Benezet which ultimately became the Raspberry Street School in Philadelphia, the School for Colored Youth which ultimately became Cheyney State College in Pennsylvania, the Aimwell School, established for daughters of poor parents not Friends, the Ayton School in York, a labor school for the children of disowned Friends. This list is suggestive, not exhaustive.

For a single very early example of a Quaker social concern or testimony for education manifesting itself, we can cite the case of Friends imprisoned in Ilchester Jail in 1662 who,

"willing to improve any opportunity for the doing of good even to their enemies, and...being well qualified for that purpose did as the lord put it into their hearts give forth a public manifestation of their purpose to teach school, and that all people that would send their children unto them, they would freely teach them to read or write and cast account, whereupon many children were sent and in a little more than a month's time the school was increased to the number of 70 scholars, which through the Lord's blessing and Friends' industry many of them profited in Learning very much....It was reported that some had gained more in two weeks' time there than in half a year else where before and many were preparing to send their children."

11. Thomas Budd, *Good Order Established in Pennsylvania and New Jersey in America: Being a True Account of the Country; with its Produce and Communities There Made in the Year 1685*, A New Edition with an Introduction and Copious Historical Notes by Edward Armstrong, New York: Fourth Edition, 1971, 43-45.

12. Thomas Woody, *Early Quaker Education in Pennsylvania,* New York, Teachers College, Columbia University, 47.

13. *Wilmington,* 3-5, 9.

14. Clyde Milner, "Quaker Education in the Carolinas," Guilford College, 1965, 8; William Rogers cites these minutes in his essay, "Friends Education in North Carolina" for *Vision 400,* Guilford College, 1995; Linda B. Selleck, *Gentle Invaders: Quaker Women Educators and Racial Issues During the Civil War and Reconstruction,* Friends United Press, Richmond, 1995, 121-22, 192.

15. *A Brief Sketch of the Schools for Black People,* Philadelphia 1867. This 32-page history is notable not only for its overview of the "Raspberry Street Schools" but as an attempt to raise money for the on-going concern. An introductory note says, "The following account . . . has been prepared for publication, under a belief that it might be serviceable in maintaining the interest of Friends in the Institution established by our religious Society . . . which, since its origin in the year 1770, has been supported to a considerable extent by the voluntary contributions of the Society, and is still in measure dependent upon the existence of a similar feeling of interest among the members for its support."

    The brief history of The Aimwell School is clearly published with the same intent and hope.

16. *Brief Sketch,* 3, 6, 11, 17.

17. Fanny Jackson-Coppin, *Reminiscences of School Life, and Hints on Teaching,* Originally published 1913 by the A.M.E. Book Concern , reprint 1987, New York, Garland, 19-23.

18. Selleck, *Gentle Invaders,* 136-44. For study of the Adelphia and Aimwell Schools, see Margaret Morris Haviland, unpublished dissertation, 1992. For study of Quaker in-

volement in charity schooling in the nineteenth century, see William Kashatus, *A Virtuous Education: Penn's Vision for Philadelphia Schools*, Pendle Hill, 1997.

19. Benjamin, *Philadelphia Quakers*, 132-33: Selleck, 133-35.

20. Benjamin, *Philadelphia Quakers*, 146, 142; Courtney Sanabria Woodfaulk, *The Jeanes Teachers of South Carolina: The Emergence, Existence and Significance of Their Work*, unpublished dissertation, 1992, 7-10.

21. Benjamin, *Philadelphia Quakers*, 137, 139-40.

22. Benjamin, *Philadelphia Quakers*, 145-47.

23. "A Letter to a Friend in the Country, Relative to the Intended School at Ackworth," 1779. All subsequent Fothergill references are from this letter.

24. Quoted in *So Numerous a Family: Two Hundred Years of Quaker Education at Ackworth*, 2.

25. Gibbs, *Children of Light*, 11, 23-24, 37, 73.

26. Gibbs, *Children of Light*, 30-32.

27. Comenius, in *The Great Didactic*, argues that a teacher can and should "preside over several hundreds of scholars" in this same way. He offers analogies which are as funny as they are inappropriate: "by one kneading of material and one heating of the oven, a baker makes many loaves and a brickmaker many bricks; a printer with one type-setting prints thousands of books. So a teacher can turn out students." Quoted in John William Adamson, *Pioneers of Modern Education in the 17th Century*, first published 1905, reprint, Teachers College, Columbia University, New York, 1971, 68. This is so out of keeping with what Comenius says the ends of education are, that we can only understand it as his attempt to solve the economic problems arising from establishing universal education, as he insists is necessary.

28. Brinton, *Quaker Education*, 85-86.

29. *Wilmington*, 9-10.

30. Edward Parrish, *An Essay on Education in the Society of Friends*, With an Account of the Proceedings on the Occasion of Laying the Cornerstone of Swarthmore College, Swarthmore College, 1866, 35; MacKaye, *Mr. Sidwell's School*, 29.

Seven

GUARDING EDUCATION: FROM WHAT
AND FOR WHAT?

Out of original Quaker principles there arose a philosophy of education which was applied most effectively in the period between 1750 and 1850. Before 1750 this philosophy was slowly taking shape in concrete applications and after 1850 it gradually became less effective due to the decay of older forms and the changes and instability in society as a whole. Yet the fundamental Quaker principles are as fertile as they ever were and just as able to generate new forms of application. [1]

GUARDING FROM

Howard Brinton identifies two particular policies as most influential in shaping this Quaker philosophy of education: *"The Creation of a Sense of Belonging to the Quaker Community, and a Religiously Guarded Education."* These he calls the positive and negative aspects of the same objective—"to bring up the young according to the Quaker way of life and to shield them from too much exposure to other ways of life."[2]

Brinton was trained in mathematics and physics as well as philosophy, and he may well want us to think of *positive* and *negative* here as complementary terms, one depending for its

power on the existence of its opposite. It is common, how-
ever, for people thinking about Quaker education in the
Quietist Period and its aftermath, to regret or deplore the
emphasis on "guarded" education. To some later Friends it
seems inexplicable, shocking or foolish that John Greenleaf
Whittier should be opposed to the study of music at
Moses Brown School, for fear music would creep into silent
worship, or that the eminent Quaker educator and scientist
John Griscom should decline to hear a lecture on
Shakespeare, saying he would be more inclined to attend
". . . if the lecture is to be given for the purpose of demonstrating that the morals of mankind would be benefitted by
an entire extermination of the writing of the great British
dramatist. . . ."[3] Samuel Tuke tells, as a success story, of
the mid-eighteenth century schoolmaster "greatly addicted
to music" as a young man, who became a Quaker and,
"laying aside his violin," established a school at Sowerby.[4]
No fiction, no drama, no art, no music, no dancing? What
were they afraid of?

It is rarely useful for addressing our present problems merely
to deplore the deficiencies of our predecessors. Instead, we
need to ask what they saw as the problems they had to face
and what resources they saw available to them for meeting
those problems. We might ask, then, what Friends of the
Quietist Period thought they had to guard *from,* what they
were guarding *for,* and *how* they thought the guarding might
best be accomplished.

In the simplest terms, Quakers of the Quietist Period did
not want to withdraw from the world, for they accepted the
imperative to be *in* but not *of* it. As merchants, as bankers, as
industrialists they profited from their reputations for probity;
they amassed both wealth and influence which gave greater
impact to their philanthropic activities. Making a livelihood,

addressing political and social problems, affecting the larger society for the better require being *in* the world. They wanted to guard themselves and their children from the *spots* of the world, the dirt and corruption of the life around them.

Worldliness does not consist solely, not even primarily, in the practice of lurid vices; it does not necessarily begin in lying, cheating, stealing, shattering the ten commandments, or what many Quaker documents call "pernicious" living or practices. Worldliness consists first in habits and attitudes. It is the cynicism which calls itself sophistication, which disparages idealism as irrelevant to the "real world," which says no principle is worth getting too worked up about. It is the tendency to cut corners here and there, to make casual compromises with principle, to accept with a shrug of resignation a choice between two evils. Described thus, worldliness is both very familiar and very troubling to us in our own lives. We too would guard our students from such worldliness, if we knew how and if the cost in other educational values were not too high.

Friends identified three particular dangers to be guarded against in bringing up the young: an unsupportive or dangerous environment, unsupportive or dangerous companions, unsupportive, indifferent, or unfaithful guardians. The environment might be a big city such as London or Philadelphia, full of enticements and enticers to the pleasures and attitudes of the seductions of the larger society. The companions might be other young people, dangerous only in that they were personally attractive but did not subscribe to the Quaker testimonies. The guardians might be indifferent teachers or families too focused on the "creaturely activities" of making money and getting ahead to inculcate the moral strengths which young Quakers would need when their time came to work in (but most emphatically not of) the world.

Dr. John Fothergill makes the case for Ackworth School
on those grounds:

> Many children amongst us sustain a grievous loss, by
> not being early and properly made acquainted with the
> principles we profess. For want of this instruction they
> become too easy a prey to the customs of the world; and
> those habitudes, which would be as a kind of hedge to
> them, and protect from many temptations, are thrown
> down, and all the allurements of vice and folly suffered
> to seduce their affections, to their ruin.[5]

Guarding For

Fothergill's language in this passage seems so apprehensive that
we are inclined to dismiss him, and Friends like him,
as simply, in the favorite disparagement of our time, "puritani-
cal"—afraid that the little Quakers will begin to have fun
and decide they like it! It is instructive, therefore, to consider
what Fothergill identifies as the chief danger to guard against.
"Perhaps there is nothing in the common course of public
education in the world," he writes, "that so unfits men for
that humble attention to the divine monitor within, . . . as *the
cultivation of a bold unfeeling disposition, under a notion of promoting manliness and courage. . . .*" (italics added) Fothergill's
first purpose, then, is to guard the peace testimony from the
flashiness associated with worldly notions of manliness.

Samuel Tuke claims that "It is a matter of almost notori-
ous observation that the degree in which the principle of
the Society, in regard to peace, has modified our training,
has had a powerful influence in the formation of the future
character of our members." Though no one is more honored
in the larger society than the brave and successful soldier,

Tuke says, and "there is not a stronger tendency in the minds of men than that of the retaliation of injuries, nor a stronger passion than that of military glory," the testimony against war has so "modified the direct circumstances of instruction or training, in our families and our schools," that even the child feeling those same tendencies, *"the little would-be hero,"* learns to embrace the testimony for himself.[6]

"Guarded education," then, is a means to recommend habits, by example and by practice, which will, in Fothergill's words, "form in the children a temper . . . equally remote from a culpable fear and servility, and an audaciousness that knows no respect for order or authority." The habits are good in themselves and will be a "hedge" against temptations. Here, in the particular understanding of what will hedge Quakers from the world, we find the dominant feature of guarded education—the insistence on the "peculiarity" of Quakers. Fothergill's paragraph on habitudes as a hedge concludes: "When they [Quaker children] cease to be distinguished from others, by their garb and deportment, they too often cease to be distinguished from the world by their morals, and the rectitude of their conduct."

THE DANGERS OF THE TIMES

It is worth dwelling briefly on what the times were like from which these Quakers wanted to guard their young. Though Howard Brinton argues that Quaker philosophy of education was applied most successfully in the period 1750-1850, he may be thinking of the American experience. John W. Harvey, writing of the same period, describes British education, including Quaker education, as having gone through a hundred years of educational stultification. ". . . In the early 1820's, the average school was a place of torpor where it was

not a place of torment, and the average school teacher a
person of narrow outlook and mediocre capacity."[7]

As historians have shown, from the middle of the eighteenth century, Quakers on both sides of the Atlantic were
increasingly exposed to the dangers of success. Wealthy
Quakers in England and America were mixing more with
the "world's people," not only in economic life but socially
and politically as well. In warning about the luxurious
life, such Friends as Woolman and Benezet are not merely
being alarmist. Woolman's "Plea for the Poor" clearly has
Quakers as a primary audience. And Benezet, in wishing
that young Quakers who did not have to work for a living
would turn their attention to teaching, rather than spend
their time either wasting money or piling up more of it, was
not exaggerating the problem.[8] Benezet and Woolman were
among the leaders, not only of anti-slavery activities in
the Religious Society of Friends, but of the movement to
disengage Quakers from political dominance in the Pennsylvania legislature in 1757, in the Seven Years War, rather than
abandon the peace testimony out of political expediency.
From our present vantage-point, we can also recognize that
the American Revolution is on the horizon, with all its tests
of British and American Quakers.

The calamity of the American Revolution, followed in
the early nineteenth century by the internal crisis of the
Separation among Friends, constituted a prolonged threat to
Quaker principles all the more dangerous because it came
so largely from the indifference of Quakers themselves. In
1761, Philadelphia Monthly Meeting answers the query on
education, "A concern subsists in many Friends for the careful Education of the Youth, . . . tho' too great Deficiency
appears in some Parents in these matters." A report in 1778
from Philadelphia Yearly Meeting urges parents "tenderly

and pressingly" to be careful about sending their children to schools whose Masters and Mistresses "do not Maintain a Religious Care to Walk and Act consistent with the Profession of Friends."

> . . . Much Corruption hath been introduced amongst us in the present Generation for want of more Care in . . . mixing in Schools for our Children where there has not been a Regulation Consistent with our holy Profession and the Principles of Truth.[9]

Strategies for Guarding the Young

Friends pursued several strategies to guard their children against the spots of the world: 1] they appealed to families to take greater responsibility for the religious education of their children; 2] they created Select Schools, open initially only to Friends' children and staffed solely by Quaker educators, where young people would enjoy the most supportive environment and companionship; 3] when possible they got their young people out of town, deliberately placing schools in rural areas where they believed the temptations would be fewer; 4] they strenuously recommended, and enforced, adherence to the testimony for plainness. Though these begin as elements in an general strategy, over time they become successive lines of defense in a rear-guard action against the dangers of worldliness.

Advice to Parents: "The Formation of Right Habits"

Samuel Tuke notes that minutes or portions of epistles on the subject of education appear from London Yearly Meeting in twenty-seven of the years from 1700 to 1738. Philadelphia Friends show a similar pre-occupation. For "the carrying on of religious instruction and the formation of right habits," Tuke says, Friends look primarily to parents and families. Families are urged to read scripture together in the home, and schoolmasters boarding with families are encouraged to call them together for that purpose. A minute of 1731 advises mothers "to take particular care to instruct [children] in the knowledge of religion and the Holy Scriptures, because it has been found that good impressions early made on the tender minds of children have proved lasting means of preserving them in a religious life and conversation."[10] Benezet even writes a basic primer for mothers to use in teaching their pre-school age children.

Schools as Family

Clearly, meetings did not believe that families were adequately discharging these responsibilities, and the very fact of Separation confirmed that judgment. Of the founding of Friends Seminary in 1784, Nancy Reid Gibbs writes, "The apparent willingness of Friends to break their own rules gave weight to arguments for a Meeting school—for only if a child were raised in accordance with Quaker testimonies would their perpetuation be assured."[11] The tone of many committee and meeting minutes suggests that select schools were founded out of a sense that the family was unable to inculcate and preserve Friends' fundamental religious convictions, and therefore the foundations on which all practical or literary education depended were in danger. The schools themselves were to be "family"; it is how Fothergill describes Ackworth, and it becomes the favorite term by which Quaker boarding schools describe themselves in the nineteenth century.

Male heads of schools are sometimes called "father," and their wives "mother." At Westtown, Haverford School, Olney—the last described as "four years at school with your cousins"—it was especially easy to think of "family" as an appropriate metaphor.

SCHOOLS IN A RURAL SETTING

In recommending Ackworth as a "safe and healthy retreat," Fothergill comments, "We need not any proofs of the difficulty of educating our youth in great cities, where evil communication ever abounds, and where the corruption of manners is almost unavoidable" Ackworth's distance from large centers of population is part of its benefit.

> . . . As we are now in possession of a house . . . where there is room for a variety of employments suitable to [the children's] ages and conditions, and where learning and good behaviour will be duly attended to, in a healthy country plentifully supplied with fuel and provisions; and to crown all, under the inspection of many judicious, valuable Friends, there is every reason to hope for success.[12]

Westtown is deliberately placed to be a day's journey to Philadelphia, for those who must go to committee meetings, but far enough away to escape city influences. In placing Haverford College in a rural setting in 1830, says William Bickley, the founders were subscribing to the pervasive American myth that country life is "sounder, more moral, more character building" than city life. "In that myth," he adds, "is imbedded the longing for what used to be, for a past that is as much a product of the imagination as it is of fact." Edward Parrish says in 1866 that Swarthmore College's location was chosen, "after a thorough examination of the rural districts surrounding Philadelphia:" about ten miles from Philadelphia, connected by train, on high land,

> . . . commanding an extensive prospect of variegated scenery, . . . a distant view of the Delaware River, the ancient town of Chester, . . . and Media, the county town, distant one and a half miles, in which, it may be remarked, the sale of liquor is prohibited by law, in all time to come.[13]

"Distinguished by their Garb and Deportment"

Brinton emphasizes that *a religiously guarded education* did not mean *a guarded religious education*, "for Friends have held that religion cannot be taught except by the Divine Teacher who works either directly within the soul or through some prophetic individual acting under a sense of direct guidance." Perhaps the best way to conceive of what was intended is to return to Fothergill's notion of "habituating" children to silence and attention, to patient waiting, and to those patterns of living, the "habitudes" which are both aided and announced by "garb and deportment." The testimony for plainness or simplicity becomes the hallmark of guarded education. The 1830 Haverford College plan proposed

> a guarded education in the higher branches of learning combining the requisite literary instruction with a religious care over the morals and manners of our scholars, enforcing plainness and simplicity of dress and deportment.

In 1831, the plan for New Garden School in North Carolina, later Guilford College, offers "the Christian and literary education of our children consistent with the simplicity of our religious profession. . . ."[14] A Report of 1832 in

Philadelphia warns, ". . . the appearance and demeanor of the Children should be so regulated as to accord with the profession of Friends. . . ."[15] Also in 1832, White Lick Quarterly Meeting of Indiana Yearly Meeting issues its rules for schools, including:

> It shall be the duty of both teachers and pupils (particularly those who are members of the religious [sic] Society of Friends) to observe plainness of apparel and endeavor to habituate themselves to using the plain Grammatical Scripture language . . .[16]

An 1837 circular describes the object of Philadelphia's Select schools as ". . . a guarded, religious education, in conformity with our principles. To effect this, it seems indispensable that plainness of dress and language be kept to. . . ." In 1846, Friends Central School's Visiting Committee minutes, "We would impressively urge upon parents and guardians of children the necessity of home culture and discipline and of their cooperation in the support of our testimonies to plainness and simplicity of dress and deportment."[17]

THE DISTINGUISHING TESTIMONIES

Samuel Tuke, as usual, makes the case most coherently. In the same paragraph in which he describes the influence on Quaker education of "the principle of the Society, in regard to peace," he continues:

> We might refer in a somewhat similar manner to the influence which our other distinguishing testimonies have had upon the methods of instruction and in the formation of character—to that against all oaths, and to that against all ostentatious display and flattery, as

severally inconsistent with the simple truth-speaking, the humility and plainness which belong to the Christian character.

It is significant that Tuke names only three distinguishing Quaker testimonies: the peace testimony, the testimony against oaths, and the testimony for plainness or simplicity. Obedience to these testimonies, he says, have exposed Friends to some trials and privations, excluded them from some circumstances common to others, and "rendered them rather conspicuous to the world at large."[18] It is hard to imagine any combination of testimonies better suited to creating a natural protective hedge. The peace testimony and the testimony against oaths are likely to become evident only in extraordinary circumstances, but plain speech, "the plain Grammatical Scripture language," and plain dress always mark one out, especially in the big city. Consider: Which young person would a contemporary drug dealer be most likely to approach, the one wearing a black leather jacket or the one in Amish-like clothes?

A Testimony Becomes a Style

Plainness can become merely a style, then a narrowing test of orthodoxy, and finally a fetish, as it clearly did for a number of Friends. What was happening at Olney in Ohio had its parallels in a number of other schools. William Taber tells of Olney School Committee members in 1912 troubled that students would say "good morning" and "good night," "which plain Friends had always avoided as being insincere and thoughtless statements." They were also concerned about the "Un-Friendly" appearance of students coming to school or leaving for home, by which they meant insufficiently plain

in dress. In the 1920s, students at Olney wore plain dress at
school but not in the family, where it was increasingly (to
use a shocking term) going out of style.

> The typical Olney graduate up into the 1940's had to be
> bi-lingual and bi-cultural—he could slip easily into the
> plain language and the earnest though subtle nuances
> of Conservative Quakerism when he came home, while
> at college or work he used the 'world's language' and
> would not be recognized as a Quaker until his ethics
> and his convictions became known.

For some Friends, all change was change for the worse.
Taber tells of a meeting for worship at Olney, during which,
". . . in the silence could be heard the happy singing of the
student dish crew below. Then a plain Friend arose and in-
toned with slow, vibrant power, 'What meaneth then this
bleating of the sheep in mine ears, and the lowing of
the oxen which I hear?'"[19]

Some Costs of Guarded Education

Campbell Stewart criticizes the emphasis on plainness as a
counsel of negation. W.C. Braithwaite says guarded education meant protection from evil influences,

> . . . but it also meant the careful inculcation of prescribed
> ideas and an approved way of life; and this training,
> however excellent, confined the mental and moral out-
> look and pruned luxurious and vigorous growth to its
> own trim patterns. It was not education at all in the
> higher sense of the word.[20]

The costs of offering this kind of education, though real, can
be over-stated. Purely from the standpoint of curriculum,

Quaker education in America does not seem to differ very much from what is offered by other schools, perhaps because a higher premium was generally placed on practical education and there were not the same obstacles to pursuing higher education as in England. The worst that can be said of guarded Quaker education in England was that it too was stuck in the hundred-year educational doldrums. Being debarred from Oxford and Cambridge only meant being spared drowsing through the deadliest, most trivial period in English university history.

The beginning of significant educational reform in England is usually dated from Thomas Arnold's appointment as Headmaster of Rugby in 1828. It does not minimize his impact to point out that Arnold's great work was raising the moral tone of his school, which was in sore need of improving, in the process pointing the way for similar improvement in other boarding schools, but that those reforms deliberately made little impact on the curriculum. At Rugby under Arnold, classics were improved and remained ascendant, science remained largely invisible, since that was the accepted way to prepare boys for university. For most of the nineteenth century, the great universities remained intellectual and moral sloughs of despond.

Some Features of Curriculum

It is enough now to note some of the chief features of the curriculum of Quaker schools in the period of guarded education. Elfrida Vipont Foulds argues that Ackworth is superior to other schools of the period for giving all students the same education, for teaching writing to all, for being a family, and for mixing physical labor with book learning as a matter of *educational* policy. Campbell Stewart agrees that "practical labor and plainness go together" and that plainness weights toward utilitarianism as well as toward ideals of service and probity. He also notes that the emphasis on plainness helped break the ascendancy of Latin in the curriculum, since the vernacular was "in the plain truth."[21]

William Bickley cites *An Account* of Haverford by the Board of Managers which proposes an institution,

> . . . in which the children of Friends shall receive a liberal education in ancient and modern literature, and the mathematical and other sciences, under the care of competent members of our own society, so as not to endanger their religious principles, or alienate them from their early principles.[22]

He concludes that from its inception Haverford was asked to accomplish contradictory ends: to provide a college education equal to the best the world offered, but to guard against that world. A similar criticism might be leveled against Swarthmore nearly four decades later. Edward Parrish promises that Swarthmore College will offer guarded education at the same time he announces the curriculum will give greater prominence to study in the natural sciences than is to be found in other colleges.[23] In general, Friends were determined that their schools would offer "literary," "liberal" education, equal in instruction and equipment to the best offered elsewhere, but with the added benefit of a "guarded" context, and if we late twentieth-century observers find meeting such complex goals hard to imagine, we must also acknowledge that our predecessors saw no unresolvable tensions. Perhaps our blind spot is that we can only regard education as "liberal" which trains children for getting into college to pursue "higher education." That is our own generation's way of joining "practical" and "liberal" learning—for no matter how earnestly we speak of learning for its own sake, we willingly measure success through standardized "achievement" tests— PSAT to SAT to GRE, MCAT or LSAT—which open doors successively into college, graduate work, or professional training.

The Hedges Are Down

> The Quaker school knew what it was doing and why. . . . The Quaker community, like every living thing, sought to reproduce itself and the school was one means in this perpetuating process.

If we view guarded education solely as a defensive strategy in a war of attrition with the world, we must conclude that it failed, and, to the extent that the outward signs of plainness became the primary test of faithfulness, failure was inevitable. For some Friends, this is the whole, sad story: As the hedges came down, from the middle of the nineteenth century to perhaps the beginning of the Second World War, Quaker education enjoyed a long, golden twilight, but now its *Quaker* future is dark.

Two of our wisest students of Quaker education and most distinguished Quaker educators, Howard Brinton and Helen Hole, give voice to this view. For Brinton,

> The older Quaker way of life . . . has . . . 'gone with the wind.' Those of us who lived in its fading twilight may experience a nostalgic longing for it but old days and ways will not come back. The dykes raised to keep out the world are all down now and the flood has come and erased the landmarks.
>
> Friends are still somewhat sensitive to the Light, internationally minded, tolerant of differing opinions.

They are more socially active than ever, but their activity tends to be more on the intellectual and deliberative level than on the deeper level in which unity with God and man is felt as a creative fact of experience.

For Helen Hole,

> The Society was profoundly influenced by the education its children received. This can no longer be said to be true. Quaker education today is, with rare exceptions, no longer the matrix out of which the ongoing life of the Society comes; rather it is a peripheral good work, or a service to the larger community. This is perhaps a legitimate motivation, but the whole matter remains a disquieting one for Friends, who need to ask themselves what we have put in the place of the earlier concept of education as spiritual preparation.[24]

But that is not the only way to understand the story.

RETHINKING GUARDED EDUCATION

If the measure of a school's purity is that it would have *no* non-Quaker students, *no* non-Quaker faculty, *no* music, drama, art, or fiction, entertain *no* ideas dangerous to traditional belief, the costs—spiritual and intellectual, not merely financial—are too high. If, as Brinton argues, the Quaker community wants to reproduce and perpetuate itself, using its schools as a means to that end, then those schools have to be something other than museums of past Quaker styles of dress and address. What benefit is it to reproduce the past, if doing so prevents us from perpetuating our strengths into the future? In education above all, it is a mistake to define virtues only by what is absent, rather than by what is present.

Some things we want to exclude because they are harmful, dangerous, mis-educative; other things we exclude because we have no room for them and they are not as valuable as something else. But what matters most is what we decide to *include* in our schools.

"Friends' Community School - A Plan"

While in Civilian Public Service camp as a conscientious objector, Leonard Kenworthy developed a plan, dated December 19, 1943, for "Friends' Community School"—he chooses the name carefully—whose aim was to "Develop Christian Citizens of the World." His plan is significant both because of how it reconceptualizes what Quaker education needs to guard, and how it might do so in a new era, and because of its influence on Iowa Conservative Yearly Meeting's School Committee as they planned re-opening Scattergood school in 1944.[25]

It is instructive how Kenworthy orders the needs impelling such a new school. The very first issue is "inroads of military mind into public school," with the possibility of compulsory military training in the future. How often, from Fothergill and Tuke to the present, affirming and maintaining the peace testimony has been a starting-point in Quaker education. Second is "dissatisfaction with many characteristics of existing Friends Schools," among which he speaks of size, "catering to non-Friends chiefly for financial reasons," and the expense and elaborateness of "inhibiting educational tradition." Most striking, from our perspective today, is the dissatisfaction he describes as "lack of adventure in race relations and educational pioneering." Third is "need for Friends schools to develop Friendly thought among members' families and develop future leaders." This is followed by an assertion which calls for further reflection: "Adherence to Friends tradition most evident in graduates of Friends Schools and Colleges."

In this identification and weighting of needs, Kenworthy was at once thoroughly traditional and thoroughly contemporary. His plan is driven by concern to preserve and deepen relevant present-day Quaker testimonies, notably the peace testimony and the testimony for equality expressed in the phrase "race relations." Though he does not speak directly of the testimony for simplicity, his plan takes it for granted, not in its older expression as "plainness" but as we are likely to understand it now, as an ordering of priorities, an avoidance of the clutter and inhibiting effect of elaborate living.[26] He also takes as a given that what he hopes to achieve educationally will be best achieved in and through a small community.

> Ideal—A day school where students could live at home in fine family atmosphere and where school could be outgrowth of community pattern. Boarding school would extend advantages of such a school to more students.

The small group, he writes, allows for mobility and flexibility in the school, permits a family atmosphere, knowing one another better, sharing of responsibility, leadership opportunities for all, both small classes and some involving the entire school ("cutting down on costs of all small classes").

For location he suggests a small town or the country, "for more wholesome life there," near a large city to allow the advantages of cultural events, week-end work camps "in industrial or conflict areas," and visitors to the school. He wants "as unique and beautiful a location as possible," including a small farm "permitting dairy, chicken farm, woods, playing fields, gardens, opportunity for expansion," "simple

rustic buildings fitting into community around school" (which
he hopes might be built by students "with expert help from
outside"), dormitories on the cottage plan, a "large home-
like central meeting place as hub of school life," and a farm
barn "with roomy hayloft for folk dancing and gym." The
school should also be near train, bus, and airplane facilities.

The student body Kenworthy envisions would be "over
50% Friends," but he also wants it to be interracial and
"international as much as possible," and attract "children of
F.O.R. and other pacifist people, children of Wider Quaker
Fellowship members, etc." He stresses the "need to strengthen
Friends' groups and their peculiar contributions to main
stream of Christianity, rather than to dilute contribution.
Other schools can be inter-denominational." And, of course,
he urges, "attempt to keep tuition low enough to attract all
economic levels of Friends' children."

His faculty would also be more than 50% Friends, including
people who have lived or traveled abroad, "if possible from
different sections of the world," with an interracial outlook,
"at least one colored member or family to give interracial
atmosphere and attract students of Negro race." He suggests
"perhaps one older couple of more maturity." For the rest, he
wants young couples raising families, to create a family atmosphere and give a sense of adventure and pioneering.
"Young people more likely to respond to new ideas," he says,
being young then himself and unable to imagine how responsive he will be for all his long life. He wants people with hobby
interests, with "other characteristics of teachers assumed— love
of young people, patience, breadth, etc.," who would not stay
more than five consecutive years without a year away from
the school "in *another type of work,* to prevent stagnation and
prevent them from becoming life teachers with certain characteristics, particularly if in boarding school."

The curriculum he outlines has a core for each of three years: the Community, the Nation, the World. The orientation of the curriculum would be very practical: in the first year, for example, "English" would focus on reading and writing for vocational uses; in "science" "the emphasis would be on the local environment both for practical purposes and for enjoyment—the geology of the area, the birds, the trees, the flowers, soil conservation as related to the school farm . . . " After this first year course,

> students would be advised to take science and math only as they needed it for vocational purposes or for special interest. As much as possible it would be related to the accounting connected with the dairy, farm and school, with the practical aspects of electricity and plumbing connected with the school. . . .

"Religion" would involve study of the contributions of various religious groups, the place of the church in worship and social service, some study of comparative religions, and "a serious attempt to develop the religious life of each pupil and of the group, experimenting with directed meditation. . . ."

Kenworthy's Plan is both a product of a particular time and a remarkable condensation of perennial themes and emphases in Quaker education. Growing out of the experience of world war, it is idealistic but not escapist. It proposes a school which will be small and family-like, in a rural location "for more wholesome life there," but close to the cultural life of, and opportunities for social service in, a city. The school will embody in its curriculum and institutional life the outward-facing testimonies for peace, for racial and international harmony and understanding, as well as the more inward-facing testimonies for simplicity and community, intrinsically and instrumentally valuable.

Community is the matrix in which young people can develop the trust and self-confidence essential for the risk-taking required in experimental education. In community everyone can learn to take responsibility, to follow or take the lead. In community we can learn to give and receive love. Simplicity gets the most out of scarce resources. It stresses acquiring practical and therefore empowering skills. It teaches us how to make do. The student who learns how to garden and to cook learns how to feed himself; the student who learns how to put up a building or fix plumbing learns how to care for her own shelter.

Certainly features of Leonard Kenworthy's Plan are open to criticism. Its curriculum is too narrowly vocational to find favor today, and its approach to race relations would probably be condemned as naive. If it is not too sanguine about the number of Friends—students and faculty—who can be recruited to the school, it does seem over-concerned about letting non-Friends in. Perhaps the strongest objections to the Plan would echo Bickley's criticism of the Haverford Plan of 1830, that it set out to accomplish contradictory ends.[27] But perhaps the times always demand paradoxical, if not contradictory, goals for education.

Kenworthy's Plan captures a vision of Quaker education where ideals are guarded and nurtured in order that they may find expression in effective practical action, where the defining testimonies of Friends can be tested in daily life and recommended to the wider world by the examples of a loving community. And it is not a Plan which merely stays on paper. We see many of its features imbedded in the experiments with education which emerge as the generation of Quaker leaders tested in the crucible of prison and Civilian Public Service asks how to make Quaker education relevant to the dangers and opportunities of the postwar world.

WORK CAMPS:
"EVALUATING AND VALIDATING IDEALISM"

The experiences of those who were conscientious objectors during the Second World War profoundly influenced subsequent Quaker educational practice. Both the men who were subject to the draft and the women who made their own witness as supporters of prison COs or as spouses of CPS men, challenged and inspired one another to idealistic experiments in community and in transforming political, social, and educational institutions. The forms which conscientious objection to war took—prison, non-combatant military service, relief work, participation as human subjects in medical experiments, service in mental hospitals, and forestry projects— shape salient features in Quaker school life in the immediate postwar period and up through the present. A simple way to describe what happened is to say that Quaker schools benefitted from the cross-fertilization of guarded education by the work camp.

Virtually all conscientious objectors in the United States were dislocated, compelled to live in total institutions (whether prisons or camps) which governed every aspect of life, and gathered into work which was frequently tedious and unrewarding. In the Civilian Public Service camps, they had to practice the disciplines of stark simplicity and perform collaborative work among independent, thorny, and quirky companions. People recalling the CPS experience describe it as a stringent test of idealism, a forced experiment in communal living, and a training-school for pacifists and social activists.

Out of patterns of relief work dating from the First World War, from AFSC projects in the Great Depression, and Civilian Public Service, emerged a form and technique which

Quaker educators looked to as a powerful tool for transforming schools and colleges—the work camp.

In the first postwar national conference on Quaker education, "Quaker Education Considered," held at Earlham
College, November 21-22, 1946, the educational value of
the work camp was a dominant theme. The conference
participants identified a number of key characteristics of
the "work camp technique": it is a "controlled experiment
in cooperative activity" where both the decisions and the
discipline of the group are "controlled by 'the sense of the
meeting.'" It is a "religiously-centered community serving
others" which provides group life with a "balance of worship, recreation, and work." Because its purpose is . . . to
start the growth of the great root systems of life in the
mind and experience of the student," the work camp "can
become an important agent in character development."
Work camp activities "get under the skin deeper that those
of the classroom and aid in developing character." Consequently, "the work camp helps to evaluate and validate
idealism."

It is worth underlining the benefits the conference
participants expected from articulating the work camp
with the classroom. Projects can have both practical and
developmental value appropriate to the age and educational level of the students. They can awaken a social conscience through giving young people a firsthand experience
of making a living in a society which perpetuates inequi-
ties based on race, class, and gender. They can generate a
spirit of service to others. In addition, particularly for college students, work camps can have a vocational benefit,
giving concrete opportunities to put knowledge and theories to the test of application, using sociological problems
as laboratory materials. "The idea is not new," says the

conference report, "but is capable of more wide, more care-fully directed, and more productive use as an effective means in a democratic society."

THE CONTROLLED EXPERIMENT

Postwar Quaker education supplements the earlier images of a Quaker school, which stressed the family or the enclosed garden, with the imagery of the laboratory and the experiment. Since the language recommending the work camp as a teaching technique depends heavily on the idea of experiment, it is appropriate to consider what the experiment was, what it was designed to test, and what was to be controlled and controlled *for*. The premise of many experiments is "what if?" Especially where human subjects are involved, we set conditions for testing responses to carefully controlled challenges.

One aspect of such an experiment, then, must be *defamiliarizing*. The circumstances are deliberately set outside the ordinary and expected, so the participants face the challenge of new tasks, group living under conditions of greater-than-usual difficulty. The romance of camping is in-extricably connected to "roughing it": overcoming physical discomforts, living in close quarters, sharing responsibilities for all aspects of communal life—cooking, gathering fuel, cleaning-up. This *plain* life provides the satisfactions of doing without familiar comforts in order to accomplish some goal, perhaps using one's body in more than usually demanding tasks. The work, and camp life, become intrinsi-cally valuable because of the very conditions established by camp life. Cooperation, mutual support, evenly-shared work are *givens* of the experiment; no one will eat or sleep comfortably unless everyone contributes to group life.

A camp which exists merely to keep itself going can be both satisfying and educative, but its chief pedagogical value lies in teaching its most important lessons tangentially, by indirection. A *work* camp cannot be merely focused on self-maintenance. Someone else must benefit from the work, in order for the experience to be fully satisfying. An aspect of the *defamiliarizing*, then, is what might be called *decentering*. Adversaries brought together to focus outside themselves, on a work project removed from their conflict, may find their understanding of one another increasing while they are not thinking about it but concentrating instead on washing dishes or building a house. In time, they must return to the substantive differences, which cannot be dish-washed away, but those differences may benefit from the shifting of focus, the decentering, which has bought time while trust and mutual growth occur. For other kinds of problems, centering on the value of the work-task, or on the benefit it gives others, can provide an unobtrusive means to shift focus from the troubled self, and even a brief moratorium from self-absorption can produce significant developmental impact.

Work is a great equalizer. Leadership comes to be shared differently, and more widely, sometimes on the basis of practical expertise, sometimes because of different physical tasks. The effective classroom teacher may need to take lessons in carpentry or painting from a student, to their mutual benefit and satisfaction. Group singing will be led by those who know the songs, games and dances taught by those with the most experience and enthusiasm. The pleasures of trading teaching-learning roles enrich the shared worship and recreation which are part of the work camp.

Postwar Quaker education is marked by numerous experiments in work camp or extended work projects, including a summer-long work camp to prepare Scattergood School to reopen in 1944, the college-wide participation in building Stout Meeting House at Earlham in 1952, and the extended work-study opportunities which built facilities at Wilmington College. Each such project was developed to achieve practical economies, but that frequently turned out to be the least important aspect of the experience. Paul Furnas, Earlham's Vice President for Business at the time, said that building Stout Meeting House as a faculty-student-alumni cooperative project probably did not cost any *more* than having it professionally-built, but nearly half a century later people still return to point with pride at some piece of the building they helped to put up.

Earlham College publications in 1948, stressing "experiment" as central to what was called "The Earlham Idea," cite the Community Dynamics Program as "tak[ing] the work camp idea." Students intending to become a new kind of social workers and community activists, found the work camps in Puerto Rico an important vocational experience. American Friends Service Committee sponsored projects, such as interns-in-industry and interns-in-mental-hospitals, *might* have had vocational value for the participants, but they were just as likely to be opportunities for college-age people to earn and save money over a summer, living cooperatively and cheaply while enjoying a balance of worship, recreation, and work with companions from diverse backgrounds but common ideals.

While sponsoring their own programs, Quaker schools and colleges also encouraged their students to broaden their experience though summer projects and weekend work camps sponsored by the American Friends Service Committee and other Quaker organizations. The outreach of such programs, bringing Quakers and non-Quakers together and enlarging the visions of all those who participated, is too great to be measured.

[Here I must record my own debt to weekend work camps sponsored by Philadelphia Yearly Meeting, which I first attended in 1951 as a public high school student totally ig-norant of Quakers. There, for the first time, I met people engaged in social action predicated on religious conviction. At the end of that weekend, I attended meeting for worship for the first time, and knew I was going to become a Quaker. All through my college years, I continued to be active in weekend work camps, as participant, sometimes as cook, and occasionally as substitute leader. My first encounter with the peace testimony, which I strenuously resisted as long as I could, came through my acquaintance with David Richie and Jim Kietzman, work camp leaders who became my mentors as I learned about the testimonies. I know first-hand, and treasure, the educative power of work camps. Every aspect of my personal and professional life and spiritual development has been shaped by the chain of experiences beginning with a work camp, and I cannot imagine what my life would have been without the Quaker faith and practice to which it introduced me.]

John Dewey tells us,

> There is more than a verbal tie between the words com-mon, community, and communication. Men [sic] live in a community by virtue of the things which they have in common; and communication is the way in which they possess things in common. What they must have in common in order to form a community or society are aims, belief, aspirations, knowledge—a common under-standing—like-mindedness as the sociologists say. . . .[28]

The report of "Quaker Education Considered" may have over-stated the potentiality of the work camp as a learning tool, making it sound like a panacea for all educational problems, but it clearly has had a powerful impact on many people over at least two generations, and what the conference called its "techniques" have been successfully generalized to apply to a wide range of teaching-learning situations.

In the late 1960s, work camps, international seminars, and other projects for reconciliation, came under a great deal of criticism for their meliorist approaches to social problems. In *The Secular City*, for example, Harvey Cox argued that they were inadequate to circumstances which required more confrontational methods to achieve social change. Douglas V. Steere questions this "patronizing attitude," arising among a number of Friends:

> While there can be no absolutizing of any social vehicle as the only means of bringing about needed social changes, it may be extremely short-sighted to deprecate the depth of the 'exposure' principle both to the Light and to the needs of one another which was so central in Woolman's thinking and which these particular vehicles have often been able to achieve.[29]

As one of those then receiving Douglas Steere's gentle remonstrance, I want to affirm the continuing wisdom of his words. Further compelling evidence of the power of workcamping can be found in the letters from participants in *Reflections and Memories—Fifty Years of workcamps*.

The workcamp techniques undergird present-day outdoor and wilderness education, often used to orient students to a school and to build a sense of common values, as well as work programs on campus, volunteer service programs, and many internships, off-campus and foreign study programs. Such programs practice economy so as to make resources stretch their farthest, and in the process recommend the values of simplicity, cooperation, and democratic decision-making. These in turn foster the values of equality, harmony, and community. The conditions which encourage group cohesiveness—a balance of work, worship, and recreation, shared decision-making—probably need a purpose beyond community-building in itself. That might be only a by-product of some other activity, important in its own right, though community might well be the longest-lasting consequence of the activity. In its own right, and as a symbol of the Quaker school's intention to reach out to the larger society, the work camp is a powerful example of an enriched concept of "guarded education."

Guarded Education Today

Two hundred years ago, "religiously guarded education," aimed to bring up the young in the Quaker way and to shield them from too much exposure to other ways of life. It was to provide a supportive environment, good companions, and caring guardians, so young people could learn the habits which would enable them to live faithful lives in the world. These goals, modified to respond to the enormous changes in Quakerism and the larger society in this century, seem remarkably appropriate today. Sociologists have described ours as a "culture of neglect," where children are concerned. Family life is threatened, destablilized, when it has not been shattered, by terrible strains, and many children are emotionally deprived and psychologically battered because the adults they must turn to for support are in the same condition. The most dangerous temptations of affluence lie readily at hand, for affluence and neglect can occur together. There is no question of completely shielding young people from too much exposure to unsupportive environments, but it is essential to offer alternatives, models of healthy lives, settings where psychological and spiritual healing can occur, reasons to hope for the future. Erik Erikson says that "trust born of care is . . . the *touchstone* of the reality of a given religion."[30] A "religiously guarded" education today must help students gain control over their inner lives. It must help them find a sense of belonging to a community of shared values. It must help them test their knowledge and convictions through direct, guided, and structured encounters with social and political problems in the world. Never has there been a greater need for schools which offer supportive environments, good companions, and caring teachers. Never has there been greater need to identify and guard what is most precious in educating the young.

NOTES

1. Brinton, *Quaker Education*, 87.

2. Brinton, *Quaker Education*, 88. Italics in the original.

3. Rufus M. Jones, *Later Periods of Quakerism*, Macmillan, London, 1921, Vol. II, 689. George Smith cites this passage in an unpublished essay, *Aspects of Quaker Education from 1740 to 1860*, September, 1993, submitted in partial fulfillment of the M.A degree at Earlham School of Religion.

4. Tuke, *Five Papers*, 78.

5. John Fothergill, *A Letter to a Friend*, 470, in *The Works of John Fothergill: with some account of his life*, Charles Dilly, London, 1784.

6. Tuke, *Five Papers*, 34-35.

7. F.S. Pollard, ed., *Bootham School 1823-1923*, J.M. Dent and Sons, London, 1926, 6-11.

8. See Woolman, *A Plea for the Poor*, and Benezet, *Letter to Samuel Fothergill*.

9. Minute of Seventh Month 31, 1778, in Brown, *Friends Select History*, 10-11.

10. Tuke, *Five Papers*, 37, 39.

11. Gibbs, *Children of Light*, 21.

12. Fothergill, *Letter to a Friend*, 472-73.

13. William Phillips Bickley, *Education as Reformation: An Examination of Orthodox Quakers' Formation of the Haverford School Association and Founding of Haverford School, 1815-1840*, unpublished dissertation, Harvard University School of Education, Ann Arbor, University Microfilms, 1983, 151-53; Parrish, *An Essay on Education*, 53-54.

14. Brinton, *Quaker Education*, 43, 45; Fothergill, *A Letter to a Friend*, 465-66.

15. The Report of the Joint Committee of four monthly meetings in Philadelphia, Fourth Month 23, 1832, in Brown, *Friends Select History*, 26-27.

16. Ethel Hittle McDaniel, *The Contribution of the Society of Friends to Education in Indiana*, Indiana Historical Society, Indianapolis, 1939, 156-57. Ethel Hittle McDaniel documents, 130, that Friends were concerned to avoid the public schools for two reasons: 1) because the schools were supported in part by fines levied against conscientious objectors to serving in the state militia, as required by the state constitution of 1816, and 2) because the public schools "powerfully militate against the Testimony of our Society . . ."

17. Circular dated Third Month 27, 1837, in Brown, *Friends Select History*, 154; *Friends Central History*, 6.

18. Tuke, *Five Papers*, 34-35.

19. William Taber, *Be Gentle, Be Plain: A History of Olney*, Olney Alumni Association, Barnesville, Ohio, 1976, 119, 134, 178. The quotation is from Samuel 15:14.

20. Campbell Stewart, *Quakers and Education*, 33, 36, citing Braithwaite, *The Beginnings of Quakerism*, 1919, 536.

21. Foulds, *History of Ackworth*, 17; Campbell Stewart, *Quakers and Education*, 29-30, 36.

22. Brinton, *Quaker Education*, 43, quoting the Haverford School Plan, 1830; Bickley, *Education as Reformation*, 139.

23. Bickley, *Education as Reformation*, 295; Parrish, *An Essay on Education*, 63-64.

24. Brinton, *Quaker Education*, 43, 88-89; Hole, *Things Civil and Useful*, 85.

25. Robert Berquist, who taught at Scattergood for 30 years, starting in 1946, called my attention to Leonard Kenworthy's Plan, which he says was sent to Sara Pemberton, "who was active in planning for reopening of Scattergood. . . ." Letter from Robert Berquist, 2-8-1995.

26. When Friends schools today try to specify the testimonies which shape them, they frequently turn to Howard Brinton's formulation and speak of community, harmony, equality, and simplicity. It is especially instructive to note Brinton's argument that the testimony for simplicity has resulted in the following educational policies: moderation in dress, speech and deportment; scholastic integrity; emphasis on practical subjects in the curriculum.

27. Bickley, *Education as Reformation*, 140, quotes a passage from *An Account*, 7, which announces Haverford's goals as "usefulness in life, providing 'religious' care over their morals and manners, and acquainting them with the great doctrines of the Christian religion." He comments, "In a single sentence they had joined secular utility, Quaker ethics, and evangelical doctrine."

28. John Dewey, *Democracy and Education: An Introduction to the Philosophy of Education*, Macmillan, New York, 1916, 1922, 5.

29. Douglas V. Steere, Introduction to *Break the New Ground*, Friends World Committee, 1969, 6; Weekend Workcamp Committee, Philadelphia Yearly Meeting, 1991.

30. Erik Erikson, *Childhood and Society*, Norton, second edition, New York, 1963, 25.

Eight

━━━◆━━━

Comenius, Pestalozzi, Froebel, Montessori and Other Educators

The seeds of knowledge, of virtue, and of piety are...naturally implanted in us; but the actual knowledge, virtue, and piety are not so given. These must be acquired by prayer, by education, and by action.

The first Thing obvious to Children is what is sensible; and that we make no Part of their Rudiments.

. . . Very little children have no greater interest than in learning how to do something with their bodies.[1]

Quakerism and Philosophy of Education

Considered in its most technical sense, *Philosophy of Education* might be said to involve three broad lines of inquiry under three old-fashioned headings: natural philosophy, social philosophy, and religious philosophy. A complete philosophy of education must consider how education happens to the human being as a physical body, as a social creature and—the aspect most disputed—as a spiritual being.

One direction philosophy of education takes is scientific or empirical, focusing primarily on *learning theory*—how the mind works, how human beings retain information and grasp

173

concepts, the physiology and psychology of human development. From empirical premises, learning theory can address
both curriculum and teaching methods. What subjects should
be taught, in what order and for what purposes? How can
subjects best be inculcated, accommodated to human minds
at different ages and different levels of comprehension?
What are the best means to encourage learning? How should
children at different developmental stages be disciplined?
Should competition or cooperation be encouraged as the
better way to learn? What are appropriate ways of rewarding
learning? Should we punish failures to learn? Is learning only
conditioned response?

It is hardly to be expected that Quakers *as* Quakers would
have made any peculiar contribution to those hard-science
elements of philosophy of education. Though there have
certainly been distinguished Quaker students of physiology,
there is no Quaker theory on how the brain functions, or
Quaker science of physiology; and while there have been quite
influential Quaker psychologists whose interest in human
development might well be inspired by their faith, there is
also no peculiarly Quaker psychology or theory of human
development. We have certainly drawn on practical experience to determine what is valuable to teach, for what reasons, and in what sequences, and our schools have tended to
encourage cooperative learning instead of competition, but
it would be hard to claim that these approaches constitute
unique contributions to educational theory.

If *learning theory* is one branch of philosophy of education,
another is comprehended in those questions which might be
thought of as either the *sociology of education* or the *ethics of
education*. Who shall be taught? Why should they be taught?
Who shall teach? How shall the teachers be taught? What
are the ends of education?

Who shall be taught? Quakers have always been committed to universal education and equal education for men and women. They have been, paradoxically, pioneers in co-education and in creating, through separated women's and men's meetings for business, opportunities for women to learn and practice leadership skills. Why should people be taught? So they may save their souls? So they may become political and cultural leaders of a society? So they may serve their society? So they may know how to live a good life? Are they to be prepared for service, for personal salvation, for ways of behaving in the world? Are they to be taught how to practice goodness, purity of life, religious fidelity, courage, "skills of being"? If those were choices in a multiple-choice question, Quakers would probably want to answer "all of the above." In their concern for educating the poor, prisoners in jails, Blacks and Indians, Quakers have historically made the means of education an expression of their social testimonies. Indeed, Quaker approaches to education justify our thinking of it as a social testimony in itself. Flawed as our witness has often been, these educational ideals have been sources of spiritual renewal again and again, in our meetings no less than in our schools. Quakers *as* Quakers have made contributions to both the sociology of education and the ethics of education, offering answers which come from their particular experiences, though they have usually found themselves sharing in a larger community of ideas.

From its beginnings, Quaker approaches to education have stressed the spiritual and the practical together, in the conviction that the ends of education are inseparable from the purposes of human life and the purposes of human communities. Anthony Benezet has described this as being concerned for educating with regard to time and to eternity. But if the test of whether Quakers have a philosophy of education rests on whether we have a unique and original theory of learning—a Quaker physiology and psychology, a sociology as well as an ethics equally unique and original—then of course we do not. Indeed, if that was what was meant by a philosophy of education, to have our own would not be merely peculiar, it would be bizarre. At any given time and place, people share in a broad community of ideas in currency, including ideas about education. Common problems may produce similar solutions. Ideas and practices get tried, discarded, lost, rediscovered, modified. They may fail to work practically in one setting and become powerful and effective under other circumstances. To trace patterns in Quaker education which might indicate a broad underlying philosophy of education in a less technical sense of that term means identifying coincidence, common inspiration, affinity, not just influence. As an illustration, we may usefully begin by bracketing William Penn's views on education between the work of Johann Amos Comenius a few decades before and John Locke's at the end of the seventeenth century.

William Penn's Views on Education

Penn's writings on education are brief and unsystematic—a section of maxims in *Some Fruits of Solitude,* 1693, "Fruits of a Father's Love," his "Advice to His Children," first published in 1726, and a letter to his wife, written in 1688 but not published until 1761, and the several versions of his Frame of Government—but they are useful as a reflection of what a university-trained aristocrat and courtier turned Quaker would consider the appropriate goals and methods of education. What is immediately evident is that he does not want for his children the kind of education he received. "We are in Pain to make them Scholars, but not *Men*! To talk, rather than to know, which is true *Canting*." In fact, he warns against trusting too much to book learning, "for much reading is an oppression of the mind and extinguishes the natural candle. . . ."

For Penn, the *subject* of education should be the natural world itself, "a great and stately *Volume* of natural things" in which "the Children of Wisdom" can read the visible and legible characters which are "the *Mark* of its Maker." In *Some Fruits of Solitude* he says "It were happy if we studied Nature more in Natural Things; and acted according to Nature; whose Rules are *few, plain,* and *most reasonable.* Let us begin where she begins, go her Pace, and close always where she ends, and we cannot miss of being good Naturalists." He urges that children be taught *things* before they learn languages and wishes that both Naturalists and "Mechanicks" would write schoolbooks in Latin for young people "that they might learn Things with Words." Instead, he says, we press children's memories too soon, making them learn words, rules, grammar, and rhetoric, "and a strange Tongue or two, that it is ten to one may never be useful to them. . . ," but "the first thing obvious to Children is what is *sensible* [i.e. what the senses tell us]; and that we make no Part of their Rudiments."

He wants his children's education to be liberal, but also useful, for "ingenuity mixed with industry is good for the body and mind too." He prefers that they be taught by tutors in the home rather than in schools. He urges teaching methods to encourage children's natural interests and abilities, which he calls their "genius," and to take account of their need for variety, play, and physical activity. "Children had rather be making of *Tools* and *Instruments* of Play; *Shaping, Drawing, Framing,* and *Building,* &c, than getting some Rules of Propriety of Speech by Heart. . . ." He hopes his children will study the useful, practical parts of mathematics—for building houses, surveying land, navigating ships—and agriculture. "To preserve a good *constitution* of body and mind," he recommends leisure time activities which will be "pleasant and profitable diversions"—"A Garden, and Elaboratory, a Workhouse, Improvements and Breeding [of livestock]. . . ." [2]

By the time Penn writes these several works, he has reason to assume that his children will be wealthy and ultimately inherit control of the province of Pennsylvania, yet the education he wants for them is notable for its down-to-earth practicality: ". . . Let my children be husbandmen and housewives; it is healthy, honest, and of good example. . . ." Good education is to be founded in the study of nature and natural things, and its methods should begin where nature does and follow at her pace; children should learn things before they learn languages.

It is worth briefly noting the affinities between Penn's ideas of the ends and methods of education and those of John Bellers, whose first proposals for a Colledge of Industry appear in 1695 and which gain the support of a number of leading Friends. George Clarke argues that Bellers' proposals "were the most serious attempts made during the late seventeenth and early eighteenth centuries to provide for a full and caring education for all children, rich and poor." [3] Bellers argues for practical education for trade and industry, especially as a way of relieving the poor, believing that educating people into good ways to make their livings "will be instrumental in finishing His Creation" by the slow modification, improvement, and eventual redemption of humankind. Like Penn, he has slight regard for scholars: "Men will grow strong with working, but not with thinking. . . ." Following what he understands to be our natural way of learning, he wants instruction in the mother tongue and words to be taught before rules of grammar, for words lie in the memory and rules in the understanding, he says, and "Children have first Memory before Understanding." He wants book-study leavened with physical labor, both for the health of the children and as a means of financial support for the college, which he wants equipped with all sorts of tools, "for every age and capacity to use," as well as a "Library of Books, a Physick-Garden for understanding of Herbs, and a Laboratory, for preparing of Medicines."[4]

COMENIUS' VIEWS ON EDUCATION

It is impossible to show any direct influence of Comenius' work on the thinking of early Friends, but some affinities among them are worth considering as an indication how similar religious convictions might lead to similar educational philosophies. Johann Amos Comenius [1592-1670] was a Bishop of the Czech Moravian Brotherhood. His most far-sighted ideas on education were not well-known until rediscovered in the mid-nineteenth century. He is studied today, ". . . as an educational statesman whose theories reflected a vision of human unity and dignity more appropriate to our day than to his. Yet it is as a writer of textbooks and organizer of schools that he was known and respected in his own day."[5] Comenius had begun work on what became his most influential book, *The Great Didactic*, in 1627 and completed it in 1632. He was in England from September 22, 1641 to June, 1642, largely through the influence of Samuel Hartlib, a devoted Comenian and the leading educationalist in England in the Commonwealth period. The English Parliament had invited Comenius to address it, but when he arrived in London, tensions with the King were especially great, and Parliament was out of session. Comenius and Hartlib published *A Reformation of Schools* in 1642, and

Hartlib published *A Continuation of Mr. J. A. Comenius'*
School Endeavours in 1648. At Hartlib's urging, John Milton
wrote his brief essay *Of Education*, 1644, which he dedicated
to Hartlib. Comenius believed that Parliament intended to
found a college in England to study his theories, and there
appears to be some evidence that he might have been offered the presidency of Harvard College. In 1658 Comenius
published the first known school picture book in history, *Orbis
Sensualium Pictus: A World of Things Obvious to the Senses
Drawn in Pictures.*[6]

Comenius believed that the seeds of knowledge, virtue,
and piety are naturally implanted in human beings. "It is not
necessary therefore, that anything be brought to a man from
without, but only that which he possesses, rolled up within
himself be unfolded and disclosed. . . ."[7] Though these seeds
are naturally planted in us, however,

> . . . the actual knowledge, virtue and piety are not so
> given. These must be acquired by prayer, by education,
> and by action. He gave us no bad definition who said
> that man was a 'teachable animal.' And indeed it is only
> by a proper education that he can become a man.

All human beings are born for the same end, to become
rational creatures, to have dominion over the earth, and to
be images of their Creator. Humans, among whom Comenius
explicitly includes women, who are ". . . also formed in the
image of God, and share in His grace and in the kingdom of
the world to come," can achieve this only by being educated.[8]
"Every human being, simply by virtue of his humanity, claims
the benefits conferred by education, irrespective of rank or
sex."[9] Comenius, like Bellers, believed that education was a
means to complete God's Creation. In *The Great Didactic*
Comenius argues that

. . . It is evident . . . that even before the Fall a school in which he might make gradual progress was opened for man in Paradise. . . . It is manifest, from the conversation of Eve with the serpent, that the knowledge of things which is derived from experience was entirely wanting. For Eve, had she had more experience, would have known that the serpent is unable to speak, and that there must therefore be some deceit.[10]

In *The Great Didactic* Comenius expounds a system of universal education based on theories of natural development which anticipate the later psychologically-based approaches to learning of Pestalozzi, Froebel, and Montessori.

Teaching according to nature meant teaching through the senses first of all, encouraging and training direct observation and investigation rather than studying books. Thus his textbook *Orbis Sensualium Pictus* appeals directly to the visual sense and simply and easily encourages learning directly from the things of the natural world. He adduces a number of principles of nature which should shape the teaching-learning process, among them: that Nature observes a suitable time for learning any particular thing; that Nature prepares the material before she gives it form; and the Natural way is to move from the universal to the particular. In practice, this would mean moving from the simple to the more complex and learning the vernacular language before the rules of grammar, "not words but *things* first." Nature in its forms moves distinctly from one point to another, and "makes no leaps but proceeds step by step," so teaching should address only one subject at a time and present studies graduated in their difficulty. All learning proceeds from within to the outer world. Comenius repeatedly stresses that *real* things should be taught before the names for them, and that learning should always be connected with what is actual and useful.[11]

Comenius' plan calls for "mother" or nursery schools up to the age of six, with a great deal of that teaching done by mothers themselves, in the home; vernacular or primary schools in every village, for boys and girls ages six to twelve; a Latin or preparatory school in every city for ages twelve to eighteen; and a university in every kingdom or province, for those eighteen to twenty-four who are studying for professions. He argues that only the state has the resources to provide universal education and make it compulsory through the primary school. Only a few countries, among them the United States, Adamson says, made the elementary school the common school for all. The common school founded in Comenius' lifetime was created by New England Puritans who had "most probably felt his influence."[12]

JOHN LOCKE AND SOME THOUGHTS CONCERNING EDUCATION

Lawrence Stone tells us that, "between about 1660 and 1800 a remarkable change in accepted child-rearing theory, in child-rearing practices, and in affective relations between parents and children" took place, a change toward "the child-oriented, affectionate and permissive mode." This movement was from the traditional Christian view, strongly reinforced by Calvinism, toward either the environmentalist view, that we are born *tabula rasa*, the biological view, that our characters and potentialities are for the most part genetically determined, to be modified to some degree by inculcating good habits , or the utopian view, according to which we are born good but corrupted by our experience in society.[13]

John Locke, the chief articulator of the environmentalist position, dominates educational theory, as he does British philosophy, for most of the eighteenth century. In 1693 he publishes an extended essay, growing out of letters of advice to a friend on how to educate his son, with the modest title *Some Thoughts Concerning Education*. Though it rests on Locke's philosophical and psychological conclusions in his *An Essay Concerning Human Understanding*, first drafted in 1671, *Some Thoughts* is less an elaboration of a philosophy than a practical manual for raising a child. Adamson tells us that Comenius anticipated Locke in believing that the human mind was like a blank tablet—Comenius also calls it malleable as wax—so humans must initially learn everything through experience. Locke's way of putting the case is that humans can have no innate ideas, though we have some natural capacities and propensities. The two great and principal actions of the mind, for Locke, are *perception* or thinking and *volition* or willing. We know through *intuition*, which is how one knows oneself, through *sensation and reflection*, which is how one begins to know the physical world and the world of others, and through *demonstration*, where we know by making logical bridges of connection between perceptions and ideas. To educate any child requires the effective managing of, which may mean cooperating with, his or her capacities for perceiving and willing. How our capacities are shaped by environment, practice, and habit working on our desires, imagination, curiosity, constitutes our education.

Locke sees human development following six principles: humans desire approbation and avoid dis-approbation; we associate reward with pleasure and punishment with pain, but these neither establish nor discourage actions but simply remain contingent; we prefer to do actions with respect to which we are free, over those which are compelled; if all their desires are satisfied, children will become overly aggressive and incapable of socialized behavior; if we are to prefer doing something, we need periodic relief from it; and if we are to know something, we must have been curious about it.[14]

Some Thoughts Concerning Education became a best-seller, going through twenty-five editions by 1800.[15] What particularly recommended it was its genial good sense and kindness toward young people and its stress on the development of moral character as more important than book-learning. Locke addresses primarily how the upper middle and aristocratic classes should be educated, so as to produce "virtuous, useful and able men in their distinct callings; though that most to be taken care of is the gentleman's calling." "'Tis virtue, then, direct virtue, which is the hard and valuable part to be aimed at in education," and its foundation is a true notion of God, the Supreme Being, Author and Maker of all things, who loves us and whom we should love and reverence. Four things are desired in a child, especially a son, though Locke also concerns himself with educating daughters, virtue, wisdom, breeding (by which he means courtesy and civility), and learning. The first three are requisites and the fourth is secondary, important only if it contributes to a pleasurable and useful life in the community. ". . . The principles of justice, generosity, and sobriety, joined with observation and industry" make an able man.[16]

Locke is very concerned that parents bind their children to them by affection and respect, which they must first show their children. "Children (nay, and men too) do most by example." Authority which rests primarily on the fear of punishment does great harm to education, he says.

> Every man must some time or other be trusted to himself and his own conduct; and he that is a good, a

virtuous, and able man, must be made so within. And therefore what he is to receive from education, what is to sway and influence his life, must be something put into him betimes; habits woven into the very principles of his nature. . . .[17]

Locke advises against overloading young children's memory with rules and precepts, "which they often do not understand, and constantly as soon forget as given." Instead, when children have done something poorly, or forgotten to do it, "make them do it over and over again till they are perfect." This procedure gives two advantages, Locke says: first, it lets the parent know whether the children are capable of doing what has been commanded—"for sometimes children are bid to do things which upon trial they are found not able to do"—and second, it develops good habits in the children which become "natural." Children's aptitudes, like those of adults, can be a little mended but not utterly transformed from what is naturally theirs, so the teacher should study their natures and aptitudes, "observe what their native stock is, how it may be improved, and what it is fit for. . . ."[18]

All of Locke's recommendations reflect this affectionate, humane good sense about children. "They must not be hindered from being children, or from playing, or doing as children, but from doing ill; all other liberty is to be allowed them." Children love to be busy, and delight in change and variety. Nothing they are to learn should be made a burden to them. If a child is required to play at spinning a top every day at the same time, ". . . see whether he will not soon be weary of any play. . . ." An effective pedagogy will provide variety and arrange lessons to be in tune with the child's readiness, but the tutor must also work to teach the child's mind mastery over itself, "habitual dominion over itself," so it is not merely at the mercy of a desire for variety and entertainment.[19]

Reading and writing are not to be hurried. The child should have alphabet blocks and other playthings with letters on them, so reading can be a game, gentle books such as Aesop's *Fables* and *Reynard the Fox*, especially if the books have pictures. Ideas come from things, he says, not sounds for things, so children should have pictures of animals with the names printed under them. Most striking, he warns against teaching reading by going through the Bible chapter by chapter, which he describes as the worst method to be found, both for reading and for learning about religion. Locke is very critical of the usual approaches to teaching languages. He recommends that a child learn English first, then French and only after that, if at all, Latin—each taught the same way, through speaking and only then through reading, emphatically *not* by writing themes, declamations or, worst of all, verses in Latin. Locke is especially critical of such overvaluing of Latin and Greek ". . . that a child should be chained to the oar seven, eight, or ten of the best years of his life, to get a language or two, which, I think, might be had at a great deal cheaper rate of pains and time, and be learned almost in playing." Children should learn about minerals, plants, and animals, the care and propagation of timber and fruit trees, geography, astronomy, and anatomy. As part of each young gentleman's education, "I would have him learn a trade, a manual trade; nay two or three, but one more particularly."[20] In virtually every particular, Locke's recommendations for content and method for educating the young would be compatible with what Penn would have wanted for his own children and with what the public school he chartered in Philadelphia offered. Locke recommends an education which puts virtue before learning, is adapted to stages of development and individual differences, is practical and science-oriented, minimizes Latin and Greek, and is preparation for the world rather than for the university. Only in those recommendations specifically concerned with educating a social elite—e.g., that dancing, fencing, wrestling, and "riding the great horse" all be a part of a gentleman's education— and perhaps the endorsement of children's playfulness, do we perceive substantial divergence from the aims of Quaker schooling as it developed in the eighteenth century. [21]

Campbell-Stewart reminds us that "The curriculum of a school at any stage of educational history is the product of historical habit with the varying influence of contemporary forces. In the case of early Friends there was also the important factor of a new effusion of faith to direct principle into practice."[22] Latin and Greek were valued as Biblical languages, and Latin for diplomacy and publishing for an international audience, as with Barclay's *Apology,* but they were useless for Friends as stepping-stones to university study. The vernacular, rather than the classics, was the basis of Quaker curriculum from the start. The vernacular stood in opposition to the hegemony of Latin, was "in the plain truth" and "the natural expression of his inward self" to every Englishman, Campbell-Stewart says. He links the early Quaker emphasis on the importance of personal activity and observation, and the use of sensory experience as a basis for education, with Comenius, Locke, Rousseau, Pestalozzi, Froebel, Montessori, "and most writers of the present day."[23]

We have no knowledge thatPenn read Locke's writings on education or would have been influenced by them if he had, though we know that the two were acquainted as far back as Penn's undergraduate days at Christ's College, Oxford and that Locke offered to intercede for Penn when he was under suspicion in the reign of William and Mary.[24] The point is not to demonstrate direct influence from Locke any more than from Comenius, each of whom has been described as the father of modern education, but to show affinities between their work and the thinking of someone who will influence Quaker education in America, and to describe developments in the earliest period of the Quaker movement which help shape a *milieu* from which Quaker educational theory and practice emerge.

John Griscom and Pestalozzianism

With Pestalozzi we can trace direct influences on Quaker education. These come through several channels, but the earliest and most influential is provided by the Quaker scientist and educator John Griscom, of whose *A Year in Europe, Comprising a Journal of Observations, . . . In 1818 and 1819*, published in 1824, Henry Barnard says, "No one volume in the first half of the nineteenth century had so wide an influence on the development of our educational, reformatory, and preventive measures, directly and indirectly, as this."[25] In his travels, Griscom focuses on several interrelated concerns, particularly research in natural science, science education, and the operation of a variety of "benevolent" institutions, among them prisons, bridewells, paupers' homes, orphanages, and schools for the poor, the blind, and the deaf-mute. One of his major preoccupations is how learning can be as widely diffused as possible, for the benefit of both society and the individual. He visits and describes a great number of institutions organized on the Lancastrian plan which, on the continent, especially in France, are described as "schools of mutual instruction" ["Ecole d'Enseignment Mutuel"]. He accepts the Lancastrian school as an efficient way to teach the poor and other disadvantaged groups and assumes the best about the system. At first, Griscom seems to be interested in the work of Pestalozzi and de Fellenberg primarily for what it has in common with the Lancastrian plan, though he concludes that "There is nothing of mechanism in it, as in the Lancastrian plan; no laying down of precise rules for managing classes, &c. It is all mind and feeling."[26] He first visits the "Institut d'education" at Hofwyl, organized by Emmanuel de Fellenberg, a disciple of Pestalozzi, which he admires because of its practical focus on agriculture, mechanic arts, and the connection of the poor with the well-to-do in a spiritual bond. De Fellenberg believed that education was least effectively organized for the highest and the lowest of the three social classes. His plan therefore involved educating boys of both those classes side by side,

> in a manner conformable to their situations, but in such a way, as to develop, to the highest extent, the best faculties of their nature; and while it preserves the proper relation between them, it should, at the same time, encourage the feelings of kindliness and sympathy on the one part, and respect and love on the other.

The rich, by observing the industry and skill of the laboring classes, would learn to respect them, and the poor, feeling their kindness, would consider them benefactors.[27]

De Fellenberg believed that agriculture and the "mechanic arts" were the best means to develop the faculties "to promote the permanent happiness of man." The children of the poor received two or more hours of instruction daily in reading, writing, and music (which de Fellenberg thought brought the mind and heart in harmony with truth), and also learned the trades of blacksmith, carpenter, wheelwright, cabinet maker, joiner, shoemaker, brass-worker. They worked in the fields during the growing season, where their labor paid for a substantial part of their living and educational costs.

> . . . They learn to read, write, and calculate, with and without the use of pencil or pen; the elements of drawing become familiar to them; and they acquire good notions of geometry, especially in relation to field surveying and its application to descriptive drawing. Botany and mineralogy constitute part of their amusements. . . . But the most admirable trait in the character of this school, is the tone of religious feeling which, it is said, pervades it.[28]

It is instructive to see what Griscom particularly emphasizes as "the leading ideas and views of human nature" which shape Pestalozzi's pedagogical method, when he visits him at Yverdun.

> He thinks there is enough in the intuitive understanding of every child to accomplish the complete growth and maturity of its faculties, if its reason be properly trained and nourished, and not warped by injudicious treatment. . . . There is a native and inherent life, which only requires to be cherished by genial treatment, to bring it into the full attainment of truth, and to the utmost perfection of its being. He therefore insists upon the greatest pains being taken to draw out this native life and to preserve it in full vigour.

For Pestalozzi, the common plans of education are too artificial and far from nature, over-emphasizing memory and neglecting the imagination. He speaks late in his life of educating the hand, the heart, and the head together. The phrases which Griscom lifts up for emphasis are especially significant for a Quaker: "native and inherent life," "native feelings of

the heart," "native powers of the mind." If these native powers
are allowed to operate, he understands Pestalozzi to be saying,
"the child is competent of itself to arrive gradually at the most
correct and important conclusions in religion and science."[29]
In Pestalozzi's *Letters to Greaves* he says, "God has given the
child a spiritual nature, that is to say, He has implanted in
him the voice of conscience; and He has done more, He has
given him the faculty of attending to this voice."[30]

Griscom only sketches in the pedagogical method itself. Very
few books are used, so "the teacher must be constantly with the
child, always talking, questioning, explaining, and repeating.
The pupils, however, by this process, are brought into very
close intimacy with the instructor." This permits close observation of each student's individual capacities, faculties, and
propensities. In a free school Pestalozzi established for both
poor boys and girls who will become teachers themselves,
Griscom observed the girls sitting around a table, sewing, while
their instructor gave them problems in arithmetic to solve.
"They are thus led on, from the most simple beginnings, to
comprehend the principles of arithmetic, and to work questions with great expertness, solely by a mental process."

Griscom observes that the success of this method depends
heavily on the personal qualities and qualifications of the teachers. Above all, he says, it requires the teacher to consider himself

> . . . as the father and bosom friend of his pupils, and to be
> animated with the most affectionate desires for their good.
> Pestalozzi himself is all this . . . His plan of teaching is
> just fit for the domestic fireside, with a father or mother
> in its centre, and a circle of happy children around them.[31]

We must look beyond Grisom for a full description of
Pestalozzi's pedagogical method, which is, above all, deeply
influenced by Rousseau, about whom Griscom has only hard

words to say: "The eye of a misanthropist, is a very miserable, distorting kind of telescope; and a heart that does not glow with the love of God and man, will serve as a very poor and delusive guide, for the head of a reformer." Griscom describes Rousseau's home as ". . . the place which he chose, as a retreat from the world which he disliked; but which he did not contribute much, I think, to mend."[32]

In their unmediated, undiluted form, Rousseau's ideas on education will not find a warm response from Quaker educators for a long time after he is safely dead, but it is Rousseau who influences Pestalozzi's dictum that the ultimate end of education is fitness for life: in *How Gertrude Teaches Her Children* Pestalozzi says "We have spelling schools, writing schools, catechism schools, and we want [need]—men's schools."[33] He believed that education should enable children to begin to practice self-instruction; he therefore grounds his teaching method on psychological principles, arranging instruction on what we would call a developmental model. This model begins with his concept of *Anschauung*, translated variously as "intuition" and "the immediate experience of objects or situations." In what seems to be a commonplace for generations of educational reformers (which perhaps must be continually repeated because it is so successfully ignored), Pestalozzi stresses that children should learn *things* before, or at least in connection with, words for things. He gave children large working vocabularies because he recognized that they used words as the thing itself, at first, a way of getting control over things. He wanted to start with the primary capacities of counting, measuring, and speaking, which give us the power to describe, as the means by which we gain accurate knowledge of sense-objects and the power to define them. His method stressed moving from the concrete to the abstract by careful, precise steps, always drawing on the child's interest and intuition. The instructor must always be on the lookout for what there is about interest which makes a task more learnable, to incorporate the secrets of informal learning into the formal. The operational meaning of *Anschauung* becomes the "object-lesson."[34]

Harry Broudy and John Palmer credit Pestalozzi with introducing such learning tools as slates and pencils and letters of the alphabet fastened on cards, and with introducing simultaneous instruction of a whole class.[35] Rusk credits him with formulating a method based on psychological principles, recognizing the practical and emotional aspects of personality, laying the basis of our present elementary school system, and reinforcing the democratic tradition in education.[36] His influence, then, is far wider than in Quaker schools alone. Pestalozzian experiments were tried early in the nineteenth century in Philadelphia and in Robert Owen's New Harmony, and Pestalozzi's friend Joseph Greaves, who became secretary of the Infant School Society in 1825, influenced those schools toward Pestalozzian principles, in addition to founding a Pestalozzian school in 1837 named Alcott House in honor of Bronson Alcott. The school system of Oswego, New York was reorganized on the Pestalozzian method in 1865.[37]

In Baltimore, Eli Lamb, head of Friends' Elementary and High School, adapted Pestalozzian methods for his schools. The 1871 school catalogue said:

> As our object is to teach *subjects*, rather than books, we are careful to urge upon each pupil the necessity of self-dependence, rather than reliance upon textbooks. To test the students' knowledge, and to accustom them to original research, questions and problems, not contained in the text-books, are frequently suggested. . . .

Primary teachers at the school introduced "object teaching" for nature study in 1871, several years before Francis Parker introduced it in the schools of Quincy, Massachusetts. As the catalogue explained the Pestalozzian theory:

> Object lessons are the easy lessons, which nature gives to the child from its infancy. The closer we follow nature in her teaching, the more likely will we be to succeed; therefore, we should teach as she does, through the medium of the senses. The first instruction should be calculated to awaken, and stimulate the mental faculties of the child, and the attention should be directed to simple, surrounding objects. That instruction must begin with real perception of things. . . . An object lesson is a systematic exercise in *thinking.* . . .[38]

It is worth returning to John Griscom, to note the two aspects of Pestalozzi's work he particularly commended: the spirit in which it was performed—"The two great instruments with which he works are faith and love."—and the combination of agricultural and mechanical with literary and scientific instruction. Griscom is interesting for how he brings science, education, and the needs of the poor together. Combining a laboring school with academic work (as earlier proposed by John Bellers and as practiced by the laboring schools established by Friends in England in the nineteenth century) is a way to balance life and to help the school pay for itself. It also rests on the assumption that science, valuable for practical reasons *and* as recreation, and industry will help save or improve the political and social order. In expressing the hope that Pestalozzi's system will be widely adopted in the United States, Griscom makes a striking application:

If white children could not at once be obtained to begin with, I would take the children of coloured people . . . Such an experiment, with persons of this description, would be highly interesting. It would put to flight the ridiculous theory of those who contend for an organic inferiority on the part of the blacks. It would in time produce examples very beneficial to our black population; and in reference to the scheme of colonization, now becoming popular, it might prove extremely important, by furnishing individuals admirably qualified by education, habits, and morals to aid in the management of an infant colony.[39]

Griscom's remarks call for two comments. First, although there is no reason to claim a causal link, the kind of schooling for black children he suggests anticipates the early days of the Quaker-sponsored School for Colored Youth, now Cheyney State University. Second, Griscom's proviso, "if white children could not . . . be obtained," inadvertently sounds a theme in the history of educational reform movements. Pestalozzi is in effect allowed to try out his utopian experiments on children of the poor, as Maria Montessori later is allowed to practice first on the mentally ill and then on slum children, because a failed experiment in those circumstances will not be a great loss. In each case, their dedication to the children they choose to serve is only fully honored when their pedagogical methods are taken up by the middle and wealthy classes for their own children.

FROEBEL AND THE KINDERGARTEN

In the institution of the kindergarten we have an example not merely of influence on Quaker education but of adoption, though whether this also represents an adoption of the elaborate philosophy behind the idea is unclear. By contrast with Pestalozzi, who says in *How Gertrude Teaches Her Children*, "Since my twentieth year I have been incapable of philosophic thoughts, in the true sense of the word," Friedrich Froebel's educational theories are heavily freighted with the idealism of Kant, Fichte, Schelling and Hegel, as well as by his direct observation of Pestalozzi's work.[40] The opening paragraph of Froebel's *The Education of Man* announces:

> The whole world—the All of the Universe—is a single great organism in which the eternal Uniformity manifests itself. This principle of uniformity expresses itself as much in external nature as in spirit. Life is the union of the spiritual with the material. Without mind or spirit matter is lifeless; it remains formless, it is mere chaos. Only through the entrance of the spiritual into the material does the cosmos originate. Spirit manifests itself in order. Every creature, every object is matter informed by spirit. . . . God is the one ground of all things. God is the all-comprehending, the all-sustaining. God is the essential nature, the meaning of the world.[41]

Froebel believes that the mind unfolds from within, according to a pre-determined pattern. The stages of early development enact a dialectic, the "law of opposites," from the inner outward in the young child, expressed most clearly in play, which he describes as ". . . the self-active representation of the inner," and from the outer inward as the young boy or girl begins to internalize what is being learned. ". . . All knowledge and comprehension of life are connected with making the internal external, the external internal, and with perceiving the harmony and accord of both."[42] To have educational value, play cannot be mere purposeless activity but must be channeled into an orderly sequence by the materials which adults provide. The very objects which the child is given, and the sequence in which they are presented—what Froebel calls the First Gift, the Second Gift, etc.—are chosen to awaken intuition of deeper meanings; each object has a formal quality which Froebel believed suggests the Divine unity. The First Gift is a soft ball, combining the unity of roundness with the yielding malleability of soft material. The child thus has a sensory experience of opposites and begins actively expressing the self by squeezing, manipulating, playing with the ball. The sphere and the cube are pure opposites, he argues, and stand in relation to one another as "unity and plurality, movement and rest, round and straight." The child plays with each pure form in turn and is then presented with a cylinder which, according to the "law of connection" combines unity complete in itself in the round surface and plurality of the sphere and cube.[43] The circle painted on the floor of the kindergarten room, around which teacher and children gather as the first exercise of the day, to sing, play, and pray together, symbolized regularity and continuity, meanings which Froebel hoped the children would absorb intuitively.[44]

As the child moves from the self-activity of play, molded by the environment which adults provide, to the stage of instruction, he or she brings the spirit of play into what will become more and more like the world of work. Froebel advocated including manual instruction in the school curriculum, as well as gardening, drawing and nature study. "Every child, boy, and youth . . . should devote daily at least one or two hours to some serious activity in the production of some external piece of work. . . ."[45] The young boy or girl engages in activities which, Robert Rusk suggests, have all the characteristic of "projects" as Kilpatrick and Dewey will later define them, "practical problems involving cooperative effort and affording intellectual and moral training."[46]

In the latter part of his life, rather than develop the implications of his system for educating adolescents, Froebel concentrated on founding kindergartens. These experiments, like Pestalozzi's, appealed on practical grounds to many who were uninformed or unconvinced of the metaphysical and philosophical premises undergirding them. It is hard for us to imagine how controversial and dangerous the kindergarten seemed to some people in the mid-nineteenth century. In 1851, the Prussian Minister of Education and Religion issued a decree forbidding them on the grounds that "kindergartens form a part of the Froebellian socialistic system, the aim of which is to teach children atheism." A comic paper in Prussia at the time talks of the kindergartens' "three-year-old demagogues."[47]

Nancy Reid Gibbs says that the kindergarten movement does not spread widely in the United States until the 1890s, though earlier "many missions and churches established the first kindergartens . . . largely for children of the poor." According to Broudy and Palmer, Mrs. Carl Schurz is said to have opened the United States' first kindergarten in 1855, Elizabeth Peabody started the first English kindergarten in 1860, and William T. Harris helped incorporate the kindergarten into the American public school system in 1873.[48] In that context we may consider how the kindergarten comes into Quaker schools. Clayton Faraday describes the kindergarten as a "new and daring idea . . . and somewhat controversial form of education" when Friends Central opened the first one in Philadelphia in 1877, immediately after the methods are demonstrated at the Centennial Exhibition. Speaking of Froebel's "radical view of the needs of young children," Gibbs says Friends Seminary was one of the earliest New York schools to open a kindergarten, in 1878, ". . . an indication, perhaps, of the congeniality of Froebel's views with the Quaker concern for the creative and individual nature of the young child." In 1883, Thomas Sidwell leased out a room in his school for a kindergarten, then advertised it: "The advantages of kindergarten preparation for school are now too well known to make repetition necessary." Eli Lamb's school in Baltimore began a kindergarten department for children aged three to seven in the same decade. Fanny Jackson-Coppin asked to open a kindergarten in the Quaker-sponsored Institute for Colored Youth in Philadelphia, in 1888, a request which met with some resistance before it was approved.

Wilmington Friends School announced its first kindergarten in 1891-92 and in the following year established a class to train kindergarten teachers in "developing the mental, moral and physical nature of the child." At Wilmington, the radicalism of kindergartens took another form, the request for a piano. Minutes of the School Committee tell a familiar story. In September, 1895: "The question was asked if a Piano was offered free of charge to the Committee for the use of kindergarten would it be accepted. . . ." A month later: "After a full and thorough discussion it was felt we were not quite ready to come to a decision today. . . ." It took three years, from 1895 to 1898, of "deliberation, doubt and perhaps dissension before Friends could bring themselves to give up the ancient testimony against music. . . ."[49]

Quaker schools are among the first to embrace the kindergarten, then, though there is no indication that they embrace the larger metaphysical framework in which Froebel and his disciples set it. Shorn of those elements, the kindergarten is another example of a pedagogy founded on a stage conception of human development; it stresses loving care of children rather than stern discipline, and it reiterates themes in both Locke and Pestalozzi affirming the psychological importance of play for a child's development. It extends the Pestalozzian emphasis on the object-lesson, joining that proud tradition which gives *things* a priority over *words*, and it encourages a range of physical activities outside the classroom such as gardening and manual training. Froebel looks back to key earlier figures whose ideas have been congenial to, or influential on, Quaker education, even as he anticipates some of the contributions of Montessori and Dewey, which will have their own impact on Quaker education. Dewey says of him: "Froebel's recognition of the significance of the native capacities of children, his loving attention to them, and his influence in inducing others to study them, represent perhaps the most effective single force in modern educational theory in effecting acknowledgement of the idea of growth."[50]

Montessori and the Children's Home

In considering the work of Maria Montessori we once again must speak primarily of strong affinities with Quaker education and general or diffuse, rather than direct, influences on Quaker schools. The affinities are so strong that many individual Quakers have expressed their concern for education by investing themselves deeply in the development of Montessori schools. Here the story to be told parallels that of Griscom, for the earliest and most influential interpretation of Montessori education in America, *A Montessori Mother*, 1912, is published by a Quaker, Dorothy Canfield Fisher, five years after the first *Casa dei Bambini* opened. It will be most instructive, therefore, to note what Fisher emphasizes in her presentation of the Montessori method.

Montessori teaching involves both a method and numbers of apparatus designed for achieving precise, graduated goals; two pieces of cloth designed for the child to practice buttoning and unbuttoning, blocks for building towers, rods of different lengths for learning arithmetic, alphabet letters cut out of sandpaper and mounted on cards. Each child chooses, or is drawn to, some exercise which is interesting and educationally challenging for him or her. "The central idea of the Montessori method," Fisher tells us, "on which every smallest bit of apparatus, every detail of technic rests solidly, is a full recognition of the fact that no human being can be educated by anyone else. He must do it himself or it is never done." In consequence, the high light of the classroom is turned away from the teacher toward the pupil, and the teacher becomes, instead of an intrusive instructor, "the scientific, observing supervisor of this mental 'playground' where the children acquire intellectual vigor, independence, and initiative as spontaneously, joyfully, and tirelessly as they acquire physical independence and vigor as a by-product of physical play." The teacher's job is to center attention on each child, observing her activity, noting growth, putting apparatus in her hands when the time is right, offering only the smallest amount of guidance to get the child started on a new interest. "The learner must do his own learning, and, this granted, it follows naturally that the less he is interfered with by arbitrary restraint and vexatious, unnecessary rules, the more quickly he will learn." Fisher quotes Montessori: "An axiom of our practical pedagogy is to aid the child only to be independent."[51]

Fisher tells us that there is no haste in this method, no adult occupations to be hindered by children's activities, no rules made solely for the adults' convenience. Consequently, children can, freely, joyously, noisily if they want, "develop themselves by action from morning to night." Because free to be absorbed in the activities of growth, to which the child is drawn instinctively, intuitively, naturally—all three words recur frequently in Fisher's book—the child takes on self-discipline and learns self-control "as a by-product of his healthy absorption in some fascinating pursuit or as a result of his instinctive imitation of older children." "The particular, vivifying truth which we must imprint on our minds in this connection is that spontaneity of action is the absolute prerequisite for any moral or intellectual advance on the part of any human being."[52]

The foundation of the system is the education of the child's senses "to rapidity, agility and exactitude, . . . for the sake of the five, finely accurate instruments which this education puts under his control." The apparatus supports ". . . systematized and ordered, graded and arranged . . . exercises which every child instinctively craves," for developing and refining the senses through practical activities. The principle of the method is that the child, given a choice, will always choose the right exercise for each stage of development. The teacher's responsibility is to give the child opportunity for completely free action, watch what the child does, and then make the right exercise and apparatus available. The child is never to be coaxed or forced into using any piece of apparatus; instead, the teacher encourages the child's "*natural* interest" through "silent object-lessons." The apparatus is always self-correcting, Fisher says, though no piece can ever be used for anything but its intended purposes—if, for example, the child wants to build towers, she can't use the measuring rods but has to be given blocks. "*. . . There is no smallest item in the Montessori training which is intended merely to amuse the child.*"[53]

Fisher singles out for attention the Montessori "lesson of silence," an exercise which began as a training for hearing but also "has a moral effect which is more important." In the busy schoolroom a sudden hush comes over everyone, and the students sit and look fixedly at the word which the directress has written on the blackboard, *Silenzio*.

> The silence becomes more and more intense. . . . It is now evident from the children's trance-like immobility that they no longer need to make an effort to be motionless. They sit quiet, rapt in a vague, brooding reverie, their busy brains lulled into repose, their very souls looking out from their wide, vacant eyes. This expression of utter peace . . . has in it something profoundly touching. In that matter-of-fact, modern schoolroom, as solemnly as in shadowy cathedral aisles, falls for an instant a veil of contemplation, between the human soul and the external realities of the world.[54]

The silence lasts for only six or seven minutes. Then the Directress steps into the next room and calls each child's name; " . . . the child joyfully goes out and throws herself into the Directress' waiting arms." This modern, scientific woman-doctor, says Fisher, has rediscovered "the mystic joys [of Quakerism] . . . and has appropriated to her system one of the most beneficial elements of the Quaker Meeting."[55]

Fisher is at pains to distinguish Montessori education from the kindergarten. In the former the emphasis is on self-generated activity, with a directress—the title is significant—observing carefully and only rarely intervening.

> No prettily-dressed, energetic, thorough-going young lady had beckoned the children away from their self-chosen occupations. There was no set circle here with the lovely teacher in the middle, and every child's eyes fastened constantly on her nearly always

delightful but also overpoweringly developed adult personality. [56]

The kindergarten, as Fisher sees it, imposes too much activity and overstimulates and fatigues the child mentally. It imposes moral coercion on the child who does not want to be social during the set hours. The Montessori method, she argues, by trusting the child's deep-rooted instincts for growth, encourages self-discipline and responsibility to grow from within. The child expresses her individuality with perfect freedom, and misbehavior is not a problem because each child is absorbed in self-chosen activities which create self-control and personal discipline. Children naturally become "little citizens" of this world, caring for themselves and one another. Montessori bases her educational theory, Fisher says, on the theory of democracy, ". . . and there is no denying that the world today is democratic."[57]

In her celebration of Montessori education, Fisher sounds a number of themes familiar in modern Quaker education: recognition that children's intellectual, physical, moral, and spiritual growth occur in stages and in supportive relation to one another; trust in the educative power of the child's natural "self-activity;" trust in a pedagogy which cooperates with each child's development; trust in science and scientific methods, and perhaps in the affinities between science and democracy, as compatible with a religious faith. These themes, to greater or less degree, also run through the work of Comenius, Locke, Pestalozzi, and Froebel, but by the beginning of the twentieth century, their authority is more and more confirmed by psychology and social science. The ground is prepared for the next, perhaps the most profound, influence on and interaction with Quaker education in England and America, Progressive Education.

NOTES

1. M.W. Keatinge, *Comenius:The Great Didactic Abridged*, New York and London, 1931, 33. Keatinge's is the first translation of *The Great Didactic* in English; *William Penn, Some Fruits of Solitude* (1693), James Newby, ed., Friends United Press, Richmond, 1978, 20; Dorothy Canfield Fisher, *Montessori for Parents* (Originally published as *A Montessori Mother* in 1912), reprint Cambridge, Robert Bentley, Inc., 1965, 52.

2. Quotations taken from *Some Fruits of Solitude*, 20-23; *William Penn's Advice to His Children*, (Containing "Letter to His Wife and Children" and "Fruits of a Father's Love") Introduction by Elizabeth Janet Gray, Friends Council on Education, 1944, 15; *The Peace of Europe . . . and Other Writings*, Introduction by Joseph Besse, Everyman's Library, 1942, 105.

3. Clarke, *Bellers*, 21.

4. Clarke, *Bellers*, 54, 63-65.

5. Harry S. Broudy and John R. Palmer, *Exemplars of Teaching Method*, Rand McNally, Chicago, 1965, 94; John William Adamson, *Pioneers of Modern Education in the Seventeenth Century*, first edition 1905, reprinted 1921, foreword by Joan Simon 1971, Teachers College Press, 1971, 47, says Comenius' ideas are rediscovered in Raumer's *Geshichte der Padagojik* (1843-51).

6. Broudy, *Exemplars*, 94-95; Adamson, *Pioneers of Modern Education*, 3-4.

7. Keatinge, *Comenius*, 27.

8. Keatinge, *Comenius*, 33, 41-42.

9. Adamson, *Pioneers of Modern Education*, 59.

10. Keatinge, *Comenius*, 34.

11. Keatinge, *Comenius*, 54-59; Adamson, *Pioneers of Modern Education*, 66.

12. Adamson, *Pioneers of Modern Education*, 78; Will S.
    Monroe, *Comenius and the Beginnings of Educational Reform*,
    Scribner's, New York, 1900, 54, claims that Samuel Hartlib
    gathered a number of thinkers interested in educational
    matters—among them John Milton "and probably the
    American Winthrop, later Governor of Connecticut, who
    was wintering in London," around Comenius when he was
    in England in 1641-42.

13. Lawrence Stone, *The Family, Sex and Marriage in England
    1500-1800*, abridged edition, Harper and Row, New York,
    1979, 254-56. Chapter nine is especially useful to read for
    this discussion. J. William Frost, *The Quaker Family in
    Colonial America: a Portrait of the Society of Friends*, St.
    Martin's Press, New York, 70, argues that ". . . a cult of
    childhood developed about the time of the [American]
    Revolution, in which, for the first time, children were
    recognized as having distinct personalities."

14. Kingsley Price, *Educational and Philosophical Thought*,
    Allyn and Bacon, Boston, 1962.

15. Stone, *Family*, 279.

16. John Locke, *On Politics and Education*, introduction by
    Howard R. Penniman, William Black, New York, 1947,
    207, 209-10, 256, 319.

17. Locke, *On Politics*, 236-37, 252.

18. Locke, *On Politics*, 245-47.

19. Locke, *On Politics*, 252, 259-60, 316.

20. Locke, *On Politics*, 331-51, 378.

21. Locke, *On Politics*, 377. See also Frost, *The Quaker Family*, 114.
    "The increasing concern that Quakers felt for children after
    1760, seen in personal letters, catechisms, and the revival of
    learning, can also be found in the textbooks. The change here
    was not as much on the conception of childhood as in an
    increasing mastery of the technique of teaching. This change

was not pioneered by nor peculiar to Friends; rather, Quakers adopted practices used in other primers."

22. Campbell-Stewart, *Quakers and Education*, 24.

23. Campbell Stewart, *Quakers and Education*, 27, 29.

24. William Wistar Comfort, *William Penn: 1644-1718 A Tercentenary Estimate*, University of Pennsylvania Press, Philadelphia, 1944, 4; Biographical Sketch of William Penn, derived from *Friends in the Seventeenth Century*, introducing *No Cross, No Crown*, Friends Book Store, Philadelphia, n.d., 55.

25. Will S. Monroe, *History of the Pestalozzian Movement in the United States*, 1907, Reprinted by Arno Press and the New York Times, 1969, 208.

26. John Griscom, *A Year in Europe. . .* , 1824, Vol I, 290.

27. Griscom, *A Year in Europe. . .* , I, 265.

28. Griscom, *A Year in Europe. . .* , I, 269.

29. Griscom, *A Year in Europe. . .* , I, 288.

30. Cited in Robert R. Rusk, *The Doctrines of the Great Educators*, revised and enlarged edition, Macmillan, New York, 1965, 226-27.

31. Griscom, *A Year in Europe. . .* , I, 290.

32. Griscom, *A Year in Europe. . .* , I, 279.

33. Rusk, *Doctrines*, 210-11, 214-17.

34. Rusk, *Doctrines*, 221, 223.

35. Broudy, *Exemplars*, 114-16.

36. Rusk, *Doctrines*, 230.

37. Monroe, *Pestalozzian Movement*, 32-33, 50-52; MacKaye, *Mr. Sidwell's School*, 28.

38. MacKaye, *Mr. Sidwell's School*, 28; Dean R. Esslinger, *Friends for Two Hundred Years: A history of Baltimore's oldest school*, Friends School, Baltimore, 58-59.

39. Griscom, *A Year in Europe. . .* , I, 276-77, 288.

40. Rusk, *Doctrines*, 261.

41. Quoted in Rusk, *Doctrines*, 266-67.

42. Rusk, *Doctrines*, 273-74.

43. Rusk, *Doctrines*, 268.

44. Broudy, *Exemplars*, 126-27.

45. Broudy, *Exemplars*, 276-78. The quotations are from Froebel's *The Education of Man*.

46. Broudy, *Exemplars*, 276.

47. H. Courthope Bowen, *Froebel and Education through Self-Activity.* 1909, 50. The Minister for Education was confusing Friedrich Froebel with his nephew, a political radical, who had published a tract entitled *High Schools for Girls and Kindergartens*, but the suspicions apparently were more widespread than that confusion alone would explain. For the three-year old demagogues, see Rusk, *Doctrines*, 261.

48. Gibbs, *Children of Light*, 63; Broudy, *Exemplars*, 127

49. Faraday, 15-16; Gibbs, *Doctrines*, 63; Mackaye, *Mr. Sidwell's School*, 36; Esslinger, *Friends for Two Hundred Years*, 73; *Wilmington*, 41.

50. Dewey, 67-68.

51. Fisher, *Montessori for Parents*, 76.

52. Fisher, *Montessori for Parents*, 31-32, 156.

53. Fisher, *Montessori for Parents*, 52-57, 86, 92-94, 98.

54. Fisher, *Montessori for Parents*, 43.

55. Fisher, *Montessori for Parents*, 45-46.

56. Fisher, *Montessori for Parents*, 20, 171-88.

57. Fisher, *Montessori for Parents*, 30, 11.

Nine

⟫⋅◈⋅⟪

Progressive Education
and Quaker Schools

It is our belief that the three ideals of democracy, Quakerism, and progressive education, and the way of life implied by them, are basically related to one another.

The two objectives of education, to advance the growth of a harmonious individual and to prepare him for a constructive relation to society, are interdependent if not identical. True service to others presupposes a sound structure of the person rendering this service.

Men and women, and boys and girls, develop creative and well-founded forms of co-operation better when they are responding to necessity than when they try to realize an idea that they think to be desirable.

Young people want schools which are realistically religious; they seek a religion that will work.[1]

Progressivism and the Progressive Era

Progressive education is one expression of the larger intellectual, social, and political ferment of the "progressive era" in the early twentieth century. As a social movement, "progressivism" seeks to address the failures of industrialism and to use the methods of science, especially the social sciences, to reform democratic institutions. It has affinities with the modernist spirit in liberal religion, which preaches the "social gospel" and which embraces scientific method and scholarly approaches to scripture known as the Higher Criticism. Even someone identified as a conservative at the 1895 Manchester Conference called by London Yearly Meeting, J. Bevan Braithwaite, affirmed the "progressive character of revelation." "The great fact of the gradual and progressive development of Divine Revelation is at once the key and the harmony of the Old and New Testaments."[2] That modernist or progressive spirit finds expression among British and American Quakers in the Manchester Conference, in the founding of Woodbrooke and later Pendle Hill, in the intellectual and spiritual leadership of such Friends as Rufus Jones, John Wilhelm Rowntree, Caroline Stephen, William C. Braithwaite, Henry J. Cadbury, and Howard Brinton.

THE PROGRESSIVE EDUCATION MOVEMENT

By the time of the First World War, Patricia Albjerg Graham reports, American educators were committed to "scientific education," experimentation, close observation of children's development, and emphasis on learning by doing. Both public and private schools were responding to the work of the social sciences and the "new psychology" of William James, E. L. Thorndike, G. Stanley Hall, and others, and to pedagogical approaches which encouraged child-centeredness, "self-activity," individual expression, and creativity as both means and ends of education. Under the pressures of new social conditions, especially industrialism, greater urbanization, and the massive influx of immigrants after the war, educators were forced to reconceptualize the aims of schools and schooling, though public school systems and private schools experienced the effects of these conditions and responded to them differently. Lawrence A. Cremin describes the willingness of public schools to assume additional responsibilities, including offering adult education and citizenship classes, health services, vocational education, and other programs to involve parents and other adults in the schools, as a distinguishing characteristic of the progressive education movement. According to Arthur Zilversmit, John Dewey "introduced the idea of the school as the 'legatee' institution, one that had to take on the socialization functions that had previously been the responsibility of institutions that were disintegrating under the pressures of industrialism."[3] As Dewey saw it, the household was once the center of

> . . . all the typical forms of industrial occupation. . . . The children, as they gained in strength and capacity, were gradually initiated into the mysteries of the several processes. . . . In all this there was a continual training of observation, of ingenuity, constructive imagination, of logical thought, and of the sense of reality acquired through first-hand contact with actualities.

Since the urban, industrialized world no longer provided such an intelligible environment as the household located in a close, stable neighborhood, the school had to recreate that environment. It had to become a little community in itself, in order to introduce the values which children had formerly learned in daily contact with the adult world of work and service. "Community is achieved through the tasks of living. To work together, people must share both the understanding of the task and their attitudes toward it." The method of science was to begin with a predicament or difficulty which impedes action, so that we become fully conscious of our situation. Then we convert the predicament into a problem, something we have defined in terms which allow us to set about solving it. We frame hypotheses, draw on previous experience and knowledge, figure out how to test our hypotheses, carry through with testing, reconceptualizing, refining our questions and hypotheses, until we have reached some solution or resolution. For Dewey, the heart of scientific method was the way it combined thinking with overt doing, "ideation (concepts) with overt physical acts. . . ." The school therefore had to replace the traditional curriculum, stressing skills of symbolization and memorizing facts and rules, with an *activity* curriculum, stressing learning by doing.[4]

For William H. Kilpatrick, Dewey's close associate, this meant turning away from mastery of bodies of subject matter in order to stress the development of character and personality traits. This could best be done through the Project Method, which places the emphasis on students' defining a question and a task of immediate interest to them, then planning how to undertake research to explore it, then working through the problem by trial and error, examining alternative explanations in the library or laboratory or field instead of consulting a textbook. The end-product might be a report, a work of art, a performance, or demonstration—a project completed rather than an examination passed. Kilpatrick asked of education:

> Does the person being taught grow as a total personality? Does he grow, as a result of the teaching, more sensitive to the possibilities inherent in life around him, so as to seize upon these fruitfully? Does he grow more disposed to take hold effectively, to bring things to pass?

Is he more persistent in his efforts? . . . Better informed, wiser about matters he works with? More creative in approach? Tending to consider what he does more thoughtfully? Does he have adequate knowledge from past and present to consider? [5]

Dewey first published *Democracy and Education: An Introduction to the Philosophy of Education* in 1916; William H. Kilpatrick published "The Project Method," in 1918. In 1919 the Progressive Education Association was founded. Its president for its first two years, 1920-22, was Arthur E. Morgan, long associated with Quakers, the chief founder of the Moraine Park country day school in Dayton and subsequently president of Antioch College. In the 1920s, Patricia Albjerg Graham tells us, a progressive school was experimental, was focused on the individual child rather than the classroom, and included in its program some of the findings of the new psychology and social sciences. In the 1930s, a progressive school "could be either one bearing down hard on individual development and creativity or one that emphasized the schools' responsibility in society." Progressive education flourished most fully in private schools; "its reforms from first to last appealed primarily to the middle and upper middle classes." [6]

In 1924 the Progressive Education Association enunciated the aim of Progressive Education as ". . . the freest and fullest development of the individual, based upon the scientific study of his physical, mental, spiritual, and social characteristics and needs." From this aim flowed the Seven Principles of Progressive Education: 1) the child's freedom to develop naturally in an environment rich in interesting material; 2) the pupil's interest and direct experience with the world as the motive of all work; 3) the teacher as a guide, not a task-master; 4) grades, written reports and tests, the scientific study of pupil development, to serve as guidance for the individual's development; 5) greater attention to all that affects the child's physical development—more room, "easier access to the out-of-doors and greater use of it;" 6) cooperation between home and school; 7) and the progressive school as a leader in educational movements, "a laboratory where new ideas, if worthy, meet encouragement. . . ." [7]

THE COUNTRY DAY SCHOOL

One particular expression of progressive education was the country day school, which a 1924 pamphlet of the Country Day School Headmasters Association describes as follows:

> Thoroughly modern in spirit, it provides a broad, sound, well balanced program of study, recitations, athletics, and miscellaneous activities. . . . When the children come to school they come to the freedom and joy of the out-of-doors, not to the restraints and fears of the city streets. The long day (often until 5 p.m.) is comfortably full of varied activities suitable to the ages of the pupils.[8]

Eugene R. Smith, one of the founders of the Progressive Education Association, the principal shaper of its Seven Principles, and founding headmaster of the Beaver Country Day School in Massachusetts, argues for "self-activity and creativeness" as school aims on essentially the same grounds that Dewey proposes: until the present industrial era, children had "natural opportunities for some kind of self-activity involving both mind and body." In the small American community,

... children had the advantage of observing most of the necessary adult activities within a comparatively close range, they imitated them in their play, took part in them in a simple way as soon as they were old enough to be of any help, and eventually worked into their future activities of adulthood as a more or less inevitable resuplt.[9]

Since those opportunities for an organic connection with the world of work had largely disappeared, the school must supply them in the framework enunciated by the Seven Principles of Progressive Education. Though moving to the country was not a requirement for being a progressive school, for some educators it clearly appeared a desirable means to facilitate the project. The country day school tries to provide all the best features of boarding-school education, but in a day-school. We may note, in passing, that Quakers were not alone in thinking that some form of guarded education involving wide open spaces, fresh air, and safety from the big city was best for the pupils' fullest development.

In 1925, when Friends Central School decided to move from central Philadelphia and become a country day school, the executive committee report recommending the move said, in part:

Conditions have changed in latter years. Friends no longer live near the school. ... Advanced educational methods today require the development of the body as well as the mind and adequate athletic facilities are essential. The best way to obtain such conditions is by means of a Country Day School. The children attend school in the morning and have their play and athletics in the afternoon. They enjoy pure air and sunshine amid

beautiful surroundings free from the dangers and allure-
ments of present city life.[10]

Qualities of the country day school had obvious appeal
to other Friends schools. In a memo to himself in 1928,
Thomas Sidwell describes his ideal: "A coeducational college preparatory country day school, primarily for American
youth, reaching down to the kindergarten, with a place
for the youth of other countries. A school aiming to keep
children in their homes as long as possible. When Wilmington
Friends moved to its "pastoral site" of Alapocas, in 1936, its
board insisted that the move did not mean the school had
become a country day school, in the sense that after-school
activities would be required. Instead, "it was a day school
in the country." A school founded in 1810 in Massachusetts,
called Friends' Academy, later became an independent non-
denominational school. As of 1953 it was called Friends'
Academy Country Day School. It closed sometime after 1960.[11]

THE WHITTIER IDEA

In 1923, Walter F. Dexter and J. Herschel Coffin began their
work as president and dean, respectively, of Whittier College.
Dexter, who had studied with Kilpatrick of Columbia
University's Teachers' College, the progenitor of the Project
Method, was professor of education, and Coffin, who had published a psychological and sociological textbook on ethics,
The Socialized Conscience and Personality in the Making, was
professor of psychology at Earlham, when they developed
together an idea of a "functional" college which was to become "The Whittier Idea."

Over a cup of tea brewed in Coffin's tiny office at Earlham,
he and Dexter questioned the value of "lectures, quizzes,

examinations, and academic machinery in general" and noted the obvious "hiatus between 'education' and life."

> Would it be possible to construct an educational program . . . based upon the native tendencies of young men and women . . . [and] actually correlate it with the concrete needs of life?[12]

The Whittier Idea rested on three principles:

1) Education must be functional. It should prepare young people to function adequately in five "life-situations:" the home-life, the vocational, the social, the avocational, and the religious or life-philosophy situation.

2) Complete education must be religious education. It should "attempt to throw into the foreground of science . . . history . . . philosophy and every other subject the spiritual interpretation that be our best insight we believe Jesus would give.

3) Education must be democratic. Democracy was an organizing principle which derived from both Quaker faith and practice and the heritage of American idealism and history. The college's objective should be the highest group welfare and "the greatest opportunity for self-realization." The college should be a community which includes every student, faculty member, and administrator, "a 'community of will' . . . based upon a spirit of friendship and good will."

The curriculum which Coffin proposed called for a sequence of required Correlation Courses through the four college years and the Project Method. The Correlation Course was to be the core of each student's program. The first year *Human Issues* course oriented the student to college work, introduced "that orderly body of knowledge touching the physical and social world in which he [she] lives," and presented the major problems of modern life. The sophomore

Correlation Course, *The Psychological Aspect of Human Issues,* considered forms of conflict between traditions and customs, introduced general psychology, and further addressed social, economic, political, and personal issues. The junior course, *The Basis of Social Progress,* dealt with forms of social organization and institutional life and the practical problems of human welfare and public health. The final capstone correlation course, *Philosophy of Christian Reconstruction,* was an introduction to philosophy. The thesis of the course was "that the religion of Jesus furnishes the only finally workable philosophy of life . . . based upon sound sociology."

Whittier's new curriculum also involved "four humanized courses in the natural sciences and mathematics" for non-science majors, the choice of a group major or departmental major, and a Project Course which accounted for one-third of the upper division work for any student who chose that option. The student's project was planned by the student and his or her professors and involved "some form of meaningful work in the community under competent professional guidance. Coordinated with this were wide reading, study, and reports."

All of college life was to be a joint undertaking, shaped by commitment to democracy, cooperation, and friendliness. The college organized a Joint Council of Control, consisting of six students appointed by the student body and four faculty members appointed by the college president, to define standards of conduct on campus, formulate policies, and recommend penalties for violations of standards. Out of its work there came an honor pact. The aim was to create "a community of will" in place of a "community of authority" for faculty and a "community of obedience for students." Dexter reported to California Yearly Meeting, "Love is now the motive of school discipline where force once ruled."[13]

How thoroughly Whittier's new curriculum of the 1920s expressed the progressive education tradition is made clear in Herschel Coffin's report on Christian Education (Preliminary Report of Commission III, Section A: Our Schools and Colleges) to the Five Years Meeting in 1935. Coffin begins by asserting that "the ideology of the Quaker is sound, [and] . . . it has a correlated philosophy of education." Quaker schools and colleges need to address themselves in fresh ways "to the two main value systems for which Quakerism has historically stood, namely the abundant life for the individual and the 'Kingdom' for society." The first object, abundant life, requires developing emotional maturity and right attitudes, harmonious home-life, economic security, and social control under democracy. The second object is democracy itself: "the induction of the young into the attitudes and the social techniques of this democratic way of life."

The heart of this educational enterprise is "functionalized education," a "functionalized curriculum" which starts with problems rather than disciplines or fields of knowledge. In place of a system of lectures, examinations, and the usual methods of studying, he argues for cooperative methods of learning, seminars. Stressing educational community and democratic participation as essential to learning, Coffin cites the progressive education principle "that education comes through *participation in significant enterprises.*" (His italics) Such participation comes through what he calls the "situation technique," where a group brings its collective attention to a *real* issue and tries to solve whatever problems its presents. To "functionalize" education might, he suggests, lead to teaching English, history, journalism, business responsibilities, and the like by having students put out a newspaper. The "situation technique," "corporate thinking," and the "project method" are three interconnected approaches to a

curriculum which would be "progressive, creative, and functional." He especially wants to distinguish general education,
which he believes students should engage in all through
high school and the first two years of college, from "liberal
education," which should be the work of the final two years.
"Liberal" for him does not mean "quantitative dissemination
of knowledge," though he expects the final two years of undergraduate work to deepen students' knowledge of disciplines
and fields, but rather a set of human relations based on freedom. "Reform, progress, freedom have meaning only in relation to personality and the relations of human personalities
to each other." Social sciences, which he calls life sciences,
are "the new humanities." Coffin urged Quaker colleges to
"find a distinctive basis in emphasizing social science, peace,
and education," an emphasis which Thomas D. Hamm reports attracted support from some faculty members at
Earlham, though President William C. Dennis found the
Coffin Report "anathema."[14]

Herschel Coffin's Report makes proposals for both Quaker
schools and colleges, especially for how the tasks of learning
should be distributed. But his proposals come at a particularly inauspicious time: The Whittier Idea finally founders
on the Great Depression, and the proposals of this 1935
report come at a time when the world of Quaker academies
is rapidly shrinking. For Coffin, clearly, progressive education's
goals and pedagogy graft perfectly onto the trunk of Christian and Quaker education.[15]

THE EIGHT-YEAR STUDY

Though progressive education influenced Quaker schools,
they also had their part in shaping progressive education. In
1925, the Progressive Education Association's president listed

fourteen schools in the Philadelphia area which were interested in progressive education, among which were Germantown Friends School, Penn Charter, and Friends Select. In addition to Arthur E. Morgan, Burton P. Fowler, who replaced Stanley R. Yarnall as head of Germantown Friends School, served as president of the association, and John A. Lester of the Friends Council on Education served as a member of the association's commission. Three Quaker schools participated in the thirty schools' eight year study (only twenty-nine completed the study), in which schools and selected colleges agreed that students would be considered for college admission on the basis of evaluations other than traditional grades and test scores: Friends Central Country Day School, George School, Germantown Friends School. Their reports at the end of the study reveal how these three schools integrated the concepts of progressive education with their understanding of Quakerism.

FRIENDS CENTRAL SCHOOL

Friends Central's report begins by making connections among the ideals of democracy, Quakerism, and progressive education: first, "is the recognition of the individual as one who possesses unique qualities and inherent worth." This principle is in the Bill of Rights, forms the basis of the Quaker testimonies, "which consider the divine or sacred element potential in each human being," and is recognized by educators "who are now attempting to plan school life to meet individual needs." All three concepts recognize

> . . . that individuals must live in harmony with one another, must unite in common enterprises for the purpose of serving the general welfare. Therefore responsi-

bility for one's neighbor, helping others to obtain the conditions requisite for a fruitful and significant life is the second common denominator of these three concepts.

The report speaks of the philosophy of the Society of Friends as having a far-reaching influence on the school's way of life: "simplicity, directness, and respect for the personality of every individual" are expected from everyone, and a weekly Friends' Meeting gives each boy and girl "time to think about his [sic] very personal and inner problems." Religious instruction is part of the curriculum, "but more important is the spiritual atmosphere of the school." All areas of school life "have been explored for their possibilities of meeting individual needs, of developing both a concern for society and habits of cooperative service."[16]

In the Eight-Year Study, Friends Central undertook substantial changes in curriculum and in its individual guidance program. For the upper school, a new core program, "The Enterprise," made social studies the central subject, to which other areas would contribute. English was to become part of the program, "with some of the literature selected to illuminate various cultural periods in history," and history was to be studied chronologically. Classes were to be taught cooperatively by instructors from different departments. Instead of textbooks, a variety of books were to be used, emphasis was to be placed on "the individual and group project method," with opportunities for consulting with authorities in various fields and a greater use of the Philadelphia community for field trips and off-campus activities.

Over time, the Enterprise was modified to approach history topically and to break too-tight links between literary and historical periods. Units developed cooperatively between English and Social Studies departments addressed such topics as "Vocational Guidance, War and Peace, Standards of Living, Minority Groups, . . . Dictatorships and Democracies, International Literature, the Drama and Social Problems." Still later, the program was further modified, to balance the emphasis on the individual's responsibilities as part of society with offerings in Human Relations "to meet more personal needs of the students."

The Enterprise influenced students and faculty beyond the courses themselves and fostered recognition of the need of "planning for the individual, developing student responsibility, and promoting social sensitivity in preparation for effective citizenship." These themes, in turn, significantly shaped how other areas of school life were organized. The individual guidance program was strengthened, with more attention given to the scientific study of each pupil's development, and a health education course stressing personality development was initiated. Students were involved in helping to plan aspects of their courses, and more individualized approaches to laboratory experiments encouraged cooperative work, interviews with outside experts, and variety in ways of writing research reports. Students were given more responsibility for planning religious life activities, and once a month there was a "Student Meeting," described as a "democratic adventure in worship." Home room assemblies were initiated and student council was given more responsibility and authority. Extracurricular activities drew more on the wider community through projects organized by the Service Club, field trips, and activities originating in Enterprise topics courses.[17]

Germantown Friends School

Germantown Friends School seems to have embraced progressive education more tentatively than Friends Central. The school claims fewer aspects of its life as having been directly affected by participation in the study. "The school has made progress with pupils of moderate academic aptitude. These now receive a better education than before, and have less occasion to feel unhappy or inferior. . . ." Honors at commencement have received less emphasis, and some teachers hope appreciation of true scholarship will increase "as we are able to escape from the influence of marks and of competition." Curricular changes "give more place to scientific interests and to practical uses of several subjects." Emphasis on history and science increases in the final six years of school, and "along with this . . . the desire to use the early years for the discovery of special interests, and the later years for the development of well-defined interests and aptitudes." The report notes that participating in the study has taught the school important things about both democracy and new ways of measuring student achievement and, in addition, enabled it to make discoveries of its own about being a Quaker school.

> We were more easily convinced that many of the old educational devices and theories were inadequate than that certain experimental new ones were the right ones for us. . . . Methods of evaluation that grow out of a pragmatist philosophy and that look to a secular democracy are likely to be challenging, but not completely satisfying.[18]

Its report, consequently, frames the eight-year experiment with the question what it means to be a Quaker school, drawing heavily on Brinton's then newly-published *Quaker Education in Theory and Practice* and its outline of ten policies reflecting the testimonies for community, harmony, equality, and simplicityto shape a scrupulous self-examination.

Affirming that "joint activity for unselfish ends is creative of community spirit of the right kind," the outline finds that the sense of community has been strengthened by "emphasis on positive interests and measures, such as the relief of suffering in wartime, the study of problems arising from our confused social order, and the numerous responsibilities which various meetings take on as routine or emergency cares." Students and graduates engage in many social service activities, particularly work camps, but reaching out into the wider community rests on a commitment to "a present-day equivalent of the older 'guarded education' . . . " Parents report that they value most "the spiritual qualities in the school atmosphere, including friendliness, toleration, integrity of scholarship, sympathy and imagination in the teaching, the spirit of sharing and of fairness in the conduct of school activities."

In the Quaker emphasis on nonviolent methods of discipline and the appeal to an inward sense of rightness, the report sees "the rightness and utility of this old Quaker and newer progressive testimony." It is especially searching on the testimony of equality in education of races and classes. Noting that the presence of a few Jewish students, "without our feeling very aware of them as different from others, marks an advance over fifteen years ago, . . . " It goes on to acknowledge "the absence of Negro children and teachers in nearly all Friends' schools," and concludes "clearly our practice lags behind our theory." The report also discusses the relation of religion to democracy:

The question is often raised whether democracy or religion can survive much longer. Friends might answer speculatively that separately neither has a good chance, but together they would command a profounder loyalty through a period of adversity than either could do alone. This attitude in our school explains the slowness with which we have been able to incorporate into our school

life many of the newer educational devices that have
been developed and justified in school situations where
the democracy aimed at was secular.[19]

GEORGE SCHOOL

George School's report announces that "the school has
taken part in the Eight-Year Study without any *fundamental*
changes in school policy or routine. There have been, however, important changes in curriculum content, in methods
of teaching, and in guidance." The most substantial curricular change reported is in what are called "Sequence Curricu-
lums" covering the final three or four years of secondary school
work. The report is clear that "the objective . . . [of each
Sequence] is not to be modern (as usually applied to those
schools which have dropped all traditional subjects), but to
serve the best interests of one type of student." Each sequence
followed a somewhat different curriculum determined by a
dominant emphasis, with students and instructors together
for three years, planning the work "in terms of the objectives
they have agreed upon, and [attempting] to evaluate results
in terms of the objectives . . . agreed upon." There was a core
of subjects common to all the sequences, but no common
body of content. A language sequence consisted of English,
Latin, French, and mathematics over three years, with
some elective options in the senior year; the social science
sequence consisted of social studies, French or German,
English, and mathematics for three years, with an option
for a science instead of mathematics in the senior year; the
mathematics-science sequence (later dropped) consisted of
mathematics, science, English, and an option of a foreign
language or social studies; the citizenship sequence consisted

of English, social studies, mathematics, and science, but no foreign language, and was designed for "slow readers and others who find such work exceedingly difficult."

Among the advantages identified in the sequence plan are that students of "similar life purposes, college or vocational goals, ambitions, interests, and abilities" are brought together; that there is considerable continuity of planning over three years; that students and teachers get to know each other well; that teachers have learned to work cooperatively; that correlation between subject fields is easier; that "teachers feel freer to explore with leisure and flexibility large areas of human concern;" that educational trips are easier to plan; and that "competition between subject fields for a pupil's time has disappeared." The sequences also make guidance more effective, and the report documents an elaborate diagnostic program for each student involving interviews, aptitude, personality, and Progressive Education Association tests, behavior ratings devised by Eugene R. Smith for the Association, teacher's reports, and a variety of other materials.

The report forthrightly describes disappointments as well as successes. Among the disappointments are the experiments in teaching mathematics and the sciences and the over-emphasis on correlating subject areas: "We had carried too far our efforts to keep the subjects out of their traditional pigeonholes. Students tired of the constant cross-referencing from field to field, so that we tended to condition them against the very thing we hoped to accomplish." (For anyone involved in cross-disciplinary experiments in colleges in the 1960s, these sentences have a poignant prescience.) Finding materials and experiences to stimulate the nonacademic student had not gone far enough. Problems of evaluation of student progress remained.

Among the benefits George School experienced from the experiment: ". . . Faculty members have developed a great deal as a result of their thinking together about their common problems. No longer are most of them content to teach one unrelated, discrete segment of the curriculum." There is less reliance on a single textbook and more emphasis on a wider variety of materials. Students use the library more often, and more effectively. Individual and group projects are more common. There is a greater tendency to think of the pupil's total personality development, not only intellectual growth , and a greater consciousness of individual differences and " . . . the complex nature of work habits and specific study skills." Mastery of information or acquisition of the tools of learning as ends in themselves are no longer regarded as the sole objectives of education.[20]

Well over half of its report focuses on William Hubben's discussion of religious life and teaching at George School. Here he explicates the two objectives of education, to advance the growth of a harmonious individual and to prepare him or her for a constructive relation to society.

> Freedom alone, of which the history of education makes so much, cannot be the ultimate goal of education; freedom must be purposeful in order to deserve a high rank. . . . The equally forceful demand, . . . that education should produce the social-minded individual, too often overlooks the fact that only a fully integrated self can function satisfactorily in the rebuilding of society.[21]

Social reconstruction, Hubben says, can only be undertaken by persons who have undergone an experience of self-reconstruction; "It is our conviction at George School that religion is the only basis for such an education." He sharply distinguishes the approaches of pragmatism or rationalism to educational reform from that of Quakerism. "Our objective in education is not knowledge only, nor motives allied with or springing from social awareness and sensitiveness. It ought to be the inner compulsion to act, which is, paradoxically, the only real freedom." He argues, therefore, for an understanding of religion as a matter of experience, not of belief, not as something set apart from life but as "a force and spirit permeating the whole of it." Religious education, then, must attempt to be an integrated part of any educational effort, enriching and being enriched by every aspect of the school's life. By its very nature, the religious life of the school provides an important "element of integration for the development of the adolescent."[22] Twice-weekly meetings for worship, assemblies, discussion groups, conferences, outreach through service projects, all supplement courses in the principles and history of religion.

> Quakerism tries to make young people see that faith is by no means identical with accepting factual or semifactual opinions about God, eternity, Jesus, or the sacraments. Since Quakerism strives to be an attitude toward life and its problems, a way of life rather than a system of thought, only tentative answers can, at times, be given.[23]

IMPACT OF THE EIGHT-YEAR STUDY

For these three schools, the invitation to experiment under the rubric of progressive education allowed for significant changes in guidance programs and in methods of evaluation for students. Germantown Friends and George School acknowledge improvements in support of less academically able students, and all three report greater sensitivity to individual differences among students. Friends Central seems more ready to acknowledge an impact on the curriculum than either of the other two schools, but a reading of only these brief reports suggests that many of the same kinds of changes occurred in all three schools: experimentation in core courses led to greater cooperation among faculty, students became more directly involved in planning aspects of their courses, the project method was more frequently employed, off-campus excursions and encounters with experts in various fields became more common, faculty thought more in cross-disciplinary terms.

As the reports for the Eight-Year Study make clear, the three Quaker schools found confirmation from progressive education for their own principles and practices: the respect for each individual and for individual differences, the integration of personal freedom with social responsibility, the valuing of community, the emphasis on cooperation rather than competition to encourage learning, trust in each child's capacity for inner-directed activity, reliance on persuasion instead of coercion in matters of discipline. For all three schools, the study encouraged rethinking of their Quaker character and the extent to which the aims of democracy as interpreted by progressive education and the aims of religiously-based education coincided and differed. Germantown Friends School and George School both sharply distinguished educational practices originating in pragmatic philosophy from those originating in religious conviction. Progressive education offered stimulating ideas and encouragement to persist in certain experiments, but for these two schools, in particular, Quakerism came far before progressive education.

By the time of the Eight-Year Study, the great battles of modernism had essentially been resolved for liberal Quakerism: to be meaningful, religion had to "work" in the world;

modern faith was compatible with science and with scientific methods of research such as the Higher Criticism of
Scripture. Howard Brinton described the Quaker meeting,
and by extension, the Quaker school, as "both a laboratory
and a training ground for the desired social order." Quakerism was open to even the most challenging aspects of modern science, and its polity was democratic; it was experiential
and "experimental;" its consistent emphasis on the practical
made it responsive to some aspects of pragmatism and in-
strumentalism as philosophy, yet it was different from these
secular approaches.

Brinton sees both affinities and fundamental differences
between the educational goals of progressive education and
those of Quakerism. The former wants schools to be like the
larger community for which they prepare students, to develop
a ". . . socially desirable way of living, . . . primarily determined by the prevailing scale of social and personal values."
Quakerism, he argues, wants its schools to prepare students
for a kind of community which is not merely reflective of or
dependent on prevailing social values. "Such a goal is not
found in the flux of society by a process of experimentation
but by an experience of that which is above the flux."[24]

Continuing Influence of
Progressive Education

Many Quaker schools in the 1920s and later, including Friends
Seminary and Sidwell Friends, described themselves as
"progressive," whether or not they had any direct connection with the Progressive Education Association. But when
any term becomes more honorific than descriptive, it is
headed for trouble. (Consider, for example, the word
"Quaker.") As "progressive" came to be more sweepingly

invoked as a term of praise, appropriated by schools and educators who saw only tricks of technique and not the underlying principles, excesses committed in its name received greater publicity. As William N. Oats, long-time head of the Friends School in Hobart, Tasmania and a leader in progressive education, describes it,

> The term 'progressive' came into disrepute because of a misconception of the meaning of the term 'child-centred.' Many parents ascribed to it the meaning suggested in the couplet
>
> > Do not thwart the little elf:
> > Let her educate herself.
>
> The little elf, unthwarted, doesn't get very far, particularly when lots of other little elves are victims of the same theory.

As early as 1918, John Dewey warned, "There is a tendency on the part of the upholders and the opponents of freedom in school to identify it with absence of social direction. . . . " And Kenneth C. Barnes, the British Quaker and pioneer in progressive education, says, "It is unfortunate that 'progressive' schools have attracted many people as teachers who are far from being mature or blessed with psychological wisdom: people who do not know themselves and are drawn to anything labelled as free in the hope of release from their hang-ups."[25]

Progressive education also shared the opprobrium attached to the term "progressive" from the beginning of the Cold War, particularly after the American presidential election of 1948, when the Progressive Party was widely viewed as appeasers and apologists for the Soviet Union. Patricia Graham reports that the Progressive Education Association, which began as an organization for private schools and some suburban public schools, had become dominated by public education systems and controlled by the big schools of education, notably Columbia University's Teachers College.[26] Certainly public education was especially vulnerable to the negative meanings attached to things "progressive." By the time the Association ended, in 1967, it had little public impact.

After the Soviet Union "conquered space" in the late 1950s, the Cold War competition extended powerfully into American education; "progressive education" was a convenient scapegoat to blame for what was perceived as American education's failure to compete. Pressure for return to traditionally-defined subject areas, for competition for grades and high scores on objective tests, and support for the educational goal of "beating the Russians" severely modified, where they did not end, programs which followed the progressive education practices emphasizing self-direction, open-endedness, and experimentation. All the more striking, therefore, is the loyalty which Quaker educators showed to the principles of progressive education, even while the schools were necessarily responding to the demands for what was called increased rigor and a return to "standards."

In 1985, Richard Mandel, then head of Friends Select School, identified two traditions influencing the school: Quakerism and progressive education. "As a Friends School we believe we have two interdependent purposes. We seek to develop the excellence of each individual, and we seek to develop the excellence of our community. . . . Quakers have evolved two well-known communal activities in which the interdependence of individual and communal growth is most clear." These are the meeting for worship, where a group gathers to seek divine inspiration, and meeting for business, where the group meets to listen to the portion of truth each individual brings to the discussion.

At Friends Select we derive our secular educational philosophy from the tradition of social progressivism which developed in the nineteenth century and which was advanced through the progressive education move- ment with which most Quaker schools aligned them- selves in the 1920s and 1930s. We believe that the purpose of education is the perfection of a democratic society. The perfect society is one in which each citizen is helped to attain his or her own individual freedom.[27]

In 1994, Norma Vogel, then principal of Green Street Friends School, described the "intersection" of two empow- ering philosophies which guide the work in Friends schools. One influence is "that of developmental psychologists such as Jean Piaget, Erik Erikson, Howard Gardner, and Eleanor Duckworth. . . . concerned with the social, physical, cognitive, and psychological ages and stages natural to the developing human organism." The second, the Religious Society of Friends, "is concerned with spiritual growth and moral ways of living." In both traditions, Vogel discerns respect for individual difference and uniqueness, willingness to let growth unfold naturally, trust in the capacity of each individual to be a seeker. She explicitly connects these principles with progressive edu- cation. The distinctive qualities of a Friends school education, she affirms, emerge from "the strength of this particular inter- section of two powerful ideologies."[28]

CODA

In the seventeenth century in Britain or the New World, anyone responsible for educating young people would have to think first about how to teach reading, writing, 'cipher- ing.' Inevitably, then and through the eighteenth century, the question would arise whether to teach Latin and Greek, as a community considered what it needed from its educated members, and how widely formal education should be made available, especially to the poor, the disadvantaged, and to females. Quaker schools addressed these fundamental questions of the age from their own perspectives, influenced by the ambiance of the times.

In the nineteenth century, Quaker boarding schools in Britain are profoundly and directly influenced by Thomas Arnold's revitalizing of Rugby, but we would be hard put to describe Arnold as a philosopher of education. Even under this powerful influence, however, Quaker schools continued to emphasize the study of natural science, though Arnold did not. The eminent Quaker educator and scientist John Griscom brought Pestalozzi's teaching methods to the attention of Quakers and others by the 1820s, and the influence went deep in a number of Quaker schools. Pestalozzi supplanted Lancaster as a model for educating large numbers of students. From the 1870s, Quaker day schools on the east coast of the United States were among the earliest to adopt kindergartens, influenced by Froebel's theories and methods for teaching the very young.

Pestalozzi, Montessori, Progressive Education, the Country Day School movement, more recently, the integrated day or open classroom—all have had and have their influence on Quaker education. Not every educational influence available in these three hundred and fifty years has made a lasting impact on Friends schools. Even the ostensibly Quaker Lancastrian education, which came to rely heavily on a system of crass reward and shaming punishment to achieve its ends, was rapidly abandoned or repudiated on grounds of principle in a number of Quaker schools. And even though Quaker schools have experimented with programmed education, none has embraced the mechanistic philosophy which, for B.F. Skinner, underlies the method.

The important affinities between Quakerism and various philosophies of education, like the influences which have persisted, such as progressive education, have many things in common, all springing from an idealism about human possibilities and a conviction that individuals grow into their best selves when supported and sustained by a healthy community. Our approaches have been synthetic and eclectic. We have sometimes invented teaching methods which others have arrived at independently; at other times, we have borrowed, adapted, modified both methods and educational purposes from whatever has seemed most effective and most in keeping with our own educational purposes.

NOTES

1. *Thirty Schools Tell Their Story*, a report of the Eight-Year Study organized by the Progressive Education Association, New York, 1943, Friends Central report 320; Report prepared by William Hubben, Director of Religious Interests at George School, 361 (hereafter *Thirty Schools*); Kenneth C. Barnes, *Energy Unbound: The Story of Wennington School*, William Session, Inc., York, 1980, 35; *Thirty Schools*, Friends Central Report, 321, quoting John A. Lester, *The Ideals of Quaker Education*, Friends Council on Education, 12.

2. J. Bevan Braithwaite, "The Attitude of the Society of Friends Towards Modern Thought" in *Report of the Proceedings of the Conference of Members of the Society of Friends, held, by direction of the Yearly Meeting in Manchester from the eleventh to the fifteenth of eleventh month, 1895*, Headley Bros., London, 1896, 214-15.

3. Patricia Albjerg Graham, *Progressive Education: From Arcady to Academe: A History of the Progressive Education Association*, Teachers College Press, New York, 1967, 1-4; Graham cites Lawrence A. Cremin, *The Transformation of the School: Progressivism in American Education, 1876-1957*, (1st ed.) Knopf, New York, 1961, viii; Arthur Zilversmit, *Changing Schools: Progressive Education Theory and Practice, 1930-1960*, University of Chicago, Chicago, 1993, 6.

4. Robert N. Bellah, Richard Madsen, William M. Sullivan, Ann Swidler, Steven M. Tipton, *The Good Society*, Knopf, New York, 1991, 151-52. The authors are citing Dewey's *The School and Society*, 1899; Broudy and Palmer, 144-46; see also Dewey's description of method in *Democracy and Education*, 192.

5. Quoted in Broudy, *Exemplar*, 149-50.

6. Graham, *Progressive Education*, 11-12; Walter Kahoe, *Arthur Morgan: A Biography and Memoir*, The Whimsie Press, Moylan, Pa, 1977, 135-36, says Arthur Morgan joined Yellow Springs Meeting in 1940.

7. Broudy, *Exemplar*, 28-30.

8. Quoted in Faraday, 46-47.

9. Eugene R. Smith, "Self-Activity and Creativeness as School Aims," *The Nation's Schools*, Vol. VII, No. 1, January, 1931, 39-40.

10. Smith, *The Nation's Schools*, 47-48.

11. MacKaye, *Mr. Sidwell's School*, 103; *Wilmington*, 70-75; John M. Bullard, *Friends' Academy 1810-1960*, A History of the First One Hundred and Fifty Years, New Bedford, 1960, 111.

12. Charles W. Cooper, *Whittier: Independent College in California*, Founded by Quakers, 1887, The Ward Ritchie Press, Los Angeles, 1967, 159-61.

13. Cooper, *Whittier*, 160-71.

14. Hamm, *Earlham College*, 149.

15. J. Herschel Coffin, *Christian Education*, Preliminary Report of Commission III, Section A, On Schools and Colleges, mimeographed report, 1935. I am indebted to my colleague Thomas D. Hamm for calling my attention to this report, which he came across in Ernest Wildman's papers in the archives at Earlham College. I had the great pleasure of being guided in my understanding by Wildman's precise underlinings and substantial marginal comments. Wildman generally thought well of Coffin's proposals, though as a chemist he did not approve of Coffin's rather cavalier treatment of the natural sciences.

16. *Thirty Schools*, 320-21.

17. *Thirty Schools*, 320-45.

18. *Thirty Schools*, 389-94, 380.

19. *Thirty Schools*, 380-88.

20. *Thirty Schools*, 346-60.

21. *Thirty Schools*, 361.

22. *Thirty Schools*, 361-64.

23. *Thirty Schools*, 371-72.

24. Brinton, *Quaker Education*, 6-10 discusses progressive education; 15.

25. William N. Oats, *Headmaster by Chance*, Aguerremendi Press, Tasmania, 1986, 176; John Dewey, *Democracy and Education*, 352; Barnes, 141.

26. Graham, *Progressive Education*, 51.

27. Brown, 230.

28. Norma L. Vogel, essay in Greene Street Friends School Newsletter, January 199.

Ten

⟨⟩◆⟨⟩

ETHICS, *Ethos*, AND A QUAKER PHILOSOPHY OF EDUCATION

. . . Keep before our eyes the fact that there can be a spiritual unity in the educational aims of Friends from nursery school through college.

A community without established customs would be like a person without habits. . . . Discipline is a method of regulating the customary, in order to free the creative faculties.

The criterion by which a Quaker school should be judged is not that it is educationally "different," but that its educational merits should spring from Quaker principles.[1]

ETHICS AND ETHOS

The connections between the two words *ethics* and *ethos* are more than etymological. Ethics is the branch of philosophy which asks what qualities we humans need to develop in ourselves as habits, strengths, or virtues, in order to create and live in a good society. An ethical system always posits definitions of goodness and expectations of coherence and consistency of action in relation to fundamental principles. Aristotle explicitly connects ethics and ethos: "Moral char-

acteristics are formed by actively engaging in particular
actions." He invites us to consider how to make such virtues
as courage, self-control, generosity, truthfulness, and justice
habitual in our lives, and how to practice friendship and love
and achieve happiness and wisdom. Building on many of
these foundations, religious ethicists ask what human
motives and actions will best serve the will of God, and how
we can develop the qualities to be a productive part of a
human community.[2]

Ethos, the Greek word for "habit," carries the weight of
both moral expectation and strongly-established custom,
then, though it is often used as simply a neutral term for
social climate. One could, for example, describe the ethos of
a racist society. In this essay, however, the word will always
be used to describe positive, healthy social climates for the
teaching-learning process, since the purpose here is to ask
how we can achieve and maintain a particular kind of ethos
in Quaker schools and colleges, an ethos of learning, of
involvement, of care, and of hope. Gray Cox argues that the
Quaker ethic is a process meant to be practiced, ". . . an
activity born of commitment and concern, . . . rooted in a
coherent set of ideas about the nature of meaning and
truth. . . ." Hugh Barbour and Arthur Roberts tell us "Quaker
social ethics was never a mere sum of particular concerns
and protests; always it was part of a totally opened life."[3] For
Quakers, the realm of ethics—how to know and follow the
will of God, and how we should behave as children of God
in what Douglas Heath identifies as our six primary roles in
the world, as workers, citizens, marital partners, parents,
lovers, and friends—and the community ethos created by
our sense of what is ethical behavior, must reinforce each
other. Ethics and ethos belong together, for where they do
not cohere, we find hypocrisy, social instability, moral and

intellectual confusion, fragmented selves and institutions, and unhealth. Studies of "burnout" show that it happens primarily to people in service professions, such as social workers, nurses, and teachers, who find their idealism so frustrated by unresponsive, bureaucratic institutions that their energies and hopes are consumed. For healthy people and institutions, ethics and ethos must reflect one another. In *The Company We Keep*, Wayne C. Booth writes,

> The word "character" comes from the Greek word for "stamp" or "mark," but it has also been used as a translation of "ethos." We might think of it as meaning "a stamped or incised ethos"—a more or less harmonious collection of characteristics that persist through time because *stamped into* the material—whatever we might take that initial "material," the unsocialized self, to be.[4]

If there is, or can be, a spiritual unity in the aims of Friends education at every level, it would seem to manifest itself less in a single comprehensive educational philosophy than in the creation of a particular kind of *atmosphere* or *climate* from which all aspects of the school life—course-work, extracurricular activities, and the interactions of students, staff, administration, and faculty—take their form and meaning. Colin Bell has called this "the smell of the school."

George D. Kuh defines a school's ethos as,

> a belief system widely shared by faculty, students, administrators, and others, . . . shaped by a core of educational values manifested in the institution's mission and philosophy, . . . an institution-specific pattern of values and principles that invokes a sense of belonging and helps people distinguish between appropriate and inappropriate behavior.

Ethos is the encoding of messages about what the institution/community values in educational, social, and personal terms. Ethos creates " a sense of intrinsic obligation." "It transforms the basis for belonging from a mere happenchance into a sense of covenanting with an ongoing reality."[5] Deeply-incised habit or character, then, stamped or imprinted into the institutional life and subsequently imprinted into the lives of those who are part of the institution—this is what we will mean by the ethos of a school.

ETHOS AND CONFLICT

To think of Quaker education in terms of ethos helps to explain both the great similarities and the differences among our schools and colleges. As Kim Hays reminds us, they are places "where moral socialization is the acknowledged goal rather than the hidden by-product of education." They are "communities that uphold particular traditions, and *tradition* is a loaded word." For a tradition to become accessible on a daily basis, she argues, a process of translation must occur, which depends on both "the practice of virtues, and the acceptance of conflict."[6]

That such conflict is essential to keep the moral tradition, and therefore the ethos, of a school vital, helps explain some disturbing impressions of Quaker schools. More than one "lifer"—the word for a student who has gone from kindergarten through high school in a Quaker school—has perceived it this way: the lower school was "most Quaker," the middle school was less so, and the upper school was "least Quaker." As would follow from that analysis, the Quaker college is "even less Quaker" than the upper school. Religion teachers in a Quaker day school express frustration with introducing Quakerism in the upper grades and suggest that perhaps the school should not try after sixth grade. Sterner critics charge that our schools and colleges are not "really Quaker," but only hide elitist, competitive academic training under a veneer of religious rhetoric.

Deferring any examination of degrees of "Quaker-ness" in different grades and schools, we can ask what it takes to achieve a consensus of opinion (using that term only in its common political sense of generally-shared agreement) about what the ethos of a Quaker school is or should be. In the lower school, such a consensus exists primarily among faculty, administration, and governing board or committee. Parents are invited to share in that already-existing consensus and to make its premises their own. When values which are assumed to be commonly agreed on turn out not to be, the conflicts tend to be pursued through disputes over the meanings of or priority among what Kim Hays calls the "magnet words," e.g. "the sacredness of the individual" and "the importance of community," in the mission statement or other expressions of the consensus.[7]

The students in the lower school are both explicitly instructed in the ethos and encouraged to internalize it. It is relatively easy to achieve young children's assent to the prevailing school ethos, especially when conforming brings reward, praise, and safety. "We respect everyone equally here," translates into "Here *you* will be respected as everyone's equal." "We solve problems non-violently because that shows respect for everyone," equals "*You* will not be hit by anyone else here." "We all work to make this a safe place for everyone," means "This will be a safe place for *you*." If the children experience dissonance between school and home, or school and neighborhood, they seem able to resolve it during school hours and on school property. It is remarkable how many worlds even very young children can learn to negotiate among.

The lower school is also a highly-controlled environment. Peer groups have far less influence than they will have later, and virtually every moment of the school day is under adult observation and influence. Never again will adult authority be so easily asserted or so willingly granted. We invest most heavily, and successfully, in socializing our youngest children. Until very recently, Earlham Professor of Psychology Nelson Bingham has pointed out, college courses in developmental psychology would all have been called "child development." The operating assumptions were that the earliest influences on a child would have the longest-lasting effects, and that not much happened developmentally again until the tumult of adolescence, by which time the foundations had better have been set. It is telling that Friedrich Froebel gave up his plan to address human development through young adulthood and decided to concentrate instead on perfecting the pedagogy of the kindergarten.

Given all those circumstances, it is not surprising if a Quaker school can give its youngest students an intensive experience with the values of Quakerism. The complex intermixture of content and learning process, affective and cognitive development, which makes up the schooling of elementary students is ideally suited for gentle inculcation of values, learning *about*, and experiential encounter with, Quaker practices. At no later point in their formal education will conditions be so favorable for the relatively unconflicted practice of such values as respect for each person, community, equality, peaceful resolution of conflict, uncompetitive, collaborative learning.

From middle school on, the pressures on the school ethos become increasingly stronger and more complex. The consensus on what constitutes good education begins to show strains on issues of subject-matter, course content, and academic achievement. Some "magnet words" repel as well as attract school constituents. Parents who have been happy to see their children's affective development encouraged in the lower school begin to require more attention to their cognitive achievements. Affective learning has certainly not been abandoned, but the tug between affective and cognitive development necessarily becomes greater. Various "outsiders" begin to have more impact on curriculum. Standardized tests become more important as "objective" measures of student achievement. Grades begin to carry more weight, as parents, children, and teachers look ahead to college applications.

Other influences become more powerful. Students feel peer pressures more intensely; they spend increasingly more time out of the supervision of adults, and they become more resistant to and independent of authority. What Alexander Astin reports of college may also be said of upper schools, "The major obstacle to student learning is social, not intellectual."[8] Every parent and teacher feels conflicted by those developments. We want our children to learn by their mistakes but are frightened as the consequences of their mistakes become more serious. We want them to think for themselves, but we wish they weren't so skeptical of our advice. We want them to beat us at arm-wrestling eventually, but not quite yet. We know rebellion is necessary for their maturity, but does it have to take the form of experimentation with alcohol and drug use, tattoos, and pierced body-parts? Not to speak of sexual experimentation (and we *mean* not to speak of it.)

Some parents may also be more in conflict with the value-commitments of the school ethos, and the breaks between worlds get harder for students to bridge. From middle school through upper school, our students and children are struggling with so many challenges to find efficacy and competence in what they do and to reconcile the needs for affiliation with the needs for independence and integrity. This is happening at the same time that the whole educational world which speaks only of subjects taken and passed, grades and standardized tests achieved, increasingly enters into, conflicts with and influences the school ethos.

It would be fatuous to pretend that Quaker schools need not take such influences into account. The experience of meeting for worship undergoes changes from the lower to the upper school as adolescent self-consciousness inhibits the openness which came so easily in the lower school. In the later years, Meeting for Worship increasingly becomes the venue for faculty to speak and for some students to act out or vent frustrations with the school. Values-commitments which might earlier have been gently diffused through the institutional life now must find expression and validation primarily through course-work. The value of compassion, which in kindergarten and the early grades might have found easy, joyful expression in caring for animals or plants, finds expression in the upper school through a service-learning course for academic credit—the only way to claim time from competing courses in English, science, and foreign language. Quakerism becomes an academic course for which papers must be written and tests passed—and a certain number of students and some parents complain either that the course takes time away from what they consider more important college-preparation work, or that it is inconsistent to grade a Quakerism course rigorously. Even the appropriate focus for such a course becomes problematic: it cannot be indoctrination, but how can it be something more than information *about* Quakers and Quakerism? Such practices and values may be stronger for being contested, but the contest is intense and often painful.

Under such intense pressures, some schools undoubtedly de-emphasize aspects of their Quaker tradition, though what makes a school or college sufficiently or "really" Quaker will always remain open to debate. If "Quaker" is taken to mean unconflicted, unambiguous, without a tinge of inconsistency, nearly perfect in word and deed, no school will qualify. But neither will any monthly, quarterly, or yearly meeting, nor any individual, with the possible exception of thee and me. (And who can be sure about thee?) Quakerism has always been perfectibilist, meaning that Quakers believe that God's grace can lead human beings closer and closer to spiritual perfection. "Be ye therefore perfect" is a commandment to persist in a direction, not to reach stasis; it does not mean making perfectionist demands on others or being a connoisseur of their shortcomings.

From the "lifer's" point of view, the upper school may seem less Quakerly, while to the student who transfers in at the ninth grade, the atmosphere may seem overwhelmingly Quaker. One has internalized values which are startlingly new to the other. Douglas Heath tells us that teachers new to Quaker schools comment on such attributes as student talkativeness, openness, expressiveness, giving, acceptance, feelings for others, imagination, fun, and deep ethical sense. He suggests that the schools' valuing of maturation of character as well as of the mind makes it easier for students to be more vulnerable and open to learning and that students participate more readily in class discussion because of their experience in the Quaker "consensual decision-making process."[9] When we have breathed that atmosphere for a long time, we may find it harder to identify its presence or "smell." It has been suggested that asking someone to describe a powerful ethos from within is like asking a fish to describe water.

According to Heath, "Researchers agree that a major effect of education can be the progressive integration of one's values. . . ." and research ". . . has confirmed that from junior high school through college, students respond to moral problems with increasingly principled judgments." Such principled judgments may not rest on the principles we would choose, or arrive at the actions we would take, but the basis of Quaker education is persuasion, not compulsion, convincement, not indoctrination, trust that good values and principles will make their way into the human heart. The ethos we create must allow for people to integrate *their* values into their lives, to discover their own sense of inner coherence and integrity. One hallmark of what Heath calls "Schools of Hope" is that they "progressively reduce their expectations and structures to test students' budding autonomy to set and carry out their own hopes in increasingly varied situations."[10] For teachers wanting to encourage more students' initiative in their own learning, "reduce the prompts" is wise advice: move from explicit to implicit; give more quizzes at the beginning and fewer as the term proceeds; over time, present fewer teacher-questions so that the students can offer theirs; lessen the external controls as students internalize their own. Inviting students to share in translating the school's magnet words may be one way of "reducing the prompts," but it may also look like an attenuation of the school's "Quaker values."

An Ethos of Learning

The discussion which follows grows from two complementary mottoes: Alfred North Whitehead's reminder, "They learn by contact," and one crystallization of Alexander Astin's many years of research, "Students learn what they study." It will draw largely on research done on higher education by George Kuh and Astin, whose findings have many strong applications to Quaker schools, and Heath's extensive studies of both schools and colleges, especially Quaker schools, in his lifelong work to develop a model of psychological health and maturity.

Kuh says that institutions marked by what he calls "an ethos of learning" share three common themes: a holistic philosophy of learning; an involving campus climate; and a climate encouraging free expression. "An educational philosophy which views students as whole persons and communicates high performance expectations is key to cultivating an ethos of learning."[11]

These findings point to a number of conclusions. A holistic philosophy of learning emerges from underlying convictions about values and purposes in life, and addresses needs of the mind, the body, the emotions, the soul. Rooted in a sense of awe, of compassion, and fellow-feeling with others and with the Creation, it fits Whitehead's definition of a religious education, "an education which inculcates duty and reverence." In Anthony Benezet's phrase, it educates "with relation to time and eternity," and is therefore practical as well as theoretical, addressing concrete problems in the larger world and helping people discover their callings by working at real jobs. It works against reliance on hierarchies of authority and draws students, faculty, administration, staff, and other constituencies into mutual responsibility for the teaching-learning process.

Direct participation in a working community sets a pattern of expectations for a variety of "learning contacts." As Kuh tells us, ". . . if expectations about learning are to affect behavior, they must be imbedded in all aspects of institutional life."[12] College students spend two-thirds to three-quarters of their waking hours outside the classroom, and a shift toward a similar division of time is occurring for upper school students in Quaker day schools. Consequently, students will have more and more educative or mis-educative experiences on their own, in conditions of relative independence and autonomy; at those times, the ethos of learning is either internalized in them, or it has little effect. Since students (and faculty) learn from what they study in courses, but also in dormitories, the dining-room, the coffee-shop, in offices and homes, we can build or damage the ethos in every encounter. Whether good or bad lessons, we learn by contact.

Holistic education holds all participants to high expectations which are linked to clear communication, consistent and steady mutual support, regular assessment of accomplishments coupled with concrete suggestions for how to improve. "An institution . . . attains one of its most important purposes when it changes students' views of themselves and of the world by raising their personal and educational aspirations and establishing clear expectations for involvement that will help students attain their goals." Holistic education requires a milieu which supports free, open, heartfelt, respectful expression, careful listening as well as careful speech. It encourages plain speaking as well as civility in the best sense of that word, behavior predicated on the sense that one is a citizen of a community. Kuh warns that an ethos of learning fosters tensions between cohesion and straightforward assessment of people's behavior, and comments " how an institution responds to conflicts between individualism and conformity is a key indication of whether an ethos of learning exists."[13]

An Ethos of Involvement; an Ethic of Care

Describing an "ethos of involvement," one which gets students actively engaged in and motivated by a wide variety of social and learning activities, Astin argues that educational effectiveness is fostered by four characteristics: "student involvement, high expectations, assessment, and feedback."[14] Kuh and his associates find that "involving colleges" offer students challenge, support, and great expectations. Such colleges are characterized by what the study calls an "ethic of membership" which holds that, "once a student chooses the institution, she or he is immediately a fully participating member of its community," by egalitarian aspirations, by a commitment to multiculturalism, and by an "ethic of care."

> Institutional agents (faculty, student affairs staff, and others such as clerical and maintenance personnel) care about students. As students sense this ethic of care, they begin to care for one another. For example, Earlham and Grinnell faculty members model involvement in the life of the community and share the excitement of participation with students both in and out of the classroom.[15]

The Kuh study cites Earlham College as challenging "the prevailing Western ethic of competition with an ethic of collaboration," perhaps an expression of all three of the ethical values care, membership, and egalitarianism. The study identifies three core assumptions and values emanating from Earlham's Quaker tradition:

> First, it is assumed that the "light of truth" can be found in each individual, and so value is placed on consensual ways of learning and knowing. . . . This belief is reflected in a strong emphasis on interdisciplinary coursework and collaborative learning techniques. . . . Collaboration rather than competition is the norm. . . . The second assumption . . . is expressed in the phrase "Let your lives speak"; knowledge is not only to be appreciated but,

more important, it is also to be lived. . . . Finally, Earlham is committed to the responsibility of the individual in the global community. This value . . . results in an emphasis on global awareness and social action throughout the student's experience at Earlham College.

The language of *Involving Colleges* is very telling: the involving college (or school) tries to ground its practice in coherent, consistent principles, ethics, of care for one another, egalitarianism, participation, membership, and collaboration. "Collaboration . . . is common in collegiate communities where distinctions are intentionally diminished."[16] Where there is a pervasive ethos of learning, both the Astin and Kuh studies reveal, students exhibit greater gains in both academic achievement and personal development than students at other institutions with similar student and institutional characteristics but lacking that ethos.

INVOLVEMENT AND CURRICULUM

In order to emphasize the significance of climate and atmosphere, researchers sometimes seem to understate the impact of the formal curriculum on students. Yet Astin's monumental work *What Matters in College* documents a great many significant correlations between student growth and experiences in courses: "Given that this study focuses on human performance in an academic setting, it is fitting that the most basic form of academic involvement—studying and doing homework—has stronger and more positive effects than almost any other involvement measure or environmental measure."[17] Students tend to become more activist and liberal over their college careers, for example, and Astin cites such *involvement variables* associated with activism as "participating in campus demonstrations, discussing racial or ethnic issues, attending racial or cultural awareness workshops, enrolling in ethnic studies courses, enrolling in women's studies courses," and participating in study-abroad programs. Activism is also related to hours per week spent in volunteer work and has positive relationships with the number of history and writing-skills courses a student takes.[18]

Astin finds student commitment to promoting racial understanding positively associated with hours per week studying or doing homework and numbers of foreign language and history courses taken. Student commitment to developing a meaningful philosophy of life he finds positively associated with the number of writing courses taken, receiving personal or psychological counseling, "and three 'hours per week' variables: attending religious services, reading for pleasure, and studying or doing homework." "Commitment to developing a meaningful philosophy of life . . . is strengthened by exposure to a peer group that emphasizes Social Activism and Community." *Involvement* measures showing the strongest positive effects on attending recitals or concerts include being a guest in a professor's home, talking with instructors out of class, having class papers critiqued by instructors, discussing racial or ethnic issues, working on independent research projects, in addition to socializing with friends and people from different ethnic or racial groups.[19]

What is particularly striking in these findings is how the *mix* of curricular and co-curricular offerings helps shape student attitudes, values, and beliefs. Why should being a guest in a teacher's home have a strong correlation with a student's going to a concert? Why should commitments to so many values and beliefs be associated with courses *taken*—in foreign languages, writing, ethnic and women's studies courses, history, and foreign study? ". . . Studying and doing homework . . . has stronger and more widespread positive effects than almost any other involvement measure or environmental measure." "Hours per week spent *studying or doing homework* (Astin's italics) produces the largest and most numerous partial correlations with student outcomes . . . "[20]

Such findings, a very small sampling of what Astin reports, remind us that curriculum is one salient manifestation of institutional ethos, as ethos is the matrix in which the curriculum is imbedded. Douglas Heath concludes that "mind's maturation can best be encouraged by . . . curricular efforts . . . when those efforts are *supported by a congruent and healthy ethos.* Conversely, character's maturation is best nurtured by a school's ethos that is *supported by an appropriate curriculum.*"[21] (Heath's italics)

"Curriculum" always sounds abstract and uninteresting, especially if all we mean by it is a catalog of courses offered and rules about what courses must be taken when. But "curriculum" also translates into *classes,* regular encounters between students and peers, students and faculty, over meaningful themes and subjects. There we know all the possibilities for passion and boredom, enlightenment and freedom, speech and silence. The classroom is the richest, fullest expression of the curriculum, and therefore it is like any other part of the teaching-learning ethos we celebrate or blame. As my colleague Gordon Thompson argues, the classroom must be the safest place in the world so that it can be the riskiest. If, at its least effective, it is where some people feel silenced, it can also be a place where people can hear their voices affirmed and supported. The classroom, the curriculum, is no more, and no less, a growing edge for true learning than service learning or international education. It is true that, as we go through school, we spend less and less of our daily time in the classroom, but that does not in itself tell us anything about how enlivening, powerful, influential over all our other hours, the classroom can be. A boat may have only a small sail and smaller rudder, but used well together they can transform the chaotic interplay of heavy wind and strong wave into a successful journey.

We cannot know the ethos of a school—certainly not its ethos for learning—separate from the curriculum, nor can there be a successful school or college which neglects curriculum, meaning both content and pedagogical matters, in the name of creating an ethos of learning. Neither can an ethic of care merely focus on the sensitive self or indulge a self-involved community; it must always attend to widening the circle of concern. "You may not divide the seamless coat of learning," says Alfred North Whitehead.[22]

"A Specific Quaker Influence Is At Work"

Kenneth Hardy's findings in 1974, that Quaker schools had educated "proportionately more productive adults than other, intellectually comparable schools," led him to conclude that "these schools are so superior in productivity, not only among the denominational schools but also among all of the schools in the entire sample, that it seems probable that a specific Quaker influence is at work." Exploring what that "specific Quaker influence" might be, Heath identifies nine qualities (found in students as well as faculty and administrators) perceived by teachers new to Quaker schools as characteristic of the schools' ethos: talkativeness, openness, expressiveness, giving, acceptance, feeling for others, imagination, fun, deep ethical sense. According to initial reports from the study of Quaker schools' effect on the moral education of students, being conducted by Friends Council on Education, the qualities which teachers and students most ascribe to the school ethos include honesty and integrity, courage, concern, caring, compassion, giving, acceptance, equality, diversity, self-reflection, community, listening, patience, openness, and responsiblity. The perceptions of teachers new to Quaker schools differed from those of new teachers "in America's foremost independent and comparable public schools," by margins of 32 to 50 percent. In addition, "the Quaker schools were perceived to be more caring, trusting and warmer by margins of 25 to 45 percent than the independent and public schools." Heath suggests that these comparisons tell us three things: that Quaker schools have highly distinctive climates and "share among themselves a widespread communion of value that we now know is essential to being a school of hope;" and if Hardy's inference of a specific Quaker influence is correct, "then valuing character's as well as mind's maturation may contribute to a student's future productivity by making it easier for students to be vulnerable and open to learning; Quaker schools, perceived as more open, accepting, and empathic, "might indeed be more responsive to their members' needs."[23]

Drawing on his own longitudinal studies of how Haverford College influenced its students' and graduates' values, Heath tells us that "to both students and alumni, while uncompromisingly intellectual, the college's core ethos was indisputably moral." A decade and more after graduation, graduates reported Haverford's continuing effect on them: "It had deepened the men's awareness of themselves as ethical persons and provided them with models of how to integrate its values and make them their own."

> The college's core values were maturity's metavalues of honesty, compassion, and respect for others, integrity, commitment, and courage," embodied in "student

generated and enforced academic and social honor codes, student freedom in self-government, faculty corporate consensual decision-making procedures, a powerful confrontational freshman English seminar that explored values through literature, and a weekly corporate meeting for meditation to which faculty and students came. . . . "24

Looking back on his own career as a college teacher in an earlier generation, Howard Brinton recalled that " . . . the Quaker colleges, Guilford, Earlham, and Haverford, in which I have taught, possessed a subtle, indefinable quality, a kind of community life centered in the higher values, independent of classroom courses, yet not wholly unrelated to them." Kuh says " . . . the spirit of the Quaker values that undergirds the Earlham mission is supported by teaching-learning processes that are collaborative through a required interdisciplinary humanities program, and by the use of consensus in the conduct of campus affairs." Heath's work on Haverford offers more extensive documentation of qualities also found in other Quaker colleges and schools, evidence of what appears to be truly a specific Quaker influence.25

Sustaining An Ethos And An Ethic

It is time to reflect on what the studies tell us about Quaker education. The studies of *effective* education document the importance of holistic approaches to teaching and learning, linked to programs and activities to encourage student *involvement*, deep and steady investment of their time and energy in the widest range of learning opportunities, of high expectations of students and regular assessment of student accomplishments coupled with concrete advice for how to improve performance, for creating an "ethos for learning." Writing in 1949, Brinton identified what he considered the two particular Quaker contributions to education, the co-educational boarding-school and the work-camp. These, he said, ". . . exhibit a common trait, they are integrated co-operative communities in which the spiritual, intellectual, and physical aspects of life become blended. To some extent they resemble an ideal family more than they resemble a community."[26] A commitment to holistic education announces that the institution not only values the development of body and mind, feelings and intellect, psyche and soul, but is committed to offering programs and activities which allow each aspect of the self, and of every self—faculty and administrators as well as students—, and the self in community, to be nourished. It is a commitment to encouraging the smudging and crossing of lines: the line between course-work and service-learning is smudged, as is the line which separates teacher from student. The lines between disciplines are regularly crossed, to create inter-disciplinary approaches to questions and issues, to look at familiar things from new perspectives, to be challenged and invigorated by seeing significant connections among disciplines or schools of thought. It is a commitment to making connections, making contacts, encouraging risk and experimentation, becoming inter-related, intimately "involved" together as companions in learning, reducing the prompts in the name of greater independence and autonomy for students, integrating thought with action and ethical convictions with ethical behavior.

The Quaker "ethos for learning" rests on a number of ethical principles and practices. Kim Hays says one Quaker goal is to change society to make it a better place for nurturing the Inner Light. "This why Quaker virtues— equality, community, simplicity, and peace—describe an environment not a person. Education at Friends schools encourages a process of eternal searching."[27] An ethic of care, of membership in a community, of egalitarianism, and of collaboration will create a strongly-inflected ethos to support the goals of holistic education, involvement, high and clear expectations, assessment, and feedback which Astin identifies as supporting effective education.

WAYS TO HARM
THE QUAKER ETHOS FOR LEARNING

The kind of ethos being described here is not peculiar to Quaker schools and colleges, but it does seem to be characteristic of Quaker education at its best. Its roots run deep into Quaker faith, and it can have great transformative power for those who participate in it. It is very easy to imagine that, because an ethos is currently powerful, it can be taken for granted as self-sustaining, but no institution's ethos is as deeply inscribed as we might wish. Even when it is very strong, it is also frail, transitory, easily damaged through neglect. A single generation can change it beyond immediate recovery. It can persist over long stretches of time only if it is continually renewed through challenge, conflict, conscious reflection, and re-affirmation through actions. Amitai Etzioni has warned,

> Values not mediated through concrete social structures tend to become tenuous, frail, and in the long run, insupportable. Although verbal formulations may remain, authentic commitment is gradually eroded. To borrow a distinction, the loss of a visible community entails the loss of the invisible one.[28]

The ethos of a Quaker school can be damaged when people embrace what they perceive to be *ends* of educational success—getting into a good college, a good graduate or professional program, a good job—but have no commitment to *means*. It can be damaged when parents send their children to what they think of as merely a "best buy" to which they are entitled but for which they have no obligation, or when teachers, administrators or school committee members secularize Quaker experience to make the school more attractive to prospective students— making "that of God in everyone" simply a metaphor for self-involved individualism, or calling meeting for worship by euphemisms to avoid the notion that *worship* might be why we gather in silent waiting. It can be damaged by well-meaning teachers who avoid confronting rule-breaking students because the spirit of friendship seems more important than the letter of mutual accountability. It can be damaged by what Hays describes as Quaker school faculty's ambivalence about and "high level of denial" of their own authority. It can be damaged by people who do not speak plainly about students' or colleagues' shortcomings for fear of injuring their self-esteem. It can also be damaged by people whose only justification for their actions is "because it is the rule."

"A Process of Eternal Searching"

George Kuh says, "The Quaker Way is not so much a system of beliefs as it is a framework for asking the right questions in the tradition of the Society of Friends."[29] It is *also* a system of beliefs, of course, but both the system and the beliefs are renewed by how they help us address changing conditions. Erik Erikson speaks to this point when he says, "Moralities sooner or later outlive themselves, ethics never; this is what the need for identity and fidelity, reborn with each generation, seems to point to."[30] The Quaker Way must be lived through and in human institutions, among which the most vital are our schools and colleges. John Reader says that the great challenge is how to incorporate the spirit of compassion into the structure of an institution. That is especially important for a Quaker school. We are called to be forever searching, but the purpose of the search is to *find*, to live conscientiously, by principle, even in a relativistic world. The Quaker Way continually tests principle and practice against one another. Whether that produces something which can be accurately called *a* philosophy of education remains open to question, as John Reader suggested, but it produces an activity which might be called *doing* Quaker philosophy of education—seeking to bring ethos and ethic together, to be lived in wholeness and integrity.

NOTES

1. Hadassah L. Holcombe "History of the Friends Council on Education," quoted by Rachel Letchworth, "Yesterday. Today—and Tomorrow?" 1971, 6; Howard Brinton, *Idea of Pendle Hill*, 26; Joseph Hutchinson, "Experiment in Education," in *Friends Schools in the Seventies*, Friends Schools Joint Committee, Friends House London 1973, 99.

2. Aristotle, *Nichomachean Ethics*, 1103a, 15-20; 1114a,10.

3. Gray Cox, *Bearing Witness: Quaker Process and a Culture of Peace*, Pendle Hill Pamphlet 262, 3-4; Hugh Barbour and Arthur Roberts, *Early Quaker Writings*, 434.

4. Wayne C. Booth, *The Company We Keep: An Ethics of Fiction*, University of Chicago, 1988, 232n.

5. George D. Kuh,"Ethos:Its Influence on Student Learning," *Liberal Education*, Fall, 1993, 22.

6. Hays, *Practicing Virtues*, 3,5.

7. Hays, *Practicing Virtues*, 6-7.

8. Kuh, *Ethos*, 30.

9. Douglas H. Heath, *Schools of Hope: Developing Mind and Character in Today's Youth*, Jossey-Bass, San Francisco, 1994, 317-18.

10. Heath, *Schools of Hope*, 256.

11. Kuh, *Ethos*, 25, 26.

12. Kuh, *Ethos*, 26.

13. Kuh, *Ethos*, 26, 28.

14. Alexander W. Astin, "Involvement: The Cornerstone of Excellence," *Change* Magazine, July/August 1985, 36.

15. George D. Kuh, John H. Schuh, Elizabeth J. Whitt, and Associates, *Involving Colleges: Successful Approaches to Fostering Student Learning and Development Outside the Classroom*, Jossey-Bass, San Francisco, 1991, 56.

16. Kuh, *Involving Colleges*, 44-45, 55-59, 292.

17. Astin, "Involvement," 376.

18. Astin, "Involvement," 116, 151.

19. Astin, "Involvement," 157, 164, 174.

20. Astin, "Involvement," 375-76.

21. Heath, *Schools of Hope*, 324.

22. Whitehead, *Aims of Education*, 11.

23. Heath, *Schools of Hope*, 317.

24. Heath, *Schools of Hope*, 225-26.

25. Brinton, "The Function of a Quaker College," The Ward Lecture, 1951, Guilford College, 19; Kuh, *Involving Colleges*, 68.

26. Brinton, "Family or Institution?", *Pendle Hill Bulletin* 49, August, 1949.

27. Hays, *Practicing Virtues*, 103.

28. Amitai Etzioni, *The Active Society: A Theory of Societal and Political Processes*, Free Press, New York, 1968, 13-14.

29. Kuh, *Ethos*, 24.

30. Erik Erikson, *Identity, Youth and Crisis*, Norton, New York, 1968, 25.

BIBLIOGRAPHY

A *Souvenir of Friends Schools*, Reprinted from *Western Work*, Oskaloosa, Iowa, 1899.

A *Brief Sketch of the Schools for Black People*, Philadelphia, 1867.

A *Gift in Trust, Wilmington Friends School*, A Celebration of our first 250 years, Wilmington: Wilmington Friends School, 1998.

A *Man and a School*, A collection of papers about George A. Walton and George School, Bucks County: George School, 1965.

Adamson, John William, *Pioneers of Modern Education in the Seventeenth Century*, Classics in Education, no. 45, New York: Teachers College Press, 1972.

An *Address to Those Who Have the Care of Children*, Philadelphia: Tract Association of Friends, 1832.

Aristotle, *Nichomachean Ethics*.

Astin, Alexander W., *What Matters in College? Four Critical Years Revisited*, San Francisco, Jossey-Bass, 1993.

Astin, Alexander W., "Involvement: The Cornerstone of Excellence," *Change Magazine*, July/August, 1985.

Barbour, Hugh and J. William Frost, *The Quakers*, New York: Greenwood Press, 1988, Richmond: Friends United Press, 1994.

Barbour, Hugh and Arthur Roberts, *Early Quaker Writings 1650-1700*, Grand Rapids, Michigan: Eerdmans, 1973.

Barclay, Robert, *Barclay's Apology in Modern English*, Dean Freiday, ed., Philadelphia, Pa: Distributed by Friends Book Store, 1980.

Barlow, F. Ralph, *Woodbrooke 1953-1978*, A Documentary Account of Woodbrooke's Third twenty five years, David B. Grey, ed, York: William Sessions Limited, 1982.

Barnes, Kenneth C., *Energy Unbound: The Story of Wennington School*, York: William Sessions, Limited, 1980.

Barry, Peter, Richard Eldridge, Elizabeth Eschalier, David B. Koth, George D. Rowe, Jr., *Buckingham Friends School, A History: 1794-1994*, Buckingham: Buckingham Friends School, 1995.

Bellah, Robert N., Richard Madsen, William M. Sullivan, Ann Swidler, Steven M. Tipton, *Habits of the Heart: Individualism and Commitment in American Life*, Berkeley: University of California Press, 1985.

Bellah, Robert N., Richard Madsen, William M. Sullivan, Ann Swidler, Steven M. Tipton, *The Good Society*, 1ˢᵗ ed. New York: Knopf: Distributed by Random House, 1991.

Bellers, John, "An Epistle to the Quarterly-Meeting of London and Middlsex," London: S.U., 1718.

Bellers, John, *"To the Lords and Commons Assembled in Parliament,"* London: Printed Sold by T. Saule, 1704.

Bellers, John, *"To The Thinking and Publick-Spirited,"* London: T. Saule, 1704.

Benezet, Anthony, *A Pattern of Christian Education*, Agreeable to the Precepts and Practice of Our Blessed Lord and Saviour Jesus Christ, illustrated under the Characters of Paternus and Eusebia, Dublin: Printed by Robert Jackson, 1783.

Benezet, Anthony, and Isaac Zane, "Some Observations Relating to the Establishment of Schools, Agreed to by the Committee, to be laid for consideration before the Yearly-Meeting" signed on behalf of the Committee 29th 9th Month, 1778, forwarded from Yearly Meeting to the attention of Quarterly, Monthly and Preparative Meetings by James Pemberton, Clerk of the Yearly Meeting, 10 Month 2nd, 1778.

Benezet, Anthony, "Letter to Samuel Fothergill," in *The Friends' Library: comprising journals, doctrinal treatises, and other writings of members of the religious Society of Friends*, Vol IX, pp. 220-22, Philadelphia: Joseph Rakestraw for the editors, 1837-50.

Benezet, Anthony, *"Some Necessary Remarks on the Education of the Youth in the Country-Parts of this, and the neighbouring Governments,"* n.d.

Benjamin, Philip S., *The Philadelphia Quakers in the Industrial Age: 1865-1920*, Temple University Press, Philadelphia, 1976.

Berquist, Robert, David Rhodes, Carolyn Smith Treadway, *Scattergood Friends School 1890-1990*, West Branch, Iowa: Scattergood School, 1990.

...*Better Than Riches: a tricentennial history of William Penn Charter School, 1689-1989*, Philadelphia: William Penn Charter School, 1988.

Bickley, William Phillips, *1947. Education as Reformation: An Examination of Orthodox,* Quakers' Formation of the Haverford School Association and Founding of *Haverford School, 1815-1840*. Unpublished dissertation, Harvard Graduate School of Education, Ann Arbor: University Microfilms, 1983.

Bjorklund, Victoria Baum, A *Century of Friends: 1877-1977*, Locust Valley, NY: published by the Board of Trustees, Friends Academy, Locust Valley, New York, 1977.

Bolam, David W., *Unbroken Community: the Story of the Friends' School, Saffron Walden, 1702-1952*, Cambridge: the Friends' School, 1952.

Bonhoeffer, Dietrich, *Life Together*, London: SLM Press, 1954.

Booth, Wayne C., *The Company We Keep: An Ethics of Fiction*, Berkeley: University of California Press, 1988.

Boulding, Elise, *Children and Solitude*, Pendle Hill pamphlet 125, Wallingford: Pendle Hill, 1962.

Bowen, H. Courthope, *Froebel and Education through Self-Activity*, New York: Scribner, 1892.

Braithwaite, J. Bevan, "The Attitude of the Society of Friends Towards Modern Thought" in *Manchester Conference, 1895*.

Braithwaite, William C., *The Beginnings of Quakerism*, 2nd ed., rev. by Henry J. Cadbury, Cambridge: Cambridge University Press, 1955.

Braithwaite, William C. "Has Quakerism a Message to the World Today?" in *Manchester Conference, 1895*.

Brinton, Howard H., "The Function of a Quaker College." The Ward Lecture, 1951, Greensboro: Guilford College, 1951.

Brinton, Howard H., "Family or Institution?" Pendle Hill Bulletin.

Brinton, Howard H., *Friends for Three Hundred Years*, Wallingford: Pendle Hill, 1965, (1952 orig.).

Brinton, Howard H., *Quaker Education in Theory and Practice*, Wallingford: Pendle Hill, 1940, fourth printing, 1967.

Brinton,Howard H., *The Pendle Hill Idea: a Quaker Experiment in Work, Worship, Study*, Pamphlet 55 (later 70), Wallingford, PA, 1950.

Brook, Peter, *The Empty Space*, New York: Antheneum, 1984.

Broudy, Harry S. and John R. Palmer, *Exemplars of Teaching Method*, Rand McNally education series. Chicago: Rand McNally 1965.

Brown, Miriam Jones, *Friends School Haverford, 1885-1985*, Exton Pa: Schiffer Publisher Co., 1985.

Brown, Thomas S. "A Theology of Education," *Quaker Religious Thought*, Quaker Theological Discussion Group, Vol X. no 2, 1968-69.

Brown, Carol H., *A Friends Select History*, Philadelphia: Friends Select School, 1989.

Budd, Thomas, *Good Order Established in Pennsylvania and New Jersey in America: Being a True Account of the Country; with its Produce and Commodities There Made in the Year 1685*, A New Edition with an Introduction and Copious Historical Notes by Edward Armstrong, Fourth Edition, New York: Burt Franklin, 1971.

Bullard, John M., *Friends' Academy 1810-1960, A History of the First One Hundred and Fifty Years*, New Bedford, Mass: Reynolds-DeWalt Printers, 1960.

Cadbury, Henry J., "Quaker Education—Then and Now," in *Two-and-a-Half Centuries of Quaker Education*, 1939.

Cadbury, Henry J., "Quaker Ideals and Education," *Friends Intelligencer*, Twelfth Month 6, 1939, no. 49.

Canby, Henry Seidel, *1878-1961. American Memoir*, Boston: Houghton Mifflin, 1947.

Clarke, George, *John Bellers, His Life, Times and Writings*, New York: Routledge Kegan Paul, 1987.

Coffin, J. Herschel, *Christian Education*, Preliminary Report of Commission III, Section A, On Schools and Colleges of Five Years Meeting of Friends, Richmond, mimeographed report, 1935.

Comenius, John, *The Labyrinth of the World and The Paradise of the Heart*, trans.& intr., Howard Lorithan and Andrea Sterk, New York: Paulist Press, 1998.

Comenius, Johann, *The Great Didactic*, see M.W. Keatinge.

Comfort, William Wistar, *William Penn: 1644-1718 A Tercentenary Estimate*, Philadelphia: University of Pennsylvania Press, 1944.

Conyers, Charline Fay Howard, *A History of the Cheyney State Teachers College, 1837- 1951*, Unpublished dissertation, New York University, Ann Arbor: University Microfilms, 1960.

Cooper, Charles W., *Whittier: Independent College in California*, founded by Quakers, 1887, Los Angeles: The Ward Ritchie Press, 1967.

Cooper, Wilmer A., *The Earlham School of Religion Story: A Quaker Dream Come True*, Richmond: Earlham School of Religion, 1985.

Cooper, Wilmer A., *The Testimony of Integrity in the Religious Society of Friends*, Pendle Hill pamphlet 296, Wallingford: Pendle Hill, 1991.

Cox, Gray, *Bearing Witness: Quaker Process and a Culture of Peace*, Pendle Hill pamphlet 262, Wallingford: Pendle Hill, 1985.

Cremin, Lawrence A., *1925. The Transformation of the School: Progressivism in American Education, 1876-1957*. [1st ed.]. New York: Knopf, 1961.

Cremin, Lawrence Arthur, *Traditions of American Education*, New York: Basic Books, 1977.

Cristol, Daniel, and Nathaniel Kahn, "Joseph Cadbury" in *Studies in Education*, Philadelphia: Germantown Friends School, Winter 1987, No. 52.

Daloz, Laurent A. Parks, Cheryl H. Keen, James P. Keen, Sharon Daloz Parks, *Common Fire: Leading Lives of Commitment in a Complex World*, Boston: Beacon Press, 1996.

Dewey, John, *Democracy and Education: An Introduction to the Philosophy of Education*, Text-book series in education. New York: Macmillan, 1916.

Dorrace, Christopher A., ed., *Reflections from a Friends Education*, Philadelphia: Friends Council on Education, 1982.

Eldridge, Richard L., "Learning as Worship," Philadelphia: Friends Council on Education, 1984.

Eldridge, Richard L., *Rites of Passage in Children*, Philadelphia: Friends Council on Education, n.d.

Erikson, Erik H., *Childhood and Society*, 2nd ed., revised and enlarged, New York: Norton, 1963.

Erikson, Erik H., *Identity, Youth and Crisis*, New York: Norton, 1968.

Esslinger, Dean R., *Friends for Two Hundred Years: a history of Baltimore's oldest school*, Baltimore: Friends School, 1983.

Etzioni, Amitai, *The Active Society: A Theory of Societal and Political Processes*. New York: Free Press, 1968.

Faraday, Clayton L., *Friends Central School 1845-1984*, Philadelphia: Friends Central School, 1984.

Fisher, Dorothy Canfield, *Montessori for Parents* (originally published as *A Montessori Mother*, 1912), reprint Cambridge: Robert Bentley, Inc., 1965.

Fothergill, John, "A Letter to A Friend in the Country, Relative to the Intended School at Ackworth, 1779," in *A Complete Collection of the Medical and Philosophical Works of John Fothergill*, London: printed for J. Walker, 1781.

Foulds, Elfrida Vipont, *Ackworth School from its foundation in 1779 to the introduction of co-education in 1946*, London: Lutterworth Press, 1959.

Fox, George, *The Journal of George Fox*, ed. John L. Nickalls, Cambridge: Cambridge University Press, 1952.

Freiday, Dean ed., *Barclay's Apology in Modern English*, Philadelphia: Friends Book Store, 1967.

Friends School in Wilmington. An account of the growth of the school from its beginnings to the present time with mention of some of the men and women who have been a part of it. [200ᵗʰ anniversary], Wilmington: Wilmington Friends School, 1948.

Froebel, Friedrich, *The Education of Man*, New York, Appelton and Co., 1900.

Frost, J. William, *The Quaker Family in Colonial America: a portrait of the Society of Friends*, New York: St. Martin's Press, 1973.

Garman, Mary, Judith Applegate, Margaret Benefiel, Dortha Meredith, *Hidden in Plain Sight: Quaker Women's Writings 1650-1700*. Wallingford: Pendle Hill,1995.

Gibbs, Nancy Reid, *Children of Light: Friends Seminary 1786-1986*. New York: Friends Seminary,1986.

Gilbert, Dorothy Lloyd, *Guilford: A Quaker College*, Greensboro: Guilford College, 1937.

Gitlin, Todd, *The Twilight of Common Dreams: Why America is Wracked by Culture Wars*. 1ˢᵗ American ed. New York: H. Holt, 1995.

Graham,Patricia Albjerg, *Progressive Education: From Arcady to Academe: A History of the Progressive Education Association*, New York: Teacher's College Press, 1967.

Greenleaf, Robert K., *Servant: Retrospect and Prospect*, Cambridge, Mass: Center for Applied Studies: distributed by Windy Row Press, Peterborough, 1970.

Greenleaf, Robert K., *The Servant as Leader*, Cambridge, Mass: Center for Applied Studies, 1970.

Greenwood, John Ormerod, *Henry Hodgkin: The Road to Pendle Hill*, Pendle Hill pamphlet 229, Wallingford: Pendle Hill, 1980.

Griscom, John, *A Year in Europe: comprising a journal of observations in England, Scotland, Ireland, France, Switzerland, the north of Italy, and Holland, in 1818 and 1819*. second edition, two vols., New York: Collins & Hanay, 1824.

Hamm, Thomas D., *Earlham College: A History, 1847-1997*. Bloomington: Indiana University Press, 1997.

Hatcher, Sadie Brown, "A History of Spiceland Academy, 1826-1921," Indianapolis: Indiana Historical Society, 1934.

Haviland, Margaret Morris, *In the world, but not of the world: the humanitarian activities of Philadelphia Quakers, 1790-1820*. Unpublished dissertation, University of Pennsylvania, Ann Arbor: University Microfilms, 1992,

Hays, Kim, *Practicing Virtues: Moral Traditions at Quaker and Military Boarding Schools*, Berkeley: University of California Press, 1994.

Heath, Douglas H., with the assistance of Harriet E. Heath, *Fulfilling Lives: Paths to Maturity and Success*, San Francisco: Jossey-Bass, 1991.

Heath, Douglas H., *The Peculiar Mission of a Friends School*, Pendle Hill pamphlet 225, Wallingford: Pendle Hill, 1979.

Heath, Douglas H., *Why a Friends School?*, Pendle Hill pamphlet 164, Wallingford: Pendle Hill, 1969.

Heath, Douglas H., *Schools of Hope: Developing Mind and Character in Today's Youth*, San Francisco: Jossey-Bass, 1994.

Hints on Education Addressed to Parents, Tract No. 17, Philadelphia: The Tract Association of Friends, n.d.

Hobart, John H., *A Quaker Headmaster: The Life and Time of Chester L. Reagan*, Moorestown: Moorestown Friends School, 1980.

Hodgkin, Violet L., *Silent Worship: The Way of Wonder*, London: Headley Bros.1919. 2nd ed. London: Swarthmore Press, 1919.

Hole, Helen G., *Things Civil and Useful*, Richmond: Friends United Press, 1978.

Hornick, Nancy Slocum, "Anthony Benezet and the Africans' School: Toward a Theory of Full Equality," *The Pennsylvania Magazine of History and Biography*, October, 1975.

Hubbard, D.G.B., *Early Quaker Education, 1650-1789*, unpublished MA thesis of University of London, 1939.

Hubben, William, *Report on Religion at George School, in George School Report, Thirty Schools Tell Their Story.*

Hughes, James L., *Froebel's Educational Laws for All Teachers*, New York: Appelton and Co., 1897.

Hutchinson, Joseph, "Experiment in Education," in *Friends Schools in the Seventies*, London: Friends Schools Joint Committee, 1973.

Jackson-Coppin, Fanny, *Reminiscences of School Life, and Hints on Teaching*, Originally published: Philadelphia: African Methodist Episcopal Book Concern, 1913. Reprinted by Garland, 1987, Intro. Shelley P. Haley, New York: G.K. Hall and Co., 1995.

James, Milton M., "The Institute for Colored Youth," *Negro History Bulletin.* Washington: Association for the Study of Negro Life and History, 1958.

Jensen, Joan M., "Not Only Ours But Others: The Quaker Teaching Daughters of the Mid- Atlantic, 1790-1850," *History of Education Quarterly*, Spring, 1984.

Jones, T. Canby, *"The Power of the Lord is Over All," The Pastoral Letters of George Fox*, Richmond: Friends United Press, 1989.

Jones, Rufus M., *Later Periods of Quakerism*, London: Macmillan, 1921.

Kahn, Nathaniel, and Daniel Cristol, "Joseph Cadbury," in Studies in Education, Philadelphia: Germantown Friends School, Winter 1987, No. 52.

Kahoe, Walter, *Arthur Morgan: A Biography and Memoir*, Moylan, Pa: The Whimsie Press, 1977.

Kashatus, William, *A Virtuous Education: Penn's Vision for Philadelphia Schools*, Wallingford: Pendle Hill, 1997.

Keatinge, M.W., *Comenius: The Great Didactic Abridged*, McGraw-Hill education classics. New York, London: McGraw-Hill Book Company, inc., 1931.

Kelsey, R.W., *Centennial History of Moses Brown School: 1819-1919*, Providence: Moses Brown School, 1919.

Kenworthy, Leonard S., *Quaker Education: a Source Book*, Kennett Square: Quaker Publications, n.d.

Klain, Zora, *Quaker Contributions to Education in North Carolina*, Philadelphia: Westbrook Publishing Co., 1925.

Kohler, Charles, *Unwillingly to School: Memoirs of the Friends School, Saffron Walden, 1924-1928*, Dorking: Kohler and Coombes, 1985.

Kuh, George D., *Involving Colleges: Successful Approaches to Fostering Student Learning and Developing Outside the Classroom*, 1st ed. San Francisco: Jossey-Bass Publishers, 1991.

Kuh, George, "Ethos: Its Influence on Student Learning," *Liberal Education*, Fall, 1993.

Lampen, John, *Wait in the Light: The Spirituality of George Fox*, London: Quaker Home Service, 1981.

Learners All: Quaker Experiences in Education, London: published for Quaker Responsibility and Education by Quaker Home Service, 1986.

Lester, John A., *The Ideals and Objectives of Quaker Education*, Philadelphia: reprinted by Friends Council on Education, n.d

Letchworth, Rachel K., *Westtown in Trust*, Westtown: Westtown School, 1975.

Letchworth, Rachel K., "Yesterday, Today—And Tomorrow? Friends Council on Education, 1931-1981," Philadelphia: Friends Council on Education, 1981.

Locke, John, *On Politics and Education*, New York: published for the Classics Club by W.J. Block, 1947.

Loukes, Harold, *Readiness for Religion*, Rufus Jones Lecture, Pendle Hill pamphlet 126, Wallingford: Pendle Hill, 1963.

MacKaye, William R. and Mary Anne MacKaye, *Mr. Sidwell's School: A Centennial History 1883-1983*, Washington, DC: Sidwell Friends School, 1984.

Manchester Conference, 1895, London Yearly Meeting (Society of Friends) Home Mission Committee. Report of the proceedings of the conference of members of the Society of Friends, held, by direction of the Yearly Meeting, in Manchester from the eleventh to the fifteenth of the eleventh month, 1895, London: Headley Brothers, 1896.

Mather, Eleanore Price, *Pendle Hill: A Quaker Experiment in Education and Community*, Wallingford: Pendle Hill, 1980.

McDaniel, Ethel Hittle, *The Contribution of the Society of Friends to Education in Indiana*, Indianapoli: Indiana Historical Society, 1939.

Milner, Clyde, "Quaker Education in the Carolinas," Greensboro: Guilford College, 1965.

Monroe, Will S., *Comenius and the Beginnings of Educational Reform*, New York: C. Scribner's sons, 1900.

Monroe, Will S., *History of the Pestalozzian Movement in the United States*, New York: Arno Press, 1969.

Moorestown Friends School: A History 1785-1985, adapted from One Hundred and Fifty Years, a History of Moorestown Friends School, 1935. Interviews by Jean Gaasch, Neil Hartman, Sandy Warg, Mary K. Williams, Elizabeth Cooper Wood, eds., Moorestown: Moorestown Friends School, 1986.

Murphy, Carol J., *The Roots of Pendle Hill*, Pendle Hill pamphlet 223, Wallingford: Pendle Hill, 1979.

Murray, Lindley, *Memoirs of the Life and Writings* in a series of letters written by himself, with a preface, and a continuation of the memoirs, by Elizabeth Frank. York: Longman, Rees, 1826.

Newby, James, ed. William Penn, *Some Fruits of Solitude* (1693), Richmond: Friends United Press, 1978.

Nickalls, John L., ed., *Journal of George Fox*, Cambridge: Cambridge University Press, 1952.

Oats, William Nicolle, *Headmaster by Chance*, Aguerremendi Press, Tasmania, 1986.

Oats, William Nicolle, *The Nurture of the Human Spirit* some thoughts on the nature and purpose of education and religion, Tasmania: The Friends School, Tasmania, 1990.

Oats, William Nicolle, *The Rose and the Waratah: the Friends School, Hobart, Formation and Development, 1832-1945*, Hobart, Tasmania: The Friends' School, 1979.

Oats, William Nicolle, *Values Education, A Three-Dimensional Model*, Tasmania, The Friends School, Tasmania, 1995.

Occasional Papers on the Meeting for Worship for Friends Schools, Philadelphia: Friends Council on Education, n.d.

On this same ground: voices from three hundred years of Abington Friends School, Jenkintown, PA: The School, 1997.

Otto, Rudolph, *The Idea of the Holy*, London: Oxford University, 1923.

Palmer, Parker J., *The Courage to Teach: Exploring the Inner Landscape of a Teacher's Life*, San Francisco: Jossey-Bass, 1998.

Palmer, Parker J., *A Place Called Community*, Pendle Hill pamphlet 212, Wallingford: Pendle Hill, 1977.

Palmer, Parker J., *Meeting for Learning: Education in a Quaker Context*, Pendle Hill Bulletin number 284, Wallingford: Pendle Hill, May, 1976.

Palmer, Parker J., *To Know as We Are Known: A Spirituality of Education*, New York: Harper & Row, 1983.

Parrish, Edward, *An Essay on Education in the Society of Friends*, Philadelphia: J.B. Lippincott, 1866.

Partners in Education: Wilmington College and Wilmington Yearly Meeting of Friends, Wilmington, OH: A Yearly Meeting Centennial Publication, 1992.

Penn, William, *William Penn's Advice to His Children* (Containing "Letter to His Wife and Children" and "Fruits of a Father's Love"), intro. Elizabeth Janet Gray, Philadelphia: Friends Council on Education, 1944.

Penn, William, *The Peace of Europe...and Other Writings*, intro. Joseph Besse, London: Everyman's Library, 1942.

Pennington, Isaac, *1616-1679. Letters of Isaac Penington*. Philadelphia: N. Kite, 1842.

Pipes, Richard, *The Russian Revolution*, 1st ed. New York: Knopf, 1990.

Polanyi, Michael, *The Study of Man*, Chicago: University of Chicago, 1958.

Poley, Irvin C., *Speaking of Teaching*, Philadelphia: Germantown Friends School, 1958.

Pollard, F.S., *Bootham School 1823-1923*, London: J.M. Dent and Sons, 1926.

Price, Kingsley, *Educational and Philosophical Thought*, Boston: Allyn and Bacon, 1962.

Punshon, John, *Testimony and Tradition: Some Aspects of Quaker Spirituality*, Swarthmore Lecture, London: Quaker Home Service, 1990.

Quaker Education Considered. Report of Friends Conference on Education, held at Earlham College, November 21-22, 1946.

Reader, John, *On Schools and Schoolmasters, some thoughts on the Quaker contribution to education*, London: Quaker Home Service, 1979.

Reagan, William J., *A Venture in Quaker Education at Oakwood School*, Poughkeepsie: Oakwood School, 1968.

Rogers, William, "Friends Education in North Carolina," *Vision 400*.

Rusk, Robert R., *The Doctrines of the Great Educators*, Rev. and enl. 3d ed. Macmillan, 1965.

Russell, Elbert, "Early Friends and Education," Philadelphia: Committee on Education of Philadelphia Yearly Meeting of Friends, 1925.

Scherer, George A., *Ernest Atkins Wildman: A Biographical Sketch*, Dublin, IN: Prinit Press, 1984.

Selleck, Linda B., *Gentle Invaders: Quaker Women Educators and Racial Issues During the Civil War and Reconstruction*, Richmond, Indiana: Friends United Press, 1995.

Sheeran, Michael J., *Beyond Majority Rule: Voteless Decisions in the Religious Society of Friends*, Philadelphia, Pa: Philadelphia Yearly Meeting of the Religious Society of Friends, 1983.

Shi, David, *The Simple Life: Plain Living and High Thinking in American Culture*, New York: Oxford University Press, 1985.

Sizer, Theodore R., ed. *The Age of the Academies*, Classics in Education, no. 22. New York: New York Bureau of Publications, Teachers College, Columbia University, 1964.

Smith, George, *Aspects of Quaker Education*, unpublished essay for the Master's degree at Earlham School of Religion, Richmond, Indiana, 1993.

Smith, Eugene R., "Self-Activity and Creativeness as School Aims," *The Nation's Schools*, Vol. VII, No. 1, January, 1931.

So Numerous a Family: 200 Years of Quaker Education at Ackworth, Ackworth, England: Ackworth School, 1979.

Soderlund, Jean R., *Quakers and Slavery: A Divided Spirit*, Princeton: Princeton University Press, 1985.

Some Account of the Aimwell School, instituted by the Society for the Free Instruction of Female Children, now incorporated under the title of "The Aimwell School Association," Philadelphia: Pile and McElroy, Printers, 1861.

Spinka, Matthew, *John Amos Comenius: that incomparable Moravian*, Chicago: The University of Chicago, 1943.

Steere, Douglas V., Intro., *Break the New Ground*, Birmingham: Friends World Committee for Consultation, 1969.

Steere, Douglas V., *On Listening to Another*, New York: Harper & Bros., 1955.

Steere, Douglas V., ed. & intro., *Quaker Spirituality: Selected Writings*, New York: Paulist Press, 1984.

Stephen, Caroline, *Quaker Strongholds*, Pendle Hill pamphlet 59, Wallingford: Pendle Hill, 1951.

Stewart, W.A. Campbell, *Quakers and Education As Seen in Their Schools in England*, London: Epworth Press, 1953.

Stoesen, Alexander R., *Guilford College on the Strength of 150 Years*, Greensboro: published by the Board of Trustees, Guilford College, 1987.

Strane, Susan, *A Whole-Souled Woman, Prudence Crandall and the Education of Black Women*, New York: Norton, 1990.

Straub, Jean, "Anthony Benezet: Teacher and Abolitionist of the Eighteenth Century," *Quaker History*, Vol. 57, No. 1, Spring 1968.

Stroud, L.J., *The History of Quaker Education in England, 1647-1903*, unpublished dissertation, University of Leeds, 1944.

Sturge and Clark, *The Mount School*, London: J.M. Dent, 1931.

Swayne, Kingdon W., *George School: The History of a Quaker Community*, Newtown: George School, 1992.

Taber, William, *Be Gentle, Be Plain, A History of Olney*, Barnesville, Ohio: Olney Alumni Association, 1976.

Thirty Schools Tell Their Story, New York: Harper, 1943.

Thompson, Henry, *A History of Ackworth School During Its First Hundred Years*, Ackworth: Ackworth School, 1879.

Thornburg, Opal, *Earlham: The Story of the College*, Richmond: Earlham College, 1963.

Tillich, Paul, *The Dynamics of Faith*. New York: Harper, 1958.

Tolles, Frederick B. and Gordon Alderfer, *The Witness of William Penn*, New York: MacMillan, 1957.

Tolles, Frederick B., *Meeting House and Counting House: The Quaker Merchants of Colonial Philadelphia, 1682-1763*, Chapel Hill: University of North Carolina, 1948, reprinted New York: Norton, 1963.

Tuke, Samuel, *Five Papers on the Past Proceedings and Experience of the Society of Friends, in Connexion with the Education of Youth*, New York: John L. Linney, 1843.

Two-and-a-Half Centuries of Quaker Education, The proceedings of the anniversary meeting held under the auspices of Friends Council of Education, Tenth Month 20, 1939, reprinted from *The Friend*, Eleventh Month 2 and 16, 1939, Vol. 113 nos. 9 and 10.

Vogel, Norma L., essay in *Newsletter*, Philadelphia: Greene Street Friends School, January 1994.

Watson, George Alston, *Ayton School: Centenary History 1841-1941*, Ashford, Kent: The School, 1941.

Whitehead, Alfred North, *The Aims of Education, and other essays*, 1929. Free Press reprinted, 1967.

Wildman, Ernest A., *Papers in Earlham College Archives*.

Williams, Susanna, "Defining Moments: Meeting for Worship in Friends Elementary Schools," unpublished essay, written for a Seminar on Quaker Education at Earlham College, Winter, 1995.

Willis, John, *On the Appointment and Classification of Teachers in the Schools of Friends*, a paper read at the annual meeting of the Friends; Educational Society, York: printed by James Hunton, 1853.

Wilson, Roger C., *Authority, Leadership and Concern*, London: Allen & Unwin, 1949.

Woodfaulk, Courtney Sanabria, *The Jeanes Teachers of South Carolina: The Emergence, Existence and Significance of Their Work*, unpublished dissertation, University of South Carolina, Ann Arbor: University Microfilms, 1992.

Woody, Thomas, *Early Quaker Education in Pennsylvania*, New York: Teachers College, Columbia University, 1920.

Woody, Thomas, *Quaker Education in the Colony and State of New Jersey*. American education—its men, ideas, and institution. New York: Arno Press, 1969.

Woolman, John, *The Journal and Major Essays of John Woolman*, Moulton, Phillips P., ed., New York, Oxford University Press, 1971.

Woolman, John, *The Works of John Woolman*, In two parts. Philadelphia, Printed by Joseph Crukshank, 1774.

Zilversmit, Arthur, *Changing Schools: Progressive Education Theory and Practice, 1930-1960*, Chicago: University of Chicago Press, 1993.

INDEX

Growing into Goodness

was composed on a Power Macintosh computer using Adobe Pagemaker 6.0 and typefaces from the Adobe Type Library: Goudy for the text with Adobe Wood Type Ornaments. Adobe Caslon was used for the cover. 60# Gladfelter Recycled paper was used for this printing of 1500 copies.

History of the Type Faces

In 1915, Frederic W. Goudy designed Goudy Old Style, his twenty-fifth type face, and his first for American Type Founders. Its recognizable features include the diamond-shaped dots on i., j., and on punctuation marks; the upturned ear of the g; and the base of E and L. Flexible enough for both text and display, it's one of the most popular typefaces ever produced.

Based on seventeenth-century Dutch old style designs, William Caslon's typefaces appeared in 1722. The designs met with instant success and became popular throughout Europe and the American Colonies. They were used for the first printings of the American Declaration of Independence and the Constitution. Adobe Caslon is based on pages printed by William Caslon between 1734 and 1770.

Book Design by
Eva Fernandez Beehler and Rebecca Kratz Mays

James — Testimonies p.54

M. McCarthy . Berkely Avenue